SMASHING IT UP

A DECADE OF CHAOS WITH

THE DAMNED

SMASHING IT UP

A DECADE OF CHAOS WITH

THE DAMNED

KIERON TYLER

OMNIBUS PRESS

London / New York / Paris / Sydney / Copenhagen / Berlin / Madrid / Tokyo

Contents

Contents

Introduction

If British punk rock was a movement, it was an outsider's movement. The Damned were its outsiders. The outsider's outsiders.

From July 6, 1976, when they first played live, a wedge was driven between themselves and brand leaders the Sex Pistols, whose manager Malcolm McLaren wanted to pay for the use of a PA they had no choice about using as they were the support band to his charges. The Damned did not fork out. Never mind that it wasn't actually called punk rock then – that came a month later – The Damned weren't paying lip service to McLaren and any ideas that they and the Pistols were united as part of a movement. The Damned's path was their own.

And so it went on. The Damned were dismissed from the Sex Pistols' December 1976 Anarchy tour. How that happened is not straightforward, but McLaren was behind the cleavage and it was he who announced "they will have to get off the tour". However, The Damned were moving faster than the headliners, setting the pace, and had already released their first single. 'New Rose' came out in October, a month before the Pistols' 'Anarchy In The U.K.'. The Damned's presence on the tour helped sell tickets but after their – instantly notorious – brush with TV host Bill Grundy, the Sex Pistols were mainstream news and their name was enough to carry the tour. The Damned were toast. Whatever they did, The Damned were always outsiders.

Yet The Damned had issued the first British punk single. Their place in history is assured. They also made British punk's first album and were the first British punk band to play America. First does not necessarily mean best, but 'New Rose' is one of the great debut singles. Eternally thrilling, it defines excitement, always turns heads and is endlessly fresh. It is one of rock's classic singles. *Damned, Damned, Damned*, the electrifying debut album, is as unforgettable.

It didn't stop there. The Damned can be defined by those firsts (and often are), but this is not all they are about. Third album *Machine Gun Etiquette*, released in 1979, and 1980's follow-up *The Black Album* are splendid. *Strawberries*, issued in 1982, captures The Damned tackling pop head-on and is another gem. So is 1985's *Phantasmagoria*. The firsts are historic markers but have little do with the music and The Damned at their most commercially successful. The debut single arrived in 1976. They hit their chart peak a whole decade later with a cover version of Barry Ryan's 'Eloise'.

Smashing It Up focuses on these ten years, travelling alongside The Damned in the decade they went from punk pioneers to pop stars.

★ ★ ★

Smashing It Up is inevitably a take on how British punk rock developed; different to and coming from a different perspective to other published books. *Smashing It Up* is one story of British punk rock. More than this, it celebrates one of Britain's great bands, the wayward Damned, the band formed in 1976 by Brian James, Rat Scabies, Captain Sensible and David Vanian.[1]

The Damned were never boring, never predictable. They endured and kept coming back when other bands would have packed it in. They split, reformed, shed members, replaced them, carried on. Self-sabotage didn't do its job. A solo Captain Sensible hit number one and, in due course, left. The Damned persevered. Part of the reason is that the key members held on to a common core belief, an ethos – usually unspoken – that The Damned prevailed.

Managers and labels came and went. Bridges were burnt. Opportunities were missed: EMI wanted to sign them in 1977 but did not. There were distractions: their first label, Stiff Records, was almost as much about marketing as it was its roster. Slogans and eye-catching packaging came before the music on the records. Band-audience, band-business and band-media relations were subjected to a scorched earth policy – they signed with one label while still contracted to another – but the band kept going.

Smashing It Up could be a textbook on how not to carve a way through the music business and has enough vignettes suggesting it might be. But The Damned made great records with great songs. Their records sold. They were in the charts. Live, they were a draw. A good or, at least, memorable show was guaranteed. In America, in 1977, they kick-started the Los Angeles punk scene. They inspired the Minneapolis band The Replacements. Rat Scabies was and is a fantastic drummer. Brian James is an idiosyncratic, superb guitarist. Captain Sensible is an exceptional musician and songwriter. David Vanian is an outstanding vocalist whose voice became more and more powerful. Instead of being a how-not-to-do-it, *Smashing It Up* shows it is possible to achieve success despite yourself while also being yourself – a version of yourself – without paying heed to how it should be done. Often, though the music was not punk, the attitude was.

An attitude which refused to recognise that others knew best. Or, putting it another way. The Damned were not going to be guided. Embracing the corporate side of the music business was never going to be easy. When that did happen, on signing with MCA in 1984 after Captain's departure, it was fine for a while but, ultimately and inevitably, ended in disarray.

The name remained the same but over the first ten years, there were three Damneds – one following the other as line-ups changed. It wasn't seamless but followed a straight line. Brian James and Rat Scabies formed the band and were joined by Captain Sensible and David Vanian: the mark one Damned – the Stiff Records' Damned – which fragmented in autumn 1977, was held together with sticking plasters for a while and hit the buffers in early 1978.

Then, later in 1978, the mark two Damned emerged. Captain switched from bass to guitar while David and Rat resumed their former roles. Bassists came and went, as did labels. A keyboard player was added, but the core trio kept mark two going.

Next, in 1984, Captain Sensible left and mark three, David and Rat's Damned, emerged: the MCA Damned, the most commercially successful version with Roman Jugg and Bryn Merrick. Slow disintegration followed and, by 1988, it was obvious the band was irredeemably in trouble. Reunions and reformations ensued.

Throughout the chopping and changing, The Damned were adept at bringing in talented new members who became essential to thriving. In 1977, additional guitarist Lu Edmonds and future Culture Club drummer Jon Moss weren't so impactful. The same applies to short-stay mark two bassist Henry Badowski. All three were integral to the story but their inputs into the music were less far-reaching than the next mark two bassists. Algy Ward and Paul Gray are key members of The Damned. As was keyboard player Roman Jugg, late on board with mark two. When Captain left, the artistically gifted Roman switched to guitar and became crucial to mark three. He also brought bassist Bryn Merrick into the mark two band after Paul Gray left.

Paul Gray and, especially, Roman Jugg had marvellous songs which The Damned recorded. They were not subsidiary members along for the ride. Without Roman's musical flair, the mark three Damned would not have left the starting gate. There were also outside contributors. The Damned were never shy about inviting friends to contribute lyrics or to help with the songwriting.

Yet The Damned are ultimately about Brian James, Captain Sensible, Rat Scabies and David Vanian. Not Brian Robertson, Ray Burns, Chris Millar and David Lett. Along with the assumed names, they took on new personae – though, as becomes apparent, little differentiates Brian James from Brian Robertson – and being in The Damned gave them license to be these characters. Though *Smashing It Up* is about the band The Damned, Brian Robertson, Ray Burns, Chris Millar and David Lett are of course here. Ray Burns' non-musical interests are defining characteristics of The Damned: his personal love of quintessentially British pursuits like cricket, the search for real ale and trainspotting. David's embedded and long-held fascinations with 1930s Hollywood horror and the glamour of the past are also essential to The Damned. Not much is cut-and-dried with The Damned, but the band is stronger than any of its members.

A version of The Damned still exists, but the chain shackled to all that had come before was broken in the wake of the success of 'Eloise'. A split was announced in 1989, but its foundations were laid in 1986. After the split, everything else was reclamation, reformation and reiteration. This doesn't mean that, say, 2001's *Grave Disorder* album is without its merits but it does mean it stands apart from what went before. The story of *Smashing It Up* is the story of that chaotic first decade.

★ ★ ★

In one form or another, The Damned have been a constant presence on the world's stages since 1976. They have made wonderful records. Their status as one of three original British punk rock bands can never be taken from them. They take their place alongside the Sex Pistols and The Clash.

Writing in the *Melody Maker* of August 7, 1976, Caroline Coon was the first onlooker to say there was a British punk rock scene and pointed to the Sex Pistols, The Clash and The Damned as its leaders. She wielded the rubber stamp. Later[2], she said, "Three bands represented the three different prongs of the punk movement. There was the personal politics of the Sex Pistols, the serious politics of The Clash and the theatre, camp, and good fun of The Damned."

Coon confirmed The Damned's indisputable place in history. Mould-breakers, they were banned and behaved badly. They made odd choices. They were eccentric, yet always developed musically and set the template for goth. When there were left turns to take, they took them. If there were prevailing trends, they were ignored. In 1980, when punk had become a cliché, they recorded the 17-minute progressive-psychedelic masterpiece 'Curtain Call'. When they recorded their second album in 1977, instead of rehashing their first – like everyone else that year – they made the dense and challenging *Music For Pleasure* with Pink Floyd's Nick Mason in the producer's seat. Uniquely, in their first decade, every time it seemed the band had killed itself off

The Damned emerged from the wreckage with their artistic strength boosted and greater commercial success.

Smashing It Up is the tale of the original band and its members. The best rock music is spawned by the combination of energy and personality, adversity and creativity, and the battles between them. From the beginning, The Damned had them all.

PROLOGUE

About Ten Years Of Worry

"Is it true you used to sleep in a coffin?" At almost ten minutes to eight on the morning of Monday February 24, 1986, presenter Anne Diamond has asked the question she has been itching to pose for the last couple of minutes.

In front of her, The Damned's singer David Vanian is sitting next to Barry Ryan on the sofa on *Good Morning Britain*, the nation's breakfast television mix of chit-chat, exercise tips, news updates and weather reports. Ryan had recorded the original of the baroque pop classic 'Eloise' in 1968 and, as the programme goes out live, The Damned's version sits at three in the charts. Their biggest hit has reached its peak position. Yet David looks ill at ease. Although arresting in his frock coat, cravat, high wing collar and swept-back hair, on-camera informality doesn't come easily.

Addressing the question about the unconventional bed, David considers his words. "Very uncomfortable. No, not really."

"What do you mean, not really?" counters Diamond.

"They're a bit small, cramped," says David.

"But you have, haven't you, you have slept in a coffin, haven't you?" Diamond's co-host Nick Owen won't let it go. "We've heard all these funny things about you."

"You used to be a gravedigger," interjects Diamond. "Is that true?"

"That's true," concedes David, who goes on to explain he enjoyed the job as he liked the isolation, being in the country and that he could get the work done quickly, leaving time to get into London and work with the band.

Finally, the awkward four minutes in the hot seat are up and The Damned are seen miming 'Eloise'.

Earlier in the encounter, Diamond was drawn to the broad grey streak in David's hair and wondered if it meant he had worry in his life. "About ten years of worry," was his response.

Ten years of worry indeed. The Damned had played live for the first time in 1976 and were instantly hailed as one of Britain's pioneering punk rock bands. This, though, was of no concern to *Good Morning Britain* a decade later. They were high in the charts and their singer was an individual sort of chap, just the type of pop star to subject to a gentle grilling as the nation readied itself for household chores or work.

And The Damned themselves were working hard. Later that week they were off to America. On the Friday, they played New York's Ritz. After that, coast-to-coast US dates, then New Zealand, Australia and Japan: two full months away from the land of *Good Morning Britain*.

In 1976, any suggestion that a decade later The Damned would be helping Britain ease itself into the week, sitting high in the charts and then jetting off for a sustained crack at the world market would have been scoffed at. However, British punk's most unruly and unstable band had long outlived the Sex Pistols. The Clash were gone too – fizzling out after November 1985's *Cut The Crap* album. The Damned were the last of the first three British punk bands standing. They were still around despite themselves.

If this was the punishment their name demanded, The Damned took it on the chin and soldiered on. Getting up early to be asked whether you slept in a coffin was a small price to pay.

CHAPTER ONE

Brian And Rat

In summer 1975, Brian Robertson was at his parents' house in Crawley. He had itchy feet. It was time to decide whether he had seen too much of Brussels, where he lived. Bastard, the band he had formed in 1972, had been based in the Belgian capital since October 1973 but, he says, "were going nowhere, people were getting married to French birds". A square meal was on offer while back in the West Sussex town where he had grown up.

He picked up a copy of *Melody Maker*, the most serious-minded of Britain's music weeklies. It looked as though business was as usual. The cover of the August 9 issue was dedicated to the news Paul Simon was scheduled to play the Royal Albert Hall in the coming December with a band featuring "well-known New York session men". Inside the cover, an article was devoted the reformation of British jazz-rock group Colosseum, whose only original member Jon Hiseman said "what we have now is quite extraordinary". Brian was a dedicated fan of the wayward Stooges, so the reanimated Colosseum and Paul Simon's stultifying session men were anathema. "I listened to The Stooges and that was action," he says. As one of the few British fans of the no-compromise Detroit outfit, he had no time for the meticulous approach to music so admired by *Melody Maker*.

The paper's values were firmly in a present which may as well have been the past. In the issue Brian was looking at, *Melody Maker*'s tip for show of the week was a headline booking at the prestigious London Palladium from 1967's 'Whiter Shade Of Pale' hit-makers Procol Harum. A two-page spread sang the praises of Pete Wingfield, then on the up after the 'Eighteen With A Bullet' single but tagged as "dues-paying musician". The article went into his past as side-man for Van Morrison and former Zombie Colin Blunstone. This is what gave him worth. In the singles review column, Rod Stewart's 'Sailing' had prime billing. The centre pages found Derek Chinnery, the head of the BBC's pop station Radio One, declaring "we reflect what the record industry throws up".

Many of the 188,000[3] readers who bought *Melody Maker* each week did so to scour its musicians-wanted small ads. Brian was amongst them as he was on the look-out for a new opportunity. Even in the back pages, the shared values were mostly those of careerism and conventionality. On page 41, an ad sought a keyboard player for a band with "commercial material". "Freaks need not apply," it cautioned. Another was placed by a "semi-pro" band looking for a "lead guitarist, strong rhythm essential".

Between them was one which caught Brian's eye. The concise, telegrammatic announcement came with a phone number to call and read:

LEAD GUITARIST and **DRUMMER** for band into
Stones / Stooges. Decadent 3rd
generation rock 'n' roll image essential
/New York Dolls style
– Michael 272 9687

"If it wasn't for that little ad in the *Melody Maker* that mentioned The Stooges, I don't know what I would have done," says Brian. "Maybe just stayed in Brussels."

He had no way of knowing it, but this was the one of two publicly visible, similarly timed notices in the *Melody Maker* telegraphing the arrival of what would become British punk rock. The Michael whose phone number was given turned out to be Mick Jones, later in The Clash, and what Brian had seen was the third ad Jones had placed looking for like-minded musicians. The second signpost appeared on September 27, 1975 after the Sex Pistols' manager Malcolm McLaren took out an ad searching for a "WHIZZ KID GUITARIST... Not worse looking than Johnny Thunders". Although his charges had no real requirement to supplement Steve Jones with a blurred photocopy of the New York Dolls' guitarist, McLaren needed the faltering band to coalesce. Drummer Paul Cook was about to leave and publicly advertising for another guitarist was McLaren's indication to the fractious group that he was serious about the band. It was a tactic to keep the band together.

While the Sex Pistols were being made to shape up in the ad he saw, Brian had already unconsciously found the roots that sprouted into both The Clash and The Damned. The three words both ads shared were "New York Dolls", the name of the band McLaren had been working with in New York in a hands-on capacity from late 1974 into 1975. After they split and on his return to London, the Sex Pistols became his prime concern. Their caretaker manager, McLaren's old friend Bernard Rhodes, was shoved aside. Before long, Mick Jones encountered the newly unoccupied Rhodes and the rest is punk history.[4]

★ ★ ★

Brian Graham Robertson was born on February 18, 1951 in Hammersmith, west London but grew up south of the capital in Crawley, West Sussex, where his family moved in 1959. Music has never branded the town, though The Cure emerged there in 1976. With Gatwick Airport to the immediate north as a local source of employment, surges in population came after the government established Crawley as a New Town in 1947.[5] Development followed. Gatwick officially became London's second airport – after Heathrow – in 1950 with even more employment.

"There were a lot of young kids around as their parents had moved out of London to buy a house," says Brian of Crawley. "Once you get to a certain age, you notice what's going on around you. I used to like to associate with kids who called themselves beats. They'd pass through Crawley. They'd get a doss bag, go around and meet other people, drink cider, smoke dope and tell stories and play songs together. They had long hair and were different. There was the mod scene on one side and the long hair thing on the other. I'd be hanging out with the mods scoring blues and hanging out with the hippies scoring dope."

In 1966, on his 15th birthday, Brian and Hazelwick Comprehensive School parted company. "I was a little bit naughty," he says of his attitude. "But really, I just didn't like school. I never went. I got called in to the headmaster's office when I'd just turned 15. He said, 'You don't want to be here, we don't want you here, why wait? Go now.'"

Music distracted attention from the classroom and came to dominate his life. He had already been given an acoustic guitar by his parents but it sat in the corner of his bedroom. The epiphany came at 14 when he saw local Rolling Stones-type band Monty Cavan & The Kingbees play a municipal hall. "They were great," he says. "Monty was a bit smooth but the band was really good. They were playing the first Stones album with a bit of Howlin' Wolf and Chuck Berry too. Next time I saw the rhythm guitarist in the street, I asked if he could teach me some things on the guitar. Particularly a thing called 'Smokey Haystack'." Brian learned this was actually Howlin' Wolf's 'Smokestack Lightning'. Equally quickly, it became obvious heading towards music was to be at the expense of a conventional career.

He marked time working in a warehouse and as a floor sweeper at Gatwick but didn't earn enough to buy an electric guitar outright, and was too young to pay for one in instalments through a higher purchase plan. His father Stan stepped in to deal with the twin obstacles. "My dad said that if I worked, he would buy it rather than me paying the ridiculous amounts of interest if he bought it on higher purchase. So, bit by bit, I paid him," says Brian. "My dad also said it would be good if I got an apprenticeship, something to fall back on." He got the guitar but did not learn a trade as his father wanted.

As well as The Rolling Stones, Brian was a fan of The Yardbirds, The Who and John Mayall, and saw bluesmen John Lee Hooker and B. B. King live. Blues Crusade, the first band he joined, were named after the

John Mayall album *Crusade*. "Heavily influenced by the first Fleetwood Mac album," says Brian of the band. "We did 'Shake Your Money Maker', 'Confessin' The Blues'."

Brian then resolved to form his own band. After finding singer and some-time bongo and sax player David Blackman though an ad placed in a shop window, Brian put together Train. Bassist Dave Searle had already been in a blues band and the drummer was Malcolm Mortimore. Indirectly, Mortimore became influential as his father played John Coltrane to Brian for the first time. "It was emotional music," says Brian. "Once you've heard Coltrane, there's no turning back."

Although Train were a local band tailored to Brian's vision of a blues-inspired outfit "we got a bit more experimental," he recalls. "Soft Machine were entering their second phase and were really interesting, after the initial thing with Daevid Allen and Kevin Ayers. Jazz was creeping in. We covered Soft Machine's 'Mousetrap':[6] I'd do the keyboard parts on my guitar."

Blackman had connections which potentially meant finding an audience beyond Crawley. John Kennet, a friend of the singer, knew Tony Stratton-Smith, who had founded Charisma Records and managed Genesis. As a result, the band got gigs. It was suggested they record a version of the American pop hit 'Witchi Tai To', which members of the Bonzo Dog Doo-Dah Band had already covered as a British single.

Train duly found themselves in a recording studio. "John Kennet was a bit of hustler and said there's this song the Bonzos' Legs Larry had done and we didn't want to put the name Train to this pop thing," explains Brian. "To me, it was just an opportunity to go into the studio. But I hated it, this guy telling me what to do. My guitar didn't sound right, it didn't sound in the control room like what I'd played." Nonetheless, 'Witchi Tai To' was issued by the independent Beacon label with the apparently Blackman-written 'Speakin' My Mind' as its B-side. Instead of Train, the labels credited the single to a band called Taiconderoga, a suggestion of Blackman's. It was 1969. Brian had made his first record.

The Train/Taiconderoga version of 'Witchi Tai To' is a straightforward if dense cover version, dominated by Brian's jagged stabs of rhythmic guitar which also carry a Jeff Beck-influenced refrain, but 'Speakin' My Mind' is something else. Hard-edged and driving, it features clipped, lacerating Hendrix-style guitar which at the two-minute point takes over the whole of the remaining 90 seconds. Brian's guitar defined both sides. The single was issued in Germany and Spain with 'Speakin' My Mind' as the A-side and sold fairly well in the former.

Despite this boost, a show at London's Lyceum supporting King Crimson and gigs around the counties south of the capital, Train were going nowhere. "We got fed up with Blackman," says Brian. "He was in the rag trade, had a shop in Redhill and had some money coming in so didn't need the band. He put his name to 'Speakin' My Mind' even though we all chipped in."

When Mortimore auditioned for and got the job with Gentle Giant[7], Brian took stock. His next band wouldn't compromise. The prime influence was *Fun House*, the second album by The Stooges. Issued in July 1970, it was a reminder that stripped-down music hit hard. It was also, with Steve Mackay's saxophone and the free-form 'L.A. Blues', overtly jazz influenced. Brian had been amongst the 300,000[8] who travelled to see Jimi Hendrix at the August 1970 Isle of Wight Festival but it didn't steer him where he was headed. "*Fun House* changed me big time," says Brian. "I heard it at a party, there was this kid who was very up on things. I said to him, 'Ivan, you're gonna know what this is.' He said, 'They're The Stooges from Detroit.' I looked at the cover and thought, 'I've got to get this.' I went up to London to find a copy." The new band he formed was called Bastard.

Bastard comprised Brian on guitar, Nobby Goff (drums), Alan Ward (vocals) and the mono-monikered Dez (bass). While the name ensured topping the charts was out of the question, Bastard's music was similarly edgy. Although Goff and Ward were previously in soul band Mustang Stampede, the drummer was a fan of Sixties R&B long-hairs The Pretty Things, the rougher and wilder counterpart to The Rolling Stones. The new band merged The Stooges with The Pretty Things.

Despite Bastard's rarefied approach, Ladbroke Grove's freak-flag-flyers The Pink Fairies were kindred spirits. Striking up relationships with Fairies road manager Boss Goodman and Pete Adam of promoters the Greasy Truckers helped get Bastard shows, including a benefit under Ladbroke Grove's flyover and July 1973's Trentishoe Whole

14

Earth Fayre. But it was tough. The gigs were intermittent. The name prevented bookings at most venues and Brian wasn't going to change it. Playing the odd free festival with the Fairies to a crowd of Hells Angels was never going to push things on.

The band's vocalist Ward worked as an engineer at north-west London's Morgan Studios. A satellite facility opened in Brussels in October 1973[9] and he intended moving there. Bastard's choice was to either break up or move to Belgium. Brian knew France loved The Flamin' Groovies, the MC5, Lou Reed and The Stooges – all of whom were on his wavelength – and Brussels was just one step removed, so finding an audience appeared possible. The band followed Ward and got a regular gig at the Café Floréo. There wasn't much money to be made, but all the beer the band wanted was there to be drunk.

Another ingredient in the pre-punk mix came to town on December 10, 1973 in the form of The New York Dolls, in Brussels to appear on a TV show. Brian had heard their first album after arriving in Belgium and made sure he met them at the studio. He and guitarist Syl Sylvain chatted about the lack of need to tune up while miming.

Like the Dolls, Brian had not yet subscribed to short hair. "When I went to Brussels mine was long and black," he remembers. "I always wore tight blue or black jeans, and back in '71 my biker leather was held together with safety pins." A change came after seeing Lou Reed at the Ançienne Belgique on May 22, 1974. "His hair was dyed blonde and short, he looked like a giant junkie monkey," continues Brian. "I looked around at the show and saw all these people with long hair and thought, 'They're not me, I want to be me.'" Pink Floyd's Syd Barrett, whose playing influenced Brian's slurring guitar style, also had an impact on the new look as press pictures from 1971 showed him with unfashionably cropped hair. Brian cut his hair.

Brian was changing. So was Bastard, but not in a way suggesting a breakthrough. Dez had returned to England shortly after the move and was replaced by local musician Yves Kengen. Demos were recorded, yet there was no interest. Bastard was losing momentum. After 20 months in Brussels, Brian was again taking stock. Back in Crawley, he saw that *Melody Maker* ad.

Calling "Michael", he immediately found common musical ground so visited him and bass player Tony James at 22 Gladsmuir Road, London N19 where Mick Jones rented a room. There was no audition, no rehearsal. There was no need. After hearing the tape of Bastard[10], it was instantly agreed Brian was in and that the trio advertise for a drummer. With that as his goal, Brian told Mick Jones and Tony James that once back in Brussels, he would tell Bastard he was leaving them and then return to London to join them in the new outfit.

"Mick and Tony were like glam rockers in a way," recalls Brian of encountering the long-haired duo. "I skipped glam as I had been in Brussels. To me, it was like a reversion to the early Sixties when you had all pretty boys dressed up, somebody writing their songs, and producers in charge. *Ziggy Stardust* had come out and it was all right, but I was never a fan of Mick Ronson's guitar playing. It was very safe. I also didn't really like what Bolan was doing, as it seemed like another rehash of Stones riffs." Nonetheless, he liked chart glam band Sweet's 'Ballroom Blitz' and was pitching in with a pair of rockers subscribing to a style he wasn't that fond of. The bond instead came through the mutual respect for the New York Dolls and The Stooges.

When Brian returned to London from Brussels and called to say he was back, he quickly learned the nascent band had acquired Bernard Rhodes as their manager and The London SS as their name: the name had been buzzing around Jones's mind since March 1975. After being ousted from working with the Sex Pistols by McLaren, Rhodes wanted his own band to manage and began nurturing the newly tagged The London SS that October. He had first encountered Jones at a show by the arty Liverpool band Deaf School. Jones was wearing a T-shirt Rhodes had designed. Mirroring McLaren's strategy for the Sex Pistols – who had a permanent rehearsal space on Denmark Street – Rhodes found a base for his new charges in the basement of The Paddington Kitchen, a café on Praed Street near Paddington Station. Coincidentally, it was a stone's throw from Bizarre Records, an independent record distributor/ mail order operation/wholesaler run by Tim Crosby and Larry DeBay, the latter a French music enthusiast whose tastes distinguished the records they promoted: by The Flamin' Groovies, MC5, The Stooges,

The Velvet Underground.[11] For Brian, it was another endorsement of his tastes. Everything he loved was coalescing.

But he wasn't sure about Rhodes. "I'd met these types of people before in Brussels and London, like second-rate boat thieves. I remember Bernie saying to me that in any one year there's only room for two bands to break through, and the Pistols are going to be one of them and you can be the other. I thought, 'Really?' I didn't like him. Bernie talked about all these people he knew: 'I saw Keith Moon the other day.' It put me off, but Mick and Tony were enamoured with it. I think with the Pistols, all Malcolm had wanted was a bunch of people out there to wear his clothes, to flog his clothes and if it caused a movement, fair enough. The best thing Bernie did was, later, take me to see the Sex Pistols."

The Sex Pistols made their impromptu stage debut on November 6, 1975. For now though, for The London SS, *Melody Maker*'s small ads were once again needed.

★ ★ ★

Chris Millar, as Brian had been, was in search of a band. The man later known as Rat Scabies had one passion. "I always loved drums," he says. "I didn't want to play with the guitarist or the bass player, it was the sound of the drums. It doesn't matter if Mickey Dolenz played in The Monkees or if it was a session man, when that break is played in 'Randy Scouse Git' it's the dynamic when it kicks in."

Hoping to find a band, he turned to *Melody Maker*'s back pages and its *Musicians Wanted* ads. The December 6, 1975 issue had one which stood out. Literally so. A display box ensured it attracted attention and that the phone number was meant to be called. It screamed:

Wild young drummer wanted
Must be aware of current New York scene
and MC5 thru to the Stooges. New
energetic kids, 18–22, rather than
seasoned pros with fixed ideals, although
obviously ability essential. Immediate
rehearsals based in central London. Must

be dedicated and look great on the above
terms. **PHONE: 485 8113**

Elsewhere in the columns, the other ads employing display boxes were after a "funky drummer" or a "keyboards player for light rock band". Another said a group of "serious Christian musicians require[d a] dedicated like-minded bass player". None were as specific as the "Wild young drummer" ad. "I had done a couple of auditions and decided I wasn't going through that nonsense again," recalls Rat. "Most of the time they were second-rate bands, 50 people want to get it and it's for some shitty group that's got a gig in a pub. I thought, 'I'm just not going through that unless they want someone really special.' After the ad had been in week after week, I realised they did."

Rat rang the number. He was asked nothing about his experience, playing or the bands he had been in. All the questioner wanted to know was whether he was au fait with New York's current music scene. At the end of 1975, barely anyone British had heard the few new records from that city. It was certain all any respondents knew about the "current New York scene" was via articles in the music weeklies. The man picking up the phone, Bernard Rhodes, had one more source: his old friend Malcolm McLaren. But Rhodes' knowledge of New York was still second hand. He had never been there.

As very few British people knew the ins-and-outs of goings-on in Manhattan, Rhodes' inquisition was borderline irrational. A year earlier, Patti Smith had issued one single on an independent label. A small amount were pressed. In 1975, it was the same for Television and their one single 'Little Johnny Jewel'. The last *Melody Maker* of November had an article on Smith, centring on her recent signing to Arista Records. In the *New Musical Express* a week earlier, Charles Shaar Murray reviewed an import copy of her debut album, *Horses*, while Jonh Ingham covered it in the *Sounds* of the same date. A little earlier, in the November 8 *NME*, Murray focused on New York in the two-page piece *Are You Alive To The Sound of '75* and covered Johnny Thunders' post-New York Dolls band The Heartbreakers, Blondie, The Ramones, The Shirts and Tuff Darts. January 1976 saw the first issue of New

18

York's *Punk* magazine hit Manhattan's shops: the month *Horses* received a UK release. Beyond Patti Smith, everything about New York's new music scene was sketched out in print only, in shorthand for British readers. Not only was their knowledge inevitably at a remove, it was mediated through the views of the music papers and their writers. If they were interested, most British music fans could only read about New York and its hot new bands.

Rat's response was to ask Rhodes what he was supposed to know about New York. The ad wanted a "wild young drummer", so he said he was the best. He also pointed out that it having been taken out in multiple issues suggested it wasn't attracting much of a response. He was called in for an audition.

★ ★ ★

Christopher John Millar was born on July 30, 1955 in Kingston, on west London's fringes. Music came early after he saw the television variety programme *Sunday Night At The London Palladium*. The swing-jazz drummer Eric Delaney and his kit with two bass drums mesmerised the eight-year-old. Delaney placed lights inside his drums and sometimes leapt over them to attack a stage-front pair of timpani. This was percussion as showmanship. "It wasn't a conscious decision," says Rat of his response. "It was a chemical reaction from the sound of the drums."

At 10, his parents – his father John, who gave Rat his middle name, was an accountant – got him his first kit from Woolworths: a set with a 14-inch bass drum without a pedal, a snare with a paper skin, one cymbal and a pair of sticks. By then, Chris was aware music was changing. Although he never lost his affection for jazz, it was no longer the main attraction. The first records he bought were singles by the stomping drummer-fronted north London beat group The Dave Clark Five and America's Sandy Nelson, whose 'Let There Be Drums' was always a touchstone. Although keen on The Beatles and The Rolling Stones, he liked The Who most of all as destruction was part of their stage act. At 12, Chris was bought a full Autocrat brand kit.

School held little interest and he left Putney's Elliot Comprehensive at 14, immediately after sitting his CSE exams.[12] He also left home on leaving school. "My parents weren't that bothered," he says. "They knew where I was, I hadn't gone missing." Chris had moved into the family home of school friends Christian and Mark Sullivan. They formed a band called Tart. He was the drummer, Christian the bassist and Mark the guitarist. At this point, he had a proper five-drum Olympic kit. Influences came from the bands they saw live like Caravan and Family, and Eric Clapton, Curtis Mayfield and Frank Zappa as well as blues: the first band Chris saw live was John Mayall's, with Duster Bennett as the support act. The Sullivans' parents allowed them to rehearse in the front room but beyond two or three local gigs, the band didn't get any further. Chris, though, had already taken his interest in music further afield and, like Brian, went to 1970's Isle of Wight Festival and saw Jimi Hendrix.

Essentially, Chris was rootless. He attempted to live rough at Gatwick Airport, close to Brian's hometown Crawley. He slept in railway stations. For a week, he was in a Crawley band called Skint. There was a job in a factory in Redhill, feeding metal rods into a machine which cut them up. It lasted one morning. There were a couple of days training as an insurance salesman, which led to three fruitless days on the job. He was also answering musicians wanted ads in *Melody Maker*. In June 1974 he was up for an audition with a band called The Delinquents. Even though he liked their name, he didn't turn up as it was in a pub in south London's dodgy Old Kent Road.

He was marking time. Drifting. But Chris got a job at Croydon's Fairfield Halls in December 1974 as a porter, where his duties included helping to set up the stage. For the January 19, 1975 appearance there by the Mahavishnu Orchestra, the venue's manager thought an orchestra as such was booked rather than John McLaughlin's jazz-fusion-prog band, so Rat was told to set up 130 music stands. Amongst the other acts he saw were Steve Marriott's All Stars and pub-style pianist Mrs Mills, who was on a bill with comedy duo Mike & Bernie Winters and all-round entertainer Roy Castle. The rollicking, good-time Mills was a revelation and a surprising influence.

"Roy Castle was sickeningly nice," recalls Rat. "Every day he'd get in early to play table tennis with the crew and help move stuff. He really was Roy Castle, this wasn't something he just did. Mike & Bernie Winters were complete dickheads, they never spoke to anyone, were never nice to anyone. Mrs Mills would arrive and get out of the Merc about 20 minutes before she would go on. Every night, she'd have the whole audience on their feet. She had it. She rocked, she was great. I'd be waiting when she went off. 'How was that?' she'd ask. She'd just blown everyone's socks off. She put everything into it, an amazing teacher who showed me how to play for the audience."

At Rat's side, also taking in this incongruous inspiration, was another Fairfield Halls employee, Ray Burns. Rat recognised him as he had seen his band, Johnny Moped's Assault & Buggery, play in 1974. Once reacquainted, the two had hit it off over their shared love of music and mutual contempt for timekeeping. Ray's main task was to clean the venue's many toilets but, for Rat, his colleague's most useful talent was finding store rooms where the pair hid to avoid working. That wasn't a problem. But arriving drunk one morning was, and Chris was sacked after four weeks at Fairfield Halls. Chris and Ray kept in touch.

Following short stints with a couple of rehearsal-only bands, Chris fetched up in Caterham and joined Tor in August 1975. Their prime mover was guitarist Simon Fitzgerald, later known as Slimey Toad. The band was filled out by Glynn Evans (guitar), Phil Mitchell (bass) and Peter Starks (vocals).[13] He stayed at Fitzgerald's house, sometimes went back to the Sullivans' in Kingston and, if really pressed, occasionally returned to his parents.

"Tor really wanted to be Jeff Beck playing *Blow By Blow*," says Rat. "Simon was really good at pushing it forward, he made silk-screen stickers. It was suddenly 'this is how a band works', the machinery where everybody had a value. He got a local artist to paint a waterfall scene on his two 4 x 4 12-inch cabs. He wanted to do peace and love and intricate things, and of course I was really against that. I used to think Tor was such a shit name that when people asked me what I'd been in I reversed it and called it Rot." The band gigged around Caterham – including Caterham Mental Hospital – Coulsdon and Croydon. They booked church halls, but found this difficult in Croydon after breaking the rules by selling beer from a barrel they had brought in. Tor were banned from playing venues owned by the parish.

Rat got some work through Fitzgerald's father, who "ran a few theatres and used to give me work. I used to go to East Grinstead and make the scenery, the flats, the signs, helping out. In return, I'd get fed, sleep on their couch." With Fitzgerald on guitar, he was the pit drummer for a pantomime staging of *Puss In Boots* at the Thameside Theatre in Grays, Essex. They also accompanied a production of *Wind In The Willows*.

Although Tor were a going concern and the theatre work was promising, Rat remained on the lookout for other opportunities and still scanned the ads in *Melody Maker*. Changes in the air meant the Jeff Beck-influenced band looked less-and-less attractive. He favoured the more direct and edgier Dr. Feelgood, Heavy Metal Kids and Pink Fairies. "I had been to a couple of *Melody Maker* auditions and I didn't like it," he says. "One was [blues-rock band] Slack Alice and there were a hundred drummers there. The next one was this rock'n'roll band The Wild Angels and it was the same thing. And I thought 'fuck this'. As I was walking out the guy asked for my number. When I rang back a couple of days later the bloke said I was in the top three. I thought that out of all these people who auditioned, that was a result – it gave me a bit of self-confidence. But I swore I'd never go through that process again." However, he did do it again.

The December 6, 1975 "Wild young drummer" ad was, as Rat realised, the fourth for the same band which had been placed since the October 25 issue. After the phone conversation with Bernard Rhodes, he arrived at the Praed Street basement to find the three musicians in The London SS: two guitarists and a bass player. A drum kit was already set up. Recalling his first encounter with Brian James, Tony James and Mick Jones, Rat says: "Mick and Tony both had really long hair and leather trousers and looked like they should be in a band like Mott The Hoople. A couple of trendy west London punters really. Brian wasn't the same, he had short hair, winkle pickers. I remember Mick trying to break a chair in a fit of anger and he couldn't do it. I don't know what he was angry about, probably his trousers. They were so bored and arrogant they had a portable TV they watched while they auditioned. Once they put the guitars on, they treated you with total disdain. Brian was only like that at the beginning."

"When I found out Brian was in Bastard it made it all seem like a very small world. I never saw them, but they were quite legendary. They played in Sussex, in Crawley. They used to play Redhill, where I lived. I was waiting for them to come around." He also discovered Mick Jones had been in The Delinquents, the band whose audition he hadn't turned up for the previous year.

At the London SS audition, a war film was airing on the TV. Brian played along with a plane dive-bombing across the screen. Rat joined in. That was it, they locked in with each other. "Rat turning up was a breath of fresh air," says Brian. "A normal geezer hitting his drums. Chris, as he was then, walked in looking a total mess. He sat down on the kit and totally demolished the thing. Smashed the fuck out of it. I thought, 'Right, this is the guy for me.' Ginger hair, an old overcoat and Doc Martens. He was the only drummer to give it anything of anything. The other two thought he didn't look rock'n'roll enough. 'You're the one for me,' I thought. Forget this little Bernie bloke. Rat was accepted until we found someone better. For me, it was round the other way. Until me and Rat found someone else, do you want to stick with the posers?"

The London SS had also pondered whether a French drummer called Roland Hot – whose friend Paul Simonon accompanied him to the rehearsal space – should be behind their kit, but once Brian encountered Rat he knew this was his choice for the band. As Tony James and Mick Jones didn't like the way Rat looked, they wouldn't commit to him joining The London SS. Cheekily, they kept asking him back for further auditions. The evening after the first, Tony James and Mick Jones were back at the basement and a rat ran across the floor. Tony James dropped a brick on it, and killed it. The deceased rodent's resemblance to that day's auditionee was noted. Next time he arrived at the basement, Chris found he was called Rat. And, after he was seen scratching, it was discovered that he had scabies. For now, and for The London SS, he had what appeared to be a short-lived nickname.

Much of the rehearsal repertoire was based around cover versions, including the Sixties garage rock nuggets 'Barracuda' (originally by The Standells), 'Night Time' (The Strangeloves), and proto-punk material like The Flamin' Groovies' 'Slow Death', the MC5's arrangement of 'Ramblin' Rose' and The Modern Lovers, 'Roadrunner'. The Rolling Stones' 'You Can't Always Get What You Want' was also tackled. While Jones had penned around five songs, Brian and Tony had co-written a drug-referencing original titled 'Portobello Reds'.[14]

Over the early weeks of 1976, Brian and Rat continued rehearsing with The London SS but were increasingly frustrated. Despite Bernard Rhodes being installed as the manager, it still wasn't much more than a bedroom band. Tony James and Mick Jones had met the Sex Pistols at their Denmark Street rehearsal room and were well aware that a metaphorical starting gun had been fired, yet were not getting The London SS off and running. A decision about who was in their band was never reached as they were so picky about clothes, hair and style in general. Rhodes had brought McLaren down to see them but he wasn't keen and, as January ended, Rhodes capriciously ejected Tony James. The London SS were rapidly over.

Brian had left Bastard and Brussels for a band which had gone nowhere, but both he and Rat knew each was a perfect fit with the other. Rat, though, was temporarily out of the picture as he was in Cwmbran, Wales working as the stage manager for a production of *The Reluctant Debutante*. Brian kept up with what was developing and, as The London SS breathed its last, accompanied Rhodes and Jones to founder of The Alternative Miss World and artistic radical Andrew Logan's Butler's Wharf warehouse on February 14, where he saw the Sex Pistols for the first time. For Malcolm McLaren this was a vital evening. Logan's parties attracted an arty crowd drawn from the fashion, media and theatre worlds even though the forbiddingly unregenerated area near Tower Bridge was often deserted during evenings and weekends.

The nature of the audience or show didn't bother the Pistols' singer Johnny Rotten, who had taken LSD before what was their ninth live performance. McLaren made sure photographers got something newsworthy as he cajoled Jordan, who worked in his shop *SEX*, to stand beside Rotten, who dutifully lifted her top to uncover her breasts.

It was the band's music that fascinated Brian. "I thought the Pistols were very interesting," he recalls. "What blew me away was that they played Stooges songs. In Bastard we played 'No Fun' and 'I Wanna Be Your Dog', but no one else did The Stooges. The Pistols looked like mods, with John who was very funny. The best bits were the attitude, which reminded me of the best mod bands. You'd wait for the bits between the numbers to see what John would come out with next."

For Brian, what had to come next was hooking up again with Rat to form a band giving the up-and-coming Sex Pistols some competition. There were interruptions, but they would get there.

CHAPTER TWO

Captain And David

When Rat returned to London from Wales after working on *The Reluctant Debutante*, he found things had rapidly changed. The Sex Pistols had been featured in *NME*. Even though they were the support band to fast-rising second-wave pub rockers Eddie & The Hot Rods[15], they scored the live review with the headliners disregarded by its writer, the paper's assistant editor Neil Spencer. The show had taken place at Soho's Marquee Club two days before Brian saw them at Butler's Wharf. It was their first time at a mainstream venue.

The review, in the February 21 issue, was headlined *Don't look over your shoulder, but the Sex Pistols are coming*. The band were quoted saying, "...actually, we're not into music, we're into chaos". The evening had not gone well. Rotten threw a chair at the PA. Spencer also noted "two scantily clad pieces dancing up front".[16] The Sex Pistols and their followers had attracted attention. For now, though, this was small beer. That week's *NME* cover star was Patti Smith, again underlining the British fascination with New York. Otherwise, the future of Genesis without Peter Gabriel and the news that John Denver was playing London's Palladium were hot topics. Aside from the Sex Pistols' coverage there were odd indications of other fascinations: two pages covered Jamaica's Toots Hibbert and his Maytals.

From the sleeve of 'New Rose' to the stage. Rat Scabies' customised, Damned-branded bass drum – with hanging rat – at the Hope & Anchor. January 2, 1977. JOHN INGHAM

The Sex Pistols' debut 100 Club appearance, with roadie Chris Millar (the future Rat Scabies) looking on (standing stage side, just right of Johnny Rotten's knee). March 30, 1976. RAY STEVENSON/REX/SHUTTERSTOCK

Continents bridged when The Ramones play Camden's Dingwalls. From left to right: Chrissie Hynde, Tommy Ramone, Chris Millar, Ray Burns (the future Captain Sensible), Dee Dee Ramone, Brian Robertson (the future Brian James), Joey Ramone and Johnny Ramone. A day later, The Damned played live for the first time. July 5, 1976. DANNY FIELDS

Posing with then-manager Andrew Czezowski's car in a previously unseen shot taken the day of recording their first demo. Brian is wearing James Williamson's – of The Stooges – sleeveless leather jacket. David's lace-up boots were bought from Kensington Market. July 23, 1976. ANDREW CZEZOWSKI

Outside North London's Pathway Studio, after recording 'New Rose', with producer Nick Lowe (left). September 20, 1976.

The 100 Club punk festival. Moments earlier, a beer glass was thrown at The Damned by an audience member later identified as Sid Vicious. September 21, 1976.

In the entrance hall of Finchley's Manor Hill Upper School: London's first multi-band all-punk bill since the 100 Club festival. David wears a *Rocky Horror Show* T-shirt. Captain has false sideburns and hippy headband. November 19, 1976.
SHEILA ROCK/REX/SHUTTERSTOCK

Brian and Rat with manager and co-head of Stiff Records Jake Riviera. December 1976. ERICA ECHENBERG/REDFERNS

Facing off at the Hope & Anchor. January 2, 1977. JOHN INGHAM

Generation X's Billy Idol and The Damned's friend Marc Bolan with Brian at the Roxy Club, during the T. Rex *Dandy In The Underworld* album launch. March 9, 1977. ANDRE CSILLAG/REX/SHUTTERSTOCK

The Damned's in-store appearance at the Bomp Records shop. There and then, the Los Angeles punk scene coalesced. April 16, 1977. JENNY LENS

Rat sets his drums alight and
Captain plays the bass at
The Starwood, Los Angeles.
April 18, 1977. JENNY LENS

"Everyone was keeping a careful eye on everyone else," says Rat of the period. "Brian wanted to know what Mick Jones was up to, Tony James wanted to know what Mick and Brian were doing. Everyone wanted to know what the Pistols were up to. The Sex Pistols were very funny, they were a cartoon. It was like a gang of grubby oiks on the other side of the fence with runny noses saying 'nah nah nah nah'. It was witty, it was charming. That's how we were allowed to adopt that attitude."

Planning was rife. Bernard Rhodes teamed the post-London SS Mick Jones with Chrissie Hynde, a former *SEX* employee, *NME* contributor and the ex-girlfriend of the paper's hippest and highest profile writer Nick Kent, who had briefly left the typewriter to rehearse with a formative Sex Pistols in 1975. Hynde had just returned to London after a spell in Paris with the New York Dolls-style band The Frenchies. With Jones, Hynde was supposed to be the core of Rhodes' putative new band School Girl's Underwear.

Rhodes' inspiration Malcolm McLaren also wanted to add bands to his roster from the ready pool of aspirants. Amongst the places the members of these bands – the hypotheticals and the up-and-running Sex Pistols – met was the Henekey's pub along Portobello Road. After one drinking session, Rat and prospective London SS singer Paul Simonon bought matching, full-length leather coats. "When I got that, I thought this is my time," says Rat. "By this point I had cut my hair, gone spiky and got out of high-street clothes."

Rat encountered McLaren at Camden Town venue Dingwalls and berated him about the current state of music, the need for change and that bands were too old. McLaren took his number. Aware of Rat's history with The London SS, he knew that a drummer needing work was a useful acquaintance. Initially, Rat's theatre experience meant he was tapped as a roadie for the Sex Pistols. At one show, at west London's Nashville Rooms, Pistols guitarist Steve Jones spat at him. Rat spat back. The distinctive band-audience interchange of gobbing was unwittingly born. "It was a laugh between two mates," says Rat of his role in creating this particular punk legacy. "It was not, 'hey everybody, this is what you do'. No one wants to get the credit for starting gobbing. It's a bit like in class, being hauled up in front of the teacher."

McLaren then tried to form a band called The Masters Of The Backside. It was to feature two singers and Chrissie Hynde and Nick Kent on guitars. As he had in 1975, with the early Sex Pistols, McLaren wanted Kent in a band he was to manage. He also wanted to create a stable: a clutch of bands which, together, formed a movement. One with the Sex Pistols as its leader. Rat was asked to be the drummer, but a bass player was needed so he immediately thought of Ray Burns, his Fairfield Halls co-worker. Although primarily a guitarist, it helped that Burns lived near McLaren's long-time friend and collaborator, the visual artist Jamie Reid – Reid was tapped to drive the prospective bassist to rehearsals.

★ ★ ★

Raymond Ian Burns was born on April 24, 1954 and brought up in Balham, south London. His family moved further from the centre of London and settled in Croydon where he attended Thornton Heath's Whitehorse Manor Junior School. At his secondary school, South Norwood's Stanley Technical, he was nicknamed Burno. Once punished for bad behaviour by being caned, he poured paint stripper on the headmaster's car as payback. Although keen on trainspotting and a regular at the busy Clapham Junction station, his main diversion was music. A cheap Spanish acoustic was his first guitar. In 1970, unlike Brian and Rat, he did not make it to the Isle of Wight Festival despite trying. Then on holiday with his parents in Herne Bay, Ray attempted to hitchhike there but got no further than Canterbury. He re-joined the family holiday and contented himself with Black Witch Climax Blues Band, the band he had formed with his younger brother Phil at the family home at 34 Edith Road, around the corner from Selhurst Station. Initially, instruments were limited to the acoustic guitar, a budget organ and a suitcase which served as drums. The impromptu combo covered hits from 1969 and 1970, like Norman Greenbaum's 'Spirit In The Sky' and The Pipkins' 'Gimme Dat Ding'. Becoming Captain Sensible was a little while off.

Black Witch Climax Blues Band then changed their name to Genetic Breakdown.[17] Captain graduated to electric guitar in early 1972, while

Phil played bass and Dave Batchelor (the later Dave Berk), switched from luggage to drums. John Skinner, renamed Xerxes by Phil, arrived as singer-saxophonist. The line-up was fluid, and the band's music did not settle on an easily digestible style.

Captain says: "We thought we were avant-garde, which meant we just couldn't play. A lot of honking, Coltrane-type saxophone. I was really into The Pink Fairies then. They had attitude, bags of it. I remember going to festivals and The Pink Fairies would be outside, playing on a truck because they thought it was wrong when people started charging to get into festivals. A people's band, totally. I also loved that fuzz organ in Soft Machine. Hugh Hopper was fantastic, very anarchic." Captain's band believed glam-jazz was the next big thing so, for a while, he became Dwayne Zenith, though he was well-aware of what it took to be a musical contender after seeing Deep Purple and The Keef Hartley Band at Croydon's Greyhound pub.

In 1974, Xerxes found he had a co-singer when the eccentric vocalist Paul Halford (later Johnny Moped) joined. Genetic Breakdown were rebranded Johnny Moped & The 5 Arrogant Superstars in May, when the band played Thornton Heath's Brigstock Arms pub. Colin Mills (the future Fred Berk) joined on bass. There was no stability: they were Johnny Moped's Assault & Buggery in summer 1974 then, in early 1975, Captain had the short-lived band Elite with Xerxes and Dave Batchelor. After that, he joined a pub-style covers band called Oasis which played working men's clubs. Their repertoire included Dawn's 'Tie A Yellow Ribbon'.

Despite his increasing proficiency as a guitarist and having music as an outlet, Captain says he "was heading towards being kind of a dosser really, sleeping under the pier, that sort of thing. I quite liked that lifestyle, a bit of petty thieving, just blundering through. Then maybe you get busted, live in a beach hut for a few months after kicking in a door."

He also had jobs which didn't last long including, from October 1974, the spell at Croydon's Fairfield Halls, when he worked with Rat. Earlier, he had worked as an usher at the concert hall and saw T.Rex there in 1971. During the pair's time at the venue, Captain wired the tea room's radio up to his cassette player and played a recording of his band's half-hour annihilation of Chuck Berry's 'Johnny B Goode' – retuning didn't make the racket go away. After Captain's dismissal from the job in February 1975, he and Rat worked together for a building contractor. Their speciality was demolishing walls.

Other skills came into play once Rat suggested Captain become the bass player in McLaren's proposed new band. Dubbed The Masters Of The Backside, it was an unconventional outfit. Captain, Chrissie Hynde – who thought Mike Hunt's Honourable Discharge was a better name – and Rat were backing the two singers: one dressed in white with dyed blonde hair called Dave White[18] and the other in black called Dave Zero. It lasted for two days over rehearsals in the hall of Christ Church, Bell Street, just off Lisson Grove. Amongst the cover versions attempted was The Troggs' Sixties garage-rocker 'I Can't Control Myself'.

"Chrissie didn't want to sing," says Captain. "So there were the two Daves, who were a mirror image of each other. Me, Chrissie and Rat were just shrieking with laughter. It was pretty wild. McLaren came back on the second day, paid for the rehearsal, paid for our food – that's why we did it. He thought it had no commercial possibilities whatsoever."

Even so, it did mean Rat and the still long-haired Captain cemented their musical partnership and took the next step towards The Damned. Brian James had not been part of The Masters Of The Backside and, as Rat concedes, "Brian had got the hump with me because I was working with Chrissie."

Any irritation was set aside when Nick Kent asked Rat for help with a band he wanted to call The Subterraneans. McLaren had brought Kent along to the first day of The Masters Of The Backside rehearsal – he left when he heard McLaren's choice of name – and Rat had kept in contact. During April, the writer and perennially would-be rocker learned he needed to magic up a band for a gig in May, so Rat brought Brian and Ray on board.

For Captain, meeting Brian for the first time at his Kilburn flat was instructive. "Rat had told he met this bloke who had some really extreme ideas about what music should be in the future," he says. Brian played Captain the MC5, New York Dolls and Stooges, and effectively reprogrammed his way of looking at music. The symbolic haircut followed.

The planned gig was unusual. Cardiff's Chapter Arts Centre was hosting the month-long *Festival of Women in the Arts*. Kent was forming a band to back his French girlfriend Hermine Demoriane who was a tightrope walker, former circus performer, had been in the art-music-performance group The Moodies, was an *International Times* contributor and an associate of the pre-Throbbing Gristle, Coum Transmissions-era Genesis P-Orridge. Whatever happened in Wales, it could not be basic rock'n'roll.

In the run-up to the Cardiff appearance they rehearsed in Kent's flat, which overlooked Leicester Square. "Nick Kent used to get so fucked up," recalls Rat. "His girlfriend was always on his case about him doing smack. He asked us to go and get Collis Browne's cough medicine." The ingredients of J Collis Browne's Mixture included the opiate laudanum and tincture of cannabis. It was addictive. And legal.

"We'd get stoned on Collis Browne's and he'd send me and Rat to get it at his local chemist," adds Brian. "They wouldn't serve him anymore."

"I was kind of fresh-faced," says Captain. "Nick said, 'Go on, have some, that'll sort you right.'"

Brian enjoyed hanging out with Kent. "I was a fan of his writing," he recalls. "It was the only thing worth reading when I was in Brussels. He helped a lot by giving exposure to people like Iggy and Syd Barrett. Nick was really good company and would tell me his stories about this, that and the other. One day we were talking about The Stooges, and he said, 'You might like this – James Williamson's jacket. He gave it to me in exchange for a Quaalude. I gave it to Stiv Bators in the end."

The sleeveless leather jacket had been worn by Williamson at The Stooges' only London show at The King's Cross Cinema (later known as The Scala) in June 1972. Brian wore it for early Damned shows. With this, The Damned had a physical link to their influences: one as totemic as the guitar Sex Pistol Steve Jones played, which was previously owned by New York Doll Syl Sylvain. In 1976, the past was never far.

Two dates in Wales were scheduled. The billing for May 25 and 26 was "Hermione Demorian (sic) and the Subterraneans". According to the local paper ad, they were to play "Songs of Random Passion and the Dance of Romance". The evening was tagged as a night of Theatre/ Music. As well as Demoraine, Kent, Brian, Captain and Rat were joined by a friend of the French front-woman named Eyno. Kent's intention was to subvert the event by supplementing cover versions like Johnny Kidd & The Pirates' 'Please Don't Touch' with the feminist-baiting 'He Hit Me (And It Felt Like A Kiss)', an obscure Phil Spector song written for The Crystals in 1962 which appeared to defend domestic abuse. The Rolling Stones' chauvinistic 'Under My Thumb' was also played and continued the theme.

For the three future members of The Damned, the shows were important as – with Brian doubling on vocals and guitar – they were given a spot to perform as a trio and debuted 'Fish', 'I Fall' and 'New Rose' in front of an audience. Brian told a nonplussed Kent that "this is what rock music's gonna be like".

It wasn't much of an audience though. The most either of the two nights attracted was, according to Rat, "two men and a dog". Which was just as well, as a Collis Browne's-dosed Captain was sick behind an onstage amplifier. A day later, on May 27, Brian and Rat accompanied Kent to see The Rolling Stones at Earls Court, on the last of their six-night run of shows there. While Princess Margaret visited the band backstage, other future punk luminaries who turned up included those who later took the names Sid Vicious, Siouxsie and Steve Severin.

Kent's Welsh adventure was a temporary distraction. Brian and Rat were still intent on forming their own band and, with Captain as their bass player, were three-quarters there. At every show they went to, the duo looked for potential candidates. The search had already come good almost two months before playing Cardiff.

★ ★ ★

On Saturday April 3, 1976, pub rock-come-roots outfit The 101ers were co-billed with the Sex Pistols at The Nashville Rooms, a west London pub with a large stage in its back room. Larger than most pub

venues, it was also better appointed: there were tables for the audience
to sit at, and the stage had a curtain. For Joe Strummer, The 101ers'
frontman, it was decisive evening. "They were light years different from
us," he said of the Sex Pistols. "It took my head off. I understood this
was serious stuff." Joe's time with his own band was now limited. Off
the stage, Brian and Rat were sniffing out the future which Strummer
had instantly realised was coming. The make-up of the audience was
as noteworthy as the band playing. A potential singer was amongst the
ever-growing Sex Pistols audience. This show was pivotal – it directly
resulted in the forming of both The Clash and The Damned.

The first person Brian and Rat approached at The Nashville was a
tall Pistols follower. "Sid walked into The Nashville and he looked
fantastic," says Rat of John Beverley, the future Sid Vicious. "He had
this lurex drape jacket on and spiky hair, he really stood out. Brian said,
'He looks like a singer, go up and talk to him.' I knew Sid through John
[Rotten] anyway."

Then, they saw another potential singer. Rat also knew this likely
candidate, as he had been Dave Zero – the all-in-black singer of the
short-lived Masters Of The Backside. "Brian said, 'He looks like a
singer as well.' He looked like one of the New York Dolls, a Thunders
haircut, backcombed and sticky-uppy." Each was buttonholed and
asked to audition for the band at the church hall where The Masters Of
The Backside had rehearsed.

"I thought if I could be in a band that had the attitude of the New
York Dolls and a guitarist that had his own sound, it would be great,"
says David of the audition. "I was supposed to get there at 11 in the
morning or 12. I knew that one other guy was coming, so I turned up
half an hour early to see him. But no one else turned up. We started
going through Iggy numbers. Brian had lyrics written out, he barked
them in my ear. He never said what he wanted, but I got the gist of it.
They said, 'That's it, you've got the job.'"

David may have been told the job was his, but the new band was a
little way from leaving the starting blocks. All was put on hold until
the other three-quarters of the future Damned completed their stint
as Nick Kent's Subterraneans. Once that was over, the singer was

welcomed back into the fold. Almost two months had passed since the audition.

On joining for real, David determined a personal rebranding was necessary. "Not as a persona so much," he says about what he was creating. "I just thought I was embarking on this journey. It wasn't a case of this is me, the real me, there – it was a case of signifying this was something. I felt like something was building right from the early New York Dolls days. Actors, designers, there was a nucleus of people that wanted to do something." He was now David Vanian.

"I remember Dave saying, 'I'll be Dave Vanian as in Transyl…,'" remembers Rat. "One of the moments that made you love him."

★ ★ ★

David Lett was born in Newcastle on October 12, 1956. He grew up north of London in Hemel Hempstead and remained living there for months after The Damned had formed. From the beginning, and when he needed it, there was a distance between him and what was happening in London.

Hemel Hempstead was, like the Crawley where Brian grew up, a New Town. The plan to build was announced in 1946 and work began on the new town centre in 1952. The development subsumed what had been a small medieval town. "It went up almost overnight," explains David. "It was a terrible place to live because when a town hasn't grown naturally it has no community, just displaced people that don't like each other. It had a bad atmosphere, quite a violent atmosphere. And of course, I was a bit odd-looking compared to the norm so it wasn't a nice place for me to be at. I was told at one point, a meeting with the school careers officer, the only thing you're fit for is working in a factory. I said I wanted to be an artist. At my school, all they cared about was football."

As well as visual art, David says his interests were fostered by "too much television, watching old movies. I was interested in Dracula and people draw the conclusion it was that [which impacted on his style]. But that wasn't the main thing, I loved Thirties movies: black eyes, white faces, so they could be seen on the screen. It was a more elegant time. I was also interested in Gene Vincent, rock'n'roll, all-black leather and black hair." His father had been in Berlin after World War II and had amassed a collection of *Weimar*-era 78s which he also loved. The music gushing from the transistor radio he had as a kid had a big impact too, especially American DJ Wolfman Jack's show on AFN – the American Forces Network Europe, which was aimed at service men and women on European postings. David grew to love girl-group The Shangri-Las and Sixties garage and psychedelic bands like The Seeds, Shadows Of Knight and The Strawberry Alarm Clock.

He had an apprenticeship with a company which made corporate films – one job was drawing images of a pipeline for an animation demonstrating how oil was pumped. But the small amount he was paid was swallowed up by the costs of travel. He marked time with a job as a warehouseman in a factory. London was the draw though, and he visited the Kensington boutique Biba. On November 26, 1973, in a midnight-blue satin jacket, he saw the New York Dolls play the shop's in-house venue The Rainbow Room – less than two weeks before Brian encountered them in Brussels. The search for anyone stylistically like-minded took him to Malcolm McLaren's King's Road shop, then trading under the name *Too Fast To Live, Too Young To Die*.

Of his look around this time, David says, "I had black hair, it was teased up a bit. Wearing black was unusual back then. You couldn't walk down the street without someone saying 'Ooh, are you going to a funeral?' I was slim, so also got the 'are you a boy or a girl' routine."

There was a period on the dole and the walk to signing-on every two weeks took him past Hemel Hempstead's Heath Lane Cemetery, where he saw someone digging. "I thought that wouldn't be a bad job," recalls David of seeing the gravedigger. "It's a job where you don't need to use your brain, you just get on with the work, the hours aren't going to be long." He went to the lodge by the gate and asked if there were any openings. After being told no – being thin, he did not look a likely candidate – he suggested a week-long try-out with no pay. He got the job and was soon appointed to a management role with responsibility for two cemeteries.

David hadn't abandoned his ambitions to work in art and when he found grave-digging was about results rather than the time taken, he hit on a strategy that would bring opportunities to go to London with his portfolio. "If there were two graves to dig, it was supposed to take all day," he explains. "But I'd be finished just after lunchtime. Then I'd go down to London. I knew if you were going to do anything, you needed to come to London. "

He found competition meant he wasn't going to get commissions for book jackets and record sleeves, and he began losing heart. But visiting London and McLaren's shop in particular brought him into a world which proved sympathetic to his outlook. "The shop was the hub," he recalls. "It was a place where like-minded people could go. Jordan, Adam Ant was later there sweeping up things. There was Helen Wellington-Lloyd, she was a very gifted portrait artist. She was a lovely person, when I used to come to London, they [McLaren and Wellington-Lloyd] had a spare room and I would use it. I got very close with Jordan for a while. When they knocked off you might end up at a gay club, where you didn't get beaten up. Ironically, it was safer."

Though he hadn't thought of being in a band, David had sung along with his girlfriend's Roxy Music records. So when McLaren told him he was putting one together David "lied. I said I'd been in a local band no one had heard of, but I'd never sung on stage or been in front of anyone." No matter. Although The Masters Of The Backside went nowhere and his Dave Zero guise was discarded, David was now recognised as a potential member of any of the bands springing up as a competitor to – or a fellow scene-maker with – the Sex Pistols. For David, the Pistols were "a raucous, out-of-tune noise. Rotten was insulting everyone. It seemed like a joke – like comedy is now, very in your face and confrontational."

And by being at The Nashville on April 3 to see them, he took the first step into a future which defined the rest of his life.

★ ★ ★

That future took a little while to come. Brian, Captain and Rat were distracted by their activities with Nick Kent. As May ended, with that out of the way, the new band began working back at Christ Church's hall. Brian chose The Damned as the band's name. Despite telling *Melody Maker* in April 1977 that he "has no idea what made him think of it" there were two sources: the 1969 Luchino Visconti film of the same title, which told the story of a wealthy German family's osmosis by and capitulation to the Nazi regime in the run–up to World War II; and the 1960 film *Village Of The Damned*, an adaptation of the John Wyndham science fiction novel *The Midwich Cuckoos*. This was about a group of telepathically linked children born to humans as a result of an alien intervention. The only way to deal with these strange offspring was to destroy them.

Brian also obliterated part of his own past by becoming Brian James rather than Brian Robertson. "I remember being with Brian in the flat in Kilburn," says Rat. "He was saying that there's been a lot of good James'es: Iggy, Williamson, Hendrix."

"I didn't want to be Brian Robertson when people started asking me what my name was," explains Brian about the name change. "I didn't want to be confused with the guitar player [of the same name] in Thin Lizzy. Before The Damned, no one was sufficiently interested in asking me. The rest had been an apprenticeship."

Each member of the band had links with Malcolm McLaren – either directly or through Bernard Rhodes – and were known to anyone in and around the Sex Pistols camp. Rat had helped decorate *ACME Attractions*, located in the King's Road indoor market Antiquarius. It had opened in 1974 was directly inspired by McLaren's *Too Fast To Live, Too Young To Die* and dealt in vintage clothing and household goods. It later moved into a shop along the King's Road, upon which it was rebranded *Boy*. Its proprietor, John Krivine, was installed as The Damned's manager. Although the link–up helped foster the idea of a new scene, the bosses of two clothes shops along the same street each having a band of their own on their books ensured competition was inescapable. On a practical level, Krivine offered his Bermondsey warehouse to The Damned as a rehearsal space, which they used as well as the hall at Christ Church.

Krivine did not last long. "We didn't like what John Krivine was doing," says Rat. "He was pulling a Malcolm stroke and wanted us to wear his clothes." The Damned's look was always do-it-yourself. David was still working for the cemetery and arrived at rehearsals in the donkey jacket which was part of his work wear.

A second manager was swiftly acquired. The Damned were still plugged into a growing network which focused on McLaren. Andrew Czezowski – who did the books for both Krivine's *ACME Attractions* and McLaren's *SEX* – took the job on.

By this point, in June 1976, Joe Strummer had split The 101ers. They played a final show on June 5 and, under the guidance of Bernard Rhodes, Strummer began rehearsing with Brian's former London SS bandmate Mick Jones, Paul Simonon, guitarist Keith Levene and (as it had been with The London SS) the first of a varying cast of drummers. After considering The Heartdrops, they chose The Clash as their name. Strummer and co now had the band which immediately became The Damned's rivals in the race to be the prime post-Sex Pistols contender. In Manchester, Buzzcocks organised a Sex Pistols show on June 4 but weren't stage ready in time themselves[19], so didn't play the bill. London was setting the pace.

In this hectic period, who might succeed the Sex Pistols as the next band identified as fundamental to the burgeoning scene was uncertain. But The Damned were front runners despite neither being the traditional frontman-plus-backing-band group – like the Sex Pistols – or a seamless unit. As four individuals, they had to be a band which bonded through a shared outlook – whether imposed or self-defined.

The Damned bonded because of two things: a recognition that musical change was needed and that Brian had the right songs, at least one of which had roots from a couple of years earlier. "The origins of 'Fan Club' come from my days with Bastard," says Brian "The basic riff of it.[20] It was ideas that had been buzzing around, and I found the right guys to play them. All of sudden they made sense where they didn't before." While in The London SS, he had played 'Portobello Reds'. It became 'Fish' which, like 'I Fall' and 'New Rose', had been performed in Cardiff with The Subterraneans.

There was common musical ground, although limited. Brian, Captain and Rat actively liked The Pink Fairies. Brian and David liked the New

York Dolls. Though Brian liked the MC5 and Stooges, much of Rat and Captain's exposure to both bands came via the guitarist after they had met him. David and Brian shared a liking for American Sixties garage bands. Captain loved Soft Machine. Without Brian imposing his vision, The Damned would not have had a unified voice. "When it started, it was Brian's band," says David. "You're playing his songs and that was great. I thought of him in a weird way as a jazz musician – he'd play and that was it, captured."

Their paths to The Damned were as different as their individual personalities and tastes. Brian had been playing in bands since the late Sixties, always searching for the right vehicle. For Rat, it was about playing and finding a band to accommodate his full-on playing style. David says, "Rat was like the Artful Dodger, a great drummer. His personality was mischievous and fun. The first time I met Captain [at The Masters Of The Backside rehearsal], he looked like Marc Bolan. He had a crushed velvet top with big sleeves, stars on cheeks, all this corkscrew hair. You could hardly see his eyes." Yet he was a skilled guitarist with a penchant for jazz-rock who had fallen into becoming a bass player. Equally, David had fallen into his role as frontman and singer but was fascinated with visual art and, although his mature baritone took some time to develop, already had a distinct, declamatory intonation. And their interest in music meant their figurative Venn diagrams had already intersected further. Brian and Rat had been at the Isle of White Festival. Captain had tried to get there. Brian and David had separately encountered the New York Dolls within two weeks of each other. The various strands guided the four members of The Damned to Bernard Rhodes, Malcolm McLaren and the members of London's first punk bands.

Each grew up beyond or on the edge of London, Brian and David in the New Towns of Crawley and Hemel Hempstead, Captain and Rat in suburban Croydon and Crawley. Despite their familiarity with Ladbroke Grove, the King's Road and central London's clubs, gigging circuit, movers and shakers, they were outsiders.

All four finally united as The Damned. This was not a band with members wearing complementary or matching outfits.

All of which made it inevitable they stood apart from any movement taking off in the Sex Pistols' wake – whether or not they were labelled as part of it.

CHAPTER THREE

The Excluded Gang

Competition between the new bands forming in the Sex Pistols' wake was inevitable. Unity was shaky and factionalism was unavoidable. Even so, the first London appearance of The Ramones brought everyone together. The New Yorkers were booked to support The Flamin' Groovies at Camden's Roundhouse on Sunday July 4 and nearby Dingwalls the following day. The Stranglers footed the bill at both dates. Rat had tried to get The Damned booked for The Roundhouse, but The Stranglers had the power of the Albion agency – who booked many of the pubs on the London gigging circuit – behind them, so his band were not going make their live debut at such a high-profile show.

Everyone, no matter the scheming, gathered on the Monday to see The Ramones. The Sex Pistols, The Clash and The Damned were at Dingwalls. Mark Perry, shortly to generate the first issue of his fanzine *Sniffin' Glue*, was at both shows – his first exposure to the evolving new scene. *Melody Maker*'s Caroline Coon was in attendance at Dingwalls, as were Chrissie Hynde and scene regular Viv Albertine. Tensions were evident though. Outside Dingwalls, The Clash's Paul Simonon spat on the ground. The Stranglers' Jean-Jacques Burnel took this as a challenge so squared up to take on the fellow bassist. In the ensuing scuffle, Stranglers follower Dagenham Dave punched Johnny Rotten. For inter-band relations, the evening at Dingwalls set the tone for what The Damned were stepping into.

A day earlier, The Clash had played their debut live show. Although supporting the Sex Pistols, it was out of plain view at Sheffield's Black Swan pub. They were not seen again until over a month later, on Friday August 13, when they played an invitation-only showcase at their Camden rehearsal room. A real audience – the ticket-buying public – first had a chance to see them on August 29 at an all-night bill with Buzzcocks and the Sex Pistols at Islington's Screen on the Green cinema. The Damned were not – and never were – so elitist or so shy. And, as Rat says, "We were already part of that excluded gang."

★ ★ ★

The day after the Dingwalls gathering, The Damned hit the stage for the first time at the 100 Club, on before the Sex Pistols – just as The Clash had been billed in Sheffield two days earlier.

Tuesday July 6, 1976 was a busy day on the London gigging calendar. Leonard Cohen was headlining the New Victoria Theatre, maverick singer-songwriter Michael Chapman was at Dingwalls and the pub circuit hosted Pacific Eardrum (at Hammersmith's Red Cow), Reggie's Rockers (The Nashville) and Strutters (Stoke Newington's The Rochester). All these were advertised, or at least listed, in the weekly guides to what was on in London. The old guard held sway. Only *Melody Maker*'s "Club Calendar" announced The Damned were on the Sex Pistols bill. This limited their audience to friends and associates, those there to see the headliners and any *MM* readers curious about the band's name. Those who were there however, witnessed London's first all-punk night out. Chrissie Hynde was at the 100 Club debut, but otherwise the audience was sparse.

As they walked on, the disembodied voice of 100 Club manager Ron Watts announced them over the PA. "Alright you cocksuckers, you'd better get your ears pinned back if you don't want to have them ripped apart because this is the start, here comes the big one, here are The Damned." Without missing a beat, as his final word died, they attacked

'1 Of The 2'. There was zero hesitancy: everything recognisably The Damned was already in place. Although 'New Rose' didn't yet have its tribal drum opening, 'See Her Tonite' was scrappy and 'So Messed Up' was subsequently reconfigured to lose its more overt Stooges references, the songs were fully formed and delivered with a preternatural assurance. Forward motion – action, attack – characterised this new band. Even the restrained 'Fan Club' and 'Feel The Pain' had the headlong drive of the rush towards a finishing line; hell-for-leather constructions grounded by bass guitar and vocals. Also extraordinary was the mesh between the guitar and drums – locked together most tightly in the middle of 'Fan Club'.[21]

McLaren got them on the bill but didn't give The Damned a break. Accounts of the actual sum vary, but it is certain he charged them more for using the PA the Pistols had hired than they were paid for the gig. The Damned did not pay up, creating a fissure with the McLaren camp. They were excluded from the scene McLaren was attempting to create. After their set, Rat introduced himself to Jonh Ingham as Kris Millar, "with a k" – the spelling was inspired by The Dudley Moore trio's drummer, Chris Karan. Connecting with Ingham was strategically key: he wrote for *Sounds*, was their man on the case with punk and, in April, had written the first Sex Pistols feature.

A member of their live debut's scant audience secured them their second gig. Shanne Bradley – later in The Nipple Erectors[22] with fellow early punk show regular Shane MacGowan – was so taken with The Damned she contacted Andrew Czezowski the next day to ask if they would play St Albans School of Art, which she attended. In March, she had organised a Sex Pistols show there.

"There was no stage," recalls Captain of the July 8 St Albans show. "It was a kind of refectory. There was a gap between us and the audience. I remember going and taking kicks at them." Although he was still Ray Burns and nicknamed "Eats", as poverty meant he was hungry and was often on the look-out something to eat, this was the first time the persona later branded Captain Sensible emerged.

"The social secretary raised his beer, trying to jolly it along," recalls David. "Captain took his beer, poured it over himself, launched himself at this guy and kicked him in the balls. That was the point at which the lunatic Captain Sensible was born."

The next show, at The Nashville on July 15, was as memorable. It was also the first time Chris Millar played as Rat Scabies. "The name had been around a while," he recalls. "I thought I can go back to *Puss In Boots* and being Chris Millar when punk is over." Booked to support blues-rock band S.A.L.T., The Damned's final song was marked by the venue's stage curtain being drawn across them. Rat's bass drum then arced through the air, past the curtain. Of the experience, *Sounds'* Jonh Ingham declared in their first review that "Scabies and James insisted on behaving like twin H-bombs." His conclusion: "the resulting melange sounded positively avant-garde". Roger Armstrong and Ted Carroll of the independent label Chiswick Records were there and, as Shanne Bradley had been, were instantly captivated. They set out to snare The Damned for their label.

Although Chiswick was an outgrowth of their mainstay – selling second-hand records to collectors – Armstrong and Carroll had their ears to the ground. Their first release was a powerful November 1975 EP by the rough-edged R&B outfit The Count Bishops. The keen grassroots awareness meant they knew bands were springing up which weren't, like The Count Bishops, pub rockers. They knew McLaren as he bought vintage records for his shop's jukebox from their own retail outlet, *Rock On* which, at this point, operated from a shop in Camden and a stall in Soho Market. Carroll's "Rock On Disco" had been billed at Pistols shows. Armstrong first saw the Sex Pistols on December 5, 1975 at Chelsea School Of Art. They had signed Joe Strummer's 101ers but there was no band to promote the 'Keys To Your Heart' single when it was issued in the final week of June, as The Clash were already taking shape. Chiswick became the first British label to try and get to grips with what would be called punk rock.

Armstrong put up the cash to record The Damned and three tracks were taped on July 23.[23] Instead of a traditional studio, the band ended up at 47a Warrington Crescent, a west London basement flat and old London SS hangout rented by future Boys member Matt Dangerfield, who had an 8-track tape recorder there. This was a makeshift set-up.

The Damned recorded the breakneck 'I Fall' and 'See Her Tonite', and the creepy-crawling, desolate 'Feel The Pain'.

The results were rough and differentiated the sound which set The Damned apart from the competitors which emerged as the year unfolded. The tight riffing of The Stooges was evident, as was the attack of the MC5. David's voice had a mid-Atlantic resonance. The chord sequence of 'See Her Tonite' nodded to that of the New York Dolls' 'Jet Boy' yet stripped-out their R'n'B and Rolling Stones roots. The Ladbroke Grove spikiness of The Pink Fairies was in the mix too. Overall though, it was evidence for a band whose prime concerns were extremes: Brian and Rat took off while Captain's bass held it all down and David's vocal cemented it as a whole. Take away any one element, and it would have fallen apart. As well as seeing them, Brian had – courtesy of Nick Kent – heard the first Ramones album, issued in America in late April. The velocity of its songs unquestionably impacted on The Damned yet their demo did not have the New Yorkers' linear thrust. The Ramones were the musical equivalent of a sprint on a level surface. The Damned added unevenly spaced hurdles of different heights to the equation.

Chiswick had paid for the session but Andrew Czezowski sent cassettes of the three tracks to Virgin Records and The Ramones' UK label Phonogram the day after they were recorded.[24] He heard nothing back from Virgin but in a speedy response dated July 27 Phonogram's Pop Product Manager Lisa Denton wrote to him saying she had "listened to it together with our A&R people but feel it would really be unfair to do anything further due to the fact that we already have The Ramones". The Damned did not become the first British punk band to sign to a major label. One band along these lines was enough for Phonogram.

Following Ingham's review and the still-live interest from Chiswick, The Damned met *Sniffin' Glue*'s Mark Perry for their first interview[25], also the fanzine's first interview. The Q&A covered influences and inspirations – The Stooges and The New York Dolls; Dave Clark and Marc Bolan – their current and past jobs – David said he was a gravedigger and Rat said he used to clean toilets. As for a mission statement, David said, "We're here to have a bit of fun."

Also raised was the question of what The Damned were and what sort of music they played. For the first three issues, *Sniffin' Glue*'s subtitle was *And Other Rock 'n' Roll Habits For Punks*. Were The Damned punk?

Rat said he didn't like the definition and, after David pointed out the word meant worthless, there was an agreement that although it could be seen why "punk" was being bandied they didn't see how it applied to the group. As for handy labels, David suggested "music for now", Brian "power music" and Rat "get up off your arse music". None stuck. "Punk" was the word in the air.

"The word punk didn't mean a thing to me," says Rat. "It was defamatory – worthless, no value – an insult. As soon as somebody said it – I remember it was Caroline Coon – it became 'this is punk rock'. It's like saying I'm into shit rock. It's pretty funny now, but I didn't see the irony then. But all it needed was some confirmation. As soon as that happened it's like a domino effect."

★ ★ ★

If The Damned, the Sex Pistols and The Clash were going to be promoted as leading a movement, it needed a name. There was only one. January 1976 had seen the first issue of *Punk* magazine hitting New York's shops. Lou Reed was featured, as were ex-New York Doll David Johansen and The Ramones. Given the British fascination with New York, punk rock looked a runner as the tag for the UK scene, but the influential London-based music press hadn't settled on a catch-all label for the new home-grown bands.

New York though was the acknowledged home of the contemporary take on punk rock – hitherto a term for Sixties garage and psychedelic bands as curated on journalist and Patti Smith guitarist Lenny Kaye's 1972 double album compilation *Nuggets* or the in-your-face gutter rock celebrated by *Creem* magazine, which had a "Punk Of The Year" category in its annual best-of poll.

In parallel, Britain's music business was willing itself into creating a punk rock. In late July 1974 *NME* ran an overview on a label trend for signing punk rock bands. "The punks are snotty and brash and frequently obnoxious…(and) come across like buccaneers of a New Town shopping precinct," wrote Chris Salewicz. He pointed to Be-Bop Deluxe, Dr. Feelgood, The Heavy Metal Kids, Nutz, the Sensational Alex Harvey Band and The Winkies, America's Blue Oyster Cult and New York Dolls as well as Japan's Sadistic Mika Band as representatives of this new wave.

Sounds' Jonh Ingham was one of the three most supportive London-based writers of what was coming, but he didn't initially latch on to the word "punk". In April 1976, he wrote the first Sex Pistols feature which, while a manifesto with Johnny Rotten quoted as saying he hated pub bands, long hair and what hippies stand for, did not use "punk".

Melody Maker's Caroline Coon was another of the three main cheerleaders. A fixture on the London's underground scene since the late Sixties, she was the founder of the drug-help charity Release and had latterly begun writing for *Melody Maker*. In the July 3 issue she co-opted Johnny Rotten into her singles review column as a commentator where he noted he had been into Captain Beefheart and that "I love The Doors, they're great." Again, no mention or sign of a new "punk" in the mainstream music press. Conspicuously, at this point, Britain had no underground press tracking the Sex Pistols. Propagation of what was dubbed punk came from a hungry overground media.[26]

London's attempts to become a trans-Atlantic counterpart to New York were most keenly tracked in *Sounds*. On July 17, Giovanni Dadomo[27] – the third propagator – devoted four pages to an *A to Z of Punk*. He noted that "a number of young London bands feature punk material in their acts". The description was scrupulous: these were not punk rock bands, they *played* punk material. His rundown mostly stuck with the *Nuggets* interpretation and was mainly dedicated to the Sixties and defunct Seventies outfits like The Stooges. The only active bands mentioned were New York's Dictators and the perennial Flamin' Groovies. A fortnight later, he reviewed the week's new singles under the headline *Punks rool!* and chose The Ramones, San Francisco's Groovies, Essex pub rockers Eddie & The Hot Rods (their cover-versions EP *Live At The Marquee* which, in August, caused *NME*'s Bob Edmands to declare "Britain is the home of punk rock") and London's

Sixties-influenced Gorillas (their debut single for The Damned-fancying Chiswick) as representatives of punk. The equal US-UK split and The Ramones aside, the remaining trio – whatever their merits – were rooted in the past and, to varying degrees, added their own twists to the Sixties. Only The Ramones had an original approach. This particular punk rock was from the past, either to be revived or used as an inspiration. In July, punk rock was not about the now.

On October 9, *Sounds* had changed tack and under the headline *Welcome to the (?) Rock Special*, Ingham said, "Punk rock as a genre in the mid-60s… has no correlation with the viciously original music of the Sex Pistols or The Clash or The Damned." On the cover, the feature was trailed as *Punks: Six-page Blitz*. The fresh bands cropping up on the London scene were listed: the Sex Pistols, The Damned (David's age was given as 17[28]), The Clash, Subway Sect, Eater and The Vibrators. The already established Eddie & The Hot Rods were shoehorned in. Manchester got a look in too with Buzzcocks. In October 1976, punk rock had become the now rather than the past.

During the ten weeks between these two different views of punk, categorisation arrived. In her *Melody Maker* singles column of July 24, Caroline Coon had mentioned the Sex Pistols, The Clash and The Damned without mentioning punk. On August 7, she wrote of "the British punk scene [that it] was well under way". For her, "British Punk Rock" was a "gloriously uninhibited melee". The Damned, she said, had declared "we are miles better than the Sex Pistols". There it was: British punk rock was codified between July 24 and August 7, 1976.[29]

Punk rock it was then for the new British bands, and punk rock was what The Damned played. Never mind that it was a recycled label and that the British music press had been willing it to be used since 1974. Malcolm McLaren had favoured the equally second-hand "new wave".

★ ★ ★

As the name game played out, The Damned ploughed on regardless and prepared to play their fifth live show at what was billed as *The 1st European Punk Rock Festival*, to be held on August 21 in Mont-de-Marsan, a French town 120km north of the border with Spain which had a 10,000-seat bull ring. Rat had turned 21 three weeks earlier. Since 1989, the arena and the town's theatres have accommodated an annual, week-long fiesta of flamenco, which attracts huge crowds, swamping the population of around 30,000. The yearly festival of bull fighting then follows. In 1976, it hosted Europe's first punk festival.

In France, and in Paris in particular, punk was not seen as a new movement but instead part of an uninterrupted lineage encompassing *Nuggets*, Lou Reed, The Stooges, The Flamin' Groovies and the New York Dolls – the archetypical, no-nonsense bands and music which informed much of the mind-set of the new British bands. A key figure in this scene was Marc Zermati, who ran the Les Halles shop *Open Market*. He first met Malcolm McLaren in 1973 when the Dolls played Paris and had been at the Sex Pistols' Butler's Wharf show in February.

Zermati was behind the festival and planned to bring Richard Hell over from New York as a headliner. Hell had been in Television, recently left The Heartbreakers (Jerry Nolan and Johnny Thunders' post-New York Dolls band) and was the spikey-haired model for McLaren's vision for the look of the band he managed.[30] His song 'Blank Generation', though unreleased, was already known on both sides of the Atlantic through cassette tapes of a demo recording. Zermati advertised Hell as being part of a one-off band called Mirrors, with ex-Brinsley Schwarz member Nick Lowe and former Ducks Deluxe drummer Tim Roper.

Tickets were sold on the basis of Mirrors appearing, but they did not. Nor did the Sex Pistols, originally Zermati's next choice. They were canned by Zermati himself after he found out their followers Sid Vicious and John Wardle (the later Jah Wobble) had assaulted and injured Nick Kent at the 100 Club on June 15. The Pistols were supposed to come as a package with The Clash but the latter pulled out, ostensibly to protest Zermati's decision but actually as they were not ready to play live again as their unsatisfactory stage debut exposed a need to take stock. The Damned became the default representatives of British music's new generation. Their decision to play further widened the fault-line between themselves and the Sex Pistols/Clash camps.

Despite being promoted as a punk rock festival, what ended up playing – The Damned excepted – was as much 1975 as it was 1976. Apart from The Damned and the Sixties/mod-inclined Gorillas, everyone who met at Victoria coach station at 10 a.m. on Thursday August 19 had feet firmly planted in the immediate past.

The fellow travellers included Nick Lowe, who had been in pub rock stalwarts Brinsley Schwarz. Sean Tyla was a former member of Ducks Deluxe, Brinsley Schwarz's competitors as pub rock's kingpins. Also on the coach were the soon-to-be defunct Pink Fairies and jazzy pub rockers Roogalator. Coon and Ingham made up the press contingent. Chiswick Records' Armstrong and Carroll drove down to see their label's bands, The Count Bishops and The Gorillas. Eddie & The Hot Rods were also playing, but made their own way to the festival. The French link with London was through Bizarre Records' Larry DeBay. In the end, disorganisation meant The Pink Fairies and Roogalator did not play, though Switzerland's Railroad, France's Shakin' Street and Bijou did.

Lowe had issued his first solo single 'So It Goes' on Dave Robinson and Jake Riviera's new independent label Stiff Records on August 14. Robinson managed Lowe (as well as Ian Dury and Graham Parker) and wanted the flexibility which came with independence. Riviera had, most recently, been Dr. Feelgood's tour manager. Stiff's next three releases were 45s by bands booked for Mont-de-Marsan: The Pink Fairies, Roogalator and The Tyla Gang. Riviera was also along for the ride to France.

En route, at an overnight stop-off in Tours, while everyone else slept, The Damned ran amok, ringing doorbells and then tearing off. At 3 a.m., back at the hotel, via the window of his third-floor room Captain tried to get into manager Andrew Czezowksi's room. A drainpipe Rat had grabbed onto detached itself from the wall and was hurled onto the roof of the adjacent building, where it smashed roof slates.

On the second day of the trip south, Rat tormented the more venerable musicians by goading them as "hippies" then "dirty hippies". "Girls" was another of his insults. Although frozen out by most of those at the front of the coach, Nick Lowe continued talking to The Damned.

Brian and David kept out of it. Although initially silent, Captain joined in the tirade which culminated in Rat tearing Lowe's Eddie Cochran T-shirt off him and reducing it to shreds.

"Mont-de-Marsan was a nightmare to get to," says Rat of the two-day journey. "Sean Tyla looked a bit angry. I remember being on this bus forever with nothing to do except wind up Nick Lowe. I tore Nick Lowe's Eddie Cochran shirt off him. It wasn't really a fight. He was sitting there with Caroline Coon, being interviewed and sounding off about the nature of rock'n'roll. I just didn't think he was qualified to give an opinion that didn't belong to him. I just saw it as an opportunity to make a bit of a fuss. I was bored – what else is there to do on a two-day drive?"

Sandwiched on the bill between Paris-based rockers Shakin' Street and Il Biaritz, who featured ex-members of the British pub rockers Bees Make Honey, The Damned hit the bull ring's makeshift stage in blazing mid-afternoon sun on Saturday. 'One Of The Two' began the set. Then came 'New Rose', before which Brian asked the audience "can you hear the guitar?" Fighting against transistor radio-poor sound, the drums and guitar of 'New Rose' were out of time with each other. Then, the bass amp failed. After that was sorted out, David ripped his shirt off to expose his porcelain-pallid torso. Against the odds, it was a powerful showing. Brian even dedicated their version of The Stooges' '1970' to "La Iggy". Gender be damned.

Eddie & The Hot Rods were the last of the British bands to go on and were followed at 3 a.m. by Passion Force, a band comprising three black US ex-servicemen who played funk and had previously backed US soul singer Arthur Conley. At 3.30 a.m., The Damned tried to take the stage again but the stage crew dismantled the drum kit as Rat began pummelling it. Prevented from playing, the band instead yelled at the crowd, shook their fists and threw beer at the remaining audience. Nick Lowe told Jonh Ingham that they were the "worst group he had seen since the Sex Pistols".

★ ★ ★

Mont-de-Marsan was a moment of delicious confusion. At this point, this punk rock embraced Lowell George-bearded types like Sean Tyla.

It also meant the mod-obsessed Gorillas and included Nick Lowe's Chuck Berry cover versions. But it was The Damned, the freshest faces there, who personified the future.

The Damned were also bestowed with one of their most memorable pieces of branding as they returned from France. Ray Burns was wearing a jacket with epaulettes looking as if it had belonged to a pilot. An egg Rat had thrown at him had dried into his hair and, as they approached the border, Larry Wallis growled "Listen, fucking Captain Sensible, you get that fucking egg out of your hair before we get to customs."

While the name Captain Sensible endured, Andrew Czezowski's patience with The Damned had come to an end. After Mont-de-Marsan, he bowed out as the band's manager. "I suppose he went off the idea when he realised how juvenile we were," says Rat. "I knew I realised."

As Czezowski – for now – made his exit from The Damned's business, Mont-de-Marsan ushered Nick Lowe, Jake Riviera and Stiff Records into their world. Lowe had been in the pop group Kippington Lodge, which was renamed Brinsley Schwarz in 1969. They split in March 1975. Lowe was then signed and swiftly dropped as a solo act by United Artists. His band's manager had been Dave Robinson. Jake Riviera – born Andrew Jakeman – had lived in France in the late Sixties, where he managed the band Variations. Back in London in 1972, after a spell in a record shop he worked as a roadie for Chilli Willi & The Red Hot Peppers, a rootsy pub-circuit band with connections to Brinsley Schwarz. Chilli Willi toured in 1975 with the soul-influenced Kokomo and Dr. Feelgood, under the banner *The Naughty Rhythms Tour*. Through this, Riviera got to know those behind the Feelgoods label, United Artists. He also became the Essex band's road manager and travelled with them to America.

"Jake was the only happening man in London," says Rat. "He had started a record company, people were talking about him. The very first time I saw Jake was at Victoria coach station before Mont-de-Marsan and he came up and knew who we were. Everyone was talking about this guy who was really, really sharp, who was changing things." Riviera had a tape of demos recorded by Richard Hell and Johnny Thunders' band The Heartbreakers which instantly caught Brian's attention.

"I never met anyone like Jake before," says Brian. "Stiff were the first people to express an interest who seemed fun. The minute we got in with Jake, he shooed everyone else away." The Damned were offered a one-off deal to make a single for Stiff. Chiswick, who they had recorded demos for, were now out of the picture.

"It was exciting to be doing something different, small labels, something challenging or anarchic," says Captain of working with Stiff. "Looking back on it, I wish I'd signed with someone bigger. They might have paid me." Despite being quick on the uptake, Stiff had little ready money so instantly taking the band into a studio was not possible.

Following Mont-de-Marsan, they had no dates booked beyond a September 3 support slot to Eddie & The Hot Roads at The Marquee, but did gain exposure from *Melody Maker* and *Sounds*' coverage of the festival. For the former's Caroline Coon, The Damned and their (supposedly) "17-year-old singer…wiped up… as far as punk rock goes". The latter's article, by Jonh Ingham, centred on The Damned but was measured, saying their performance "hit several peaks".

For British punk rock on its home turf, the Sex Pistols' show at Islington's Screen on the Green cinema on August 29 was the next sign it wasn't strictly necessary to play standard venues or with non-scene bands. McLaren's quartet was billed with Manchester's Buzzcocks, their first time in London, and The Clash, playing in public for the first time since their July 4 live debut in Sheffield. The Damned were not approached to perform, confirming their outsider status; they were excluded from the in-crowd.

Having lost Czezowski, The Damned looked outside punk's inner, King's Road-centred circle for a manager. Ron Watts got the job. As the booker of the 100 Club, High Wycombe's Nag's Head and a major supporter of the Sex Pistols, he knew what was going on. But he was not an Andrew Czezowski, John Krivine, Malcolm McLaren or Bernard Rhodes. "Ron Watts swung the deal by buying us a hamburger at *Wimpy*," says Captain. "I thought, I'm definitely going with this one."

Stiff were still in the picture though. With their limited budget, the label booked The Damned into Islington's Pathway Studio on Monday September 20, where The 101ers had recorded 'Keys To Your Heart'. Nick Lowe was their producer.

An 8-track facility, Pathway was usually used to record demos. The Sex Pistols' first demo, recorded in May, was, conversely, tracked at the higher-spec 16-track Majestic Studio in south London. The Damned's single was made at the bargain-basement end of the music business in a studio which looked like a potting shed. 'I Fall' was Captain's choice for the A-side but he was outvoted and the band taped 'New Rose'. 'Help' was the B-side. Two hours were spent on recording. The same on mixing. The cost to Stiff was £46. The finished master was on a reused reel of tape and recorded over tracks by DP Costello, the future Elvis Costello.

Any financial or time constraints had no impact on what was captured. Together, The Damned and Nick Lowe created a single which more than justified the music press' hoo-hah about the changes coming to British music. Though 'New Rose' was much as it was since first being played live, Rat's new full-barrel drum intro gave it an opening which meant everyone hearing it had to pay attention. Since the mod era, no British single had such drive. More than this, it had a tune; a proper pop tune.

While of the now, the past was not hidden. David's spontaneous, spoken "Is she really going out with him" intro borrowed a phrase from the New York girl group The Shangri-Las' 1964 single 'Leader Of The Pack'. The Shangri-Las were a favourite of the New York Dolls, who had chosen their producer Shadow Morton to work on their first album. The main 'New Rose' riff re-wrote that of the Dolls' 'Personality Crisis'. While 'Help' was a Beatles cover version, the direct and recent inspiration to reconfigure it came from The Ramones. Yet the single sounded like nothing else and was thrillingly new.

"I was astonished," says Captain of his reaction to the first playback. "I thought it was so good. Whenever we went to see a band, I'd jump on stage in between the bands and 'I'd just like to announce we've made this fabulous recording with this marvellous new band The Damned. We're absolutely brilliant.'"

"Nick Lowe captured the live sound really well," adds Brian. "It stands up. There's nothing to date it. 'Help' was something we did live, and obviously something that people latched onto because it was the way The Beatles should have done it."

"Pathway Studios was so small you could barely fit someone into the room," notes Rat. "I was awed by 'New Rose', what Nick had done, what it sounded like. It sounds like jet fighters, the excitement. I thought studios are great, you can do anything. It was fucking brilliant. Nick's real art was knowing that was the take, the unquantifiable art of a producer, the taste of knowing what to go with."

"'New Rose' sounded great," agrees David. "As soon as you hear those drums, it's magic. It had the fallout of the Sixties' stuff. We thought 'Help' might get in *Guinness Book of Records* as the shortest song. It's a satirical nod in the direction of those times. Nick Lowe was just a nice chap, I think he was bemused by the whole thing but he liked it, he could see where it was coming from. He must have seen similarities to early rockabilly."

The Damned were on a high. They had just recorded British punk rock's first single and instantly and rightly knew it was magnificent. David had quit his job at the graveyard. In London's West End, celebration of a different sort was taking place. Their time in the studio coincided with the first day of what was advertised as a *Punk Special* at the 100 Club. Day one featured bands billed as Suzie & the Banshees, Sub Way Sect, Clash and Sex Pistols. The first two were making their stage debuts.

The Banshees were an off-the-cuff grouping comprising Pistols followers and friends Siouxsie, Marco Pirroni, Steve Spunker (later Steve Severin) and Sid Vicious. Subway Sect were managed by Bernard Rhodes and used The Clash's Camden rehearsal room. Although what became known as *The 100 Club Punk Festival* was a major public-facing event, the first day showcased scene insiders.

Day two was different. The *Punk Special* was originally conceived as a one-day event and advertised as such. But the amount of bands under consideration meant it spilled over into a second day. The Damned were booked for day two. On before them were Parisians Stinky Toys (originally scheduled for the one-day event, the day before) and The

Vibrators (a pub band who had just gone punk), who were joined by session guitarist Chris Spedding (the producer of the first Sex Pistols demo) to run through his 1975 hit single 'Motor Bikin''. Buzzcocks were on after The Damned.

For The Damned, the show was the antithesis of the previous day's euphoric recording session. The Vibrators jeered them. David's microphone was cutting out. One of Brian's guitar strings snapped and 15 minutes into their set they had to have an enforced break. Once they got going again, a beer glass thrown towards them from the audience hit one of the venue's stage-side columns and shattered, showering shards of glass onto the crowd. Rat reacted by leaping out from behind his drums and David castigated whoever had thrown it. A piece of glass had pierced the eye of a friend of his there to see his band, necessitating an ambulance.

The glass had been thrown by Sid Vicious, who was arrested. Earlier in the evening, while backstage, he had threatened Stinky Toys with a knife: one was found on his person by police. Caroline Coon, trying to defend his rights as an arrestee while he was forcibly removed from the venue by police, was also hustled off. Vicious was held at Ashford Remand Centre and the case reached court the next year.

More than anything else to date, the events during The Damned's 100 Club festival appearance reinforced the impression that punk rock and violence went hand-in-hand, a conclusion which had basis in fact. Vivienne Westwood had started a fight at a Sex Pistols show at The Nashville on April 3 when she set about an audience member. Johnny Rotten left the stage to lend a hand and it got his band onto the cover of *Melody Maker*. Vicious and John Wardle, aka Jah Wobble, had attacked Nick Kent at the 100 Club on June 15. Although his misbehaviour was less high profile and in a media-free environment, Captain kicked a spectator at St Albans on July 8. Rat had instigated a set-to with Nick Lowe on the way to Mont-de-Marsan. After the 100 Club episode, London's venues actively began avoiding booking punk rock bands. It wasn't a co-ordinated ban, but the shutters were already coming down.[31]

Even though he still managed The Damned, the 100 Club's Ron Watts ceased booking punk bands there. He reset the venue's default to blues, jazz and soul. A Sex Pistols show advertised for October 26 was pulled. The Stranglers and Vibrators still played The Nashville as they weren't quite punk[32] but when The Damned wanted to play a benefit there on October 16 for the audience member injured at the 100 Club, the venue would not have them. Eddie & The Hot Rods substituted.

As wariness about punk rock took hold, The Damned prepared for the release of their single in a newly charged climate. The mainstream music press stoked punk, as did *Sniffin' Glue*. Record labels were coming alive to the possibility there was something to sell. In the mainstream, the London daily newspaper *The Evening Standard* summed it up on September 23 in their review of the 100 Club festival where they pointed to "a great deal of interest from the music press and Britain's leading record companies. Less partisan observers [though] are unsure whether it [punk rock] adds up to a new cultural phenomenon or a giant confidence trick." Six weeks later, after 'New Rose' was out, the paper tagged The Damned as the "self-possessed demons of the punk rock scene".

For those outside the scene, the new cultural phenomenon now had another of its principal characters.

CHAPTER FOUR

First Punx On Wax

Punk rock was being shunned by London's pub venues but its music press supporters were not letting up on publicising what they saw as the future. *Melody Maker* made the 100 Club punk festival front-page news on October 2. The central image of the issue's cover was of David at the event, his begloved left hand outstretched, in a leather jacket, with swept-back hair, eye shadow and beads: a Gene Vincent from the dark side.

That same week, Johnny Rotten took the cover of *NME*. A week later, *Sounds'* collage-style cover superimposed a photo of Eric Clapton on a Sex Pistols gurning their way along Carnaby Street, one of the former hubs of Swinging London a decade earlier. No matter that the Sex Pistols and The Damned did not have records out, and that their audiences were small.

The Sex Pistols signed with EMI on October 8.[33] Their debut single 'Anarchy In The U.K.' arrived in shops on November 27. The music business magazine *Music Week* reported the liaison as "Sex Pistols join establishment". *Sounds* reacted similarly and said "Anarchy meets establishment". Stiff Records duly announced The Damned's live set was going to include a new song titled "Anarchy Courtesy Of EMI". It was them, not Rotten and co though, who became, as *Sounds* put it, the "first punx on wax". 'New Rose' was issued on October 26, a fortnight after David's 20th birthday[34] and seven years on from 1969, when Brian had played on his last single with the band credited as Taiconderoga.

Satirical made-up song titles aside, EMI were actually only a couple of steps removed from The Damned. Stiff had contracted their pressing plant to manufacture 'New Rose', the label's sixth single. Of the Pistols' deal with EMI, Captain says, "I used to look at the Pistols and think, 'What are they doing that for?' Then we heard 'Anarchy' and thought ooh, that's a bit turgid. I always rated Rotten but didn't think much of the band."

But it was Rotten and co who scored national headlines within a week of 'Anarchy''s release. What had been a scene mostly of concern to the music press and a limited number of fans was national news. The Damned did not escape the fallout.

★ ★ ★

British punk rock's debut single was issued by an independent label and initially available only either by mail order from Stiff or through outlets serviced by the distributor Bizarre Records, who had shipped 1,200 within a week of receiving copies. Two thousand were initially pressed and it came in a picture sleeve. A poster with early copies bought from Stiff helped sales, and it was claimed 4,000 had been sold by the beginning of November.

Despite the varying sales figures bandied, the demand was genuine and Stiff set up a distribution deal with United Artists: Jake Riviera had been tour manager of UA band Dr. Feelgood, and Lowe had been in Brinsley Schwarz, who were signed to UA. The connections were vital to getting 'New Rose' to the world. For the one-off deal, United Artists' sales force took the orders and the single then reached shops through their distributor, EMI. While Stiff was independent and it was not possible to argue that, like the Sex Pistols, The Damned were joining the establishment, 'New Rose' nonetheless reached shops courtesy of EMI.

Just as the business side blurred matters, double standards were being applied to The Damned. Given her unalloyed support for the band,

Caroline Coon's mind-set was probably unwitting but her perspectives on The Damned, The Clash and violence in relation to each were at odds. In the *Melody Maker* of November 13, she interviewed Brian and David. Under the heading *Violent World of the Damned*, the article began with Brian saying "the violence has been blown up out of all proportion to what there really is". Despite Brian's assertions, the opening paragraphs of the full-page article dealt with the violence and aggression.

On the opposite page of the same issue, she introduced readers to The Clash with the headline *Down and Out and Proud*. As that interview took place, bassist Paul Simonon was reported to have fired a replica pistol at a dog. Ironically, Joe Strummer's onstage pronouncement to an audience of "all of you think violence is tough – why don't you go home and collect stamps. That's much tougher" began the piece. Despite Simonon's behaviour, his band was not interrogated for their thoughts about violence. Unlike The Damned.

The Damned were not analysing the media attitudes though. 'New Rose' had been greeted with almost universal praise. In *Sounds*, Jonh Ingham said the single was "so hot it's a wonder the vinyl doesn't melt". *NME*'s Charles Shaar Murray had reservations: "the song ain't great shakes but the band sound very good and they can only improve with practice". *Sniffin' Glue* said The Damned had "come up with a killer. The energy on 'New Rose' is frightening." For *Melody Maker*, Coon brought Marc Bolan in to offer his thoughts on that week's singles. The Damned were also to hand and sat "silently as he appraises their debut single". Bolan declared "the energy level is dynamite, the attitude is positive rather than moody-positive. It has the same feel as The Stones' 'I Wanna Be Your Man'. You have to sit up, take notice." "A hit," concluded Coon.[35]

A more ambivalent view came from *Zigzag*, the independent music monthly slanted towards singer-songwriters, America's west coast and all points between. In 1977 the magazine underwent a makeover to embrace punk and the prime mover in the shift of focus was writer Kris Needs. In 1976, of 'New Rose' and before the magazine's wholesale shift to punk, he said he did not "understand how a band so posey and energy-less on stage made such an outstanding debut single. They should lose that singer who looks like [TV sitcom star] Terry Scott imitating Dracula and sings flat."

On the day 'New Rose' was released, The Damned supported the on-the-up soul-infused pub rockers Graham Parker & The Rumour at the Victoria Palace Theatre. They were the first of the punk bands to be booked at a mainstream London venue. Rat wore a pair of tartan Bay City Rollers trousers[36] and an Adolf Hitler mask. Later that evening, 'New Rose' was heard nationally for the first time when John Peel played it on his late-night BBC Radio 1 show.

Nick Kent was at the Victoria Palace and judiciously acknowledged that "having once been in a group with three of the four members, and through much personal involvement over the past six months, I'm certainly not in any position to turn out some dutifully objective critique." Despite the scrupulousness, he concluded the show was the "best I've heard them so far. They'll be very, very big."

The booking came through Stiff's Dave Robinson, who managed the headliners. He had previously run a studio at the Islington pub the Hope & Anchor, which helped access to the pub rock circuit. Even though they had not yet formally signed with the label – a "handshake deal" sufficed instead of a contract[37] – Stiff opened doors for The Damned. Inevitably, Jake Riviera replaced Ron Watts as the band's manager.

"Jake was so enthusiastic," says David. "He was really into driving things forward, not like the record industry men in suits, where it's not about the music, it's about the dollar. He had a vision that it was not going to be five minutes and it's over. Jake was a tough taskmaster. I was just there for the ride. You didn't think about tomorrow, we were totally green in so many ways."

Although reports of the amount 'New Rose' had sold differed, The Damned were becoming a big deal. *Sounds* put them on the cover on November 6, despite not carrying an accompanying article. A tour was required to help build the profile. After the 100 Club punk festival, there were odd dates outside London but nothing coordinated. The issue about punk bands being unwelcome at venues had to be considered, as did uncertainties about how much of an audience there was outside London. Filling, say, the Hope & Anchor's basement was not the same as trying to draw a crowd in the north-east of England. The traditional strategy was followed: in mid-October, it was announced that The Damned were supporting The Flamin' Groovies on a national tour.[38]

It looked a perfect match. The Groovies were acknowledged godfathers of punk, were currently on the same label as The Ramones and had just reissued their 1971 punk-sympatico *Teenage Head* album. The San Francisco band had already encountered the burgeoning British scene while playing London in July – despite the in-crowd's focus on their support band, The Ramones. The Damned would benefit from this as the audience for the San Francisco band was one primed for straight-ahead, no-frills rock'n'roll. Nine dates were scheduled: the first was Redcar's Coatham Bowl on November 11[39]; the last on November 21 at Croydon's Greyhound. London saw the bands on November 14 at The Roundhouse. However, The Flamin' Groovies had recently adopted a mid-Sixties Beatles look and sound. Raunchy classics which resonated with punkish spirit like 'Slow Death' and 'Teenage Head' were elbowed in favour of recreating the beat group and folk rock eras. Whatever, The Damned were the first of the new British punk bands to undertake a UK tour – a major accomplishment.

"They were scared as hell," says Captain of The Flamin' Groovies' reaction to The Damned. "They didn't like us, didn't like the audience. They didn't like what was going on in Britain at the time. When we walked through their dressing room they used to cower, it was weird."

"They were going through this real weird thing of Beatles jackets and old Beatles songs," adds Brian, whose view of this version of the Groovies remains robust. "It was, 'fuck me where's "Slow Death"? People were coming to see us to find out what it was about and the Groovies were going down like a bunch of shit."

For Rat, whatever the headliners thought, the opening date proved a triumph for The Damned. "We finished them off. It was Redcar," he recalls. "Brian would play their records, blinding gems. Then we met them and it was a tragedy. They really didn't want to talk to us. We went and played this show and kicked their arses. The crowd didn't want the Groovies and booed them off stage. I don't know to this day why that audience liked us. You'd get maybe 10 per cent of the crowd liking it and the rest saying this is shit, it's not Quo. We played and the audience went mental. They demanded an encore. I was astounded. We had been taken on our merits. We went and played and they liked us."

After Redcar, faced with almost two more weeks of this disconnect The Flamin' Groovies bailed out. Three days later, at The Roundhouse, they didn't turn up. The Troggs, booked for that date only, became the headliners over The Damned. It was announced that guitarist Cyril Jordan and vocalist Chris Wilson had heavy colds. The latter said The Damned "are the worst musicians we've played with". Stiff said, "The Damned agreed to play the tour in order to give the concerts some modern credibility. They are not interested in supporting or bailing out living legends." The tour was over.

With enforced spare time, the band returned to Pathway Studios to begin recording their debut album with Nick Lowe. Backing tracks were completed between November 3 and 11. A less conventional item was introduced into their itinerary on the 19th when they played Manor Hill Upper School in Finchley. Although they were booked to play Uxbridge that evening they also made it to north London for a bill trailed as "Punks at the High School". With Slaughter & The Dogs and Eater also playing, despite being at a school, it was London's first all-punk bill since the 100 Club festival.

This bizarre concert came about as Rat Scabies' protégé, the 13-year old drummer Roger Bullen aka Dee Generate, had just joined Eater. Otherwise, the band's ages were 15 and 17. The band's guitarist and singer attended Manor Hill Upper School and, as unlikely as it was, put the show on there.

Bullen's stepfather, a friend of Tor's guitarist Simon Fitzgerald, had asked Rat to give him drum lessons. "All I did was show him a few tricks," says Rat. "I used to work him real hard and he did it, and got there. Eater originally had a drummer that couldn't play, I was asked if I knew anyone. I didn't go down and insist they hire my boy. I never thought of myself as being a patron to the arts. The important point about Eater was they were the youngest kids, the next generation."

★ ★ ★

The next attempt at touring was equally short, sharp, even more fraught and much higher profile. It began as what was meant to be a punk package tour, announced the week The Damned set off to play with the living legends from San Francisco.

The Sex Pistols had issued their debut single, 'Anarchy In The U.K.', on November 26 and were to hit the road in the wake of its release and co-headline with The Ramones. The bill was to be bulked out with New York's Talking Heads and the unhip partnership of Chris Spedding and The Vibrators. The tour was announced in *NME*[40] and *Sounds* on November 13. It was trailed as a punk-rock package tour running from November 29 or December 1 (depending on which paper was read) to December 19. The Damned were not invited along.

They also did not feature in the first television programme overview of punk, an episode of the London-region *London Weekend Show* that was broadcast on November 28 (a promotional tie-in screened two days after the release of 'Anarchy').[41] The elision of The Damned from the evolving narrative on punk rock continued.

A week after the press announcements, the tour had suddenly transformed. There were to be no Ramones, Talking Heads or the Spedding/Vibrators union. Ramones manager Danny Fields declared, "We never said we were playing" and that "only three venues in a list of about 20 cities were confirmed." Their label boss Seymour Stein said "the tour was not handled as professionally as we liked. At one point we were told there were 20 dates, at another six. We expect to be told the truth. We did not pull out because of the Sex Pistols' image." For a controversy stoking McLaren, "The Ramones were just scared of playing with the Pistols because of their violent image."

The fresh version of the tour now featured just one band from the original line-up: the Sex Pistols. The hurriedly assembled new bill featured them as headliners with The Damned, The Clash and The Heartbreakers, the New York band featuring former New York Dolls Jerry Nolan and Johnny Thunders – all of whom were presumably not scared of the Sex Pistols. This was duly advertised as the *Anarchy In The U.K. Tour*. Press ads had The Damned as "special guests" and noted 'New Rose' was "available from even your dumbest dealer" while 'Anarchy In

The U.K.' was "available from your cleverest". The 19 dates began in December 3 in Norwich and ended December 26 in London.

One week The Damned were not invited. The next they were. However it was looked at, two bands on the bill with records out was more of a draw than one. "McLaren needed The Damned," says Brian. To generate ticket sales, The Damned were grudgingly shoehorned into the *Anarchy* tour.

The Damned, though, had done something the Sex Pistols had not, and would never do. On November 30, they entered the BBC's Maida Vale studio to record a session for the *John Peel Show*. The five tracks were broadcast on a special punk-only show on December 10, which also featured an airing of the by-then banned 'Anarchy In The U.K.'.

The Sex Pistols appearance on the *Today* show on December 1 and the subsequent fallout do not need revisiting, but it is worth stressing that what made national headlines and turned punk rock into a bête noir was a live appearance on a regional news and chat programme.[42] *Today* was not seen beyond the London area. The Damned themselves did not see it as they were with The Clash and The Heartbreakers at Harlesden's Roxy Cinema rehearsing for the tour, focussing on perfecting the changeovers between each band. "We had a dress rehearsal. The Pistols came in, they had just done the Bill Grundy show," recalls Brian. "The next day they were headlines."

The headlines led to cancellations and wariness from licensing authorities, promoters and venues. Before this, The Damned's involvement in the *Anarchy* tour had come at the last minute and, even if the Bill Grundy appearance had not happened, their relationship with McLaren was going to be – as it had been – fraught.

"The competition was between the managers," says Captain. "I always got on well with Mick Jones and Johnny Rotten, but the managers were deadly rivals."

"The Pistols would always take the piss out of Malcolm and say, 'We're not supposed to talk to you guys,'" adds Brian. "John would keep on his own though. With The Clash, they became very diffident. Like they'd been told by Bernie don't mix with the guys from The Damned, even Mick. It was odd."

McLaren wanted to charge The Damned £1,000 to use their tour bus and for transporting their equipment along with that of the other bands. It was a cost Stiff was not going to pay. With their EMI money, the Sex Pistols were able to stay in chain hotels. The Damned were to travel on their own and their overnight accommodation was cheap bed and breakfast establishments. The separate travelling arrangements meant communication between the two camps was bound to be scrambled or, more likely, non-existent.

Norwich, the intended first date, was cancelled outright. The second, in Derby, was also scratched, but in more byzantine circumstances. Local councillors wanted to see the bands for themselves and demanded what amounted to auditions. Malcolm McLaren used the request as a means to ditch The Damned from the tour.

On the day of the Derby show, their tour manager Rick Rogers[43] was invited to McLaren's hotel where he met him and Bernard Rhodes in a room. He was told the local council wanted to audition the Sex Pistols, which they wouldn't do. The other bands should play though: would he confirm The Damned will? Rogers checked it was a joint decision made by all involved, was told it was and that The Damned were to headline over The Heartbreakers and The Clash. McLaren also told Rogers that if they played they could join the rest of the bands on the tour coach rather than using their own van. McLaren deceived Rogers, and then spun it that The Damned said they would do the audition. Rogers, who was duped, was subsequently dismissed from Stiff.

According to Captain, "We were locked up in this B&B in Derby and our tour manager Rick Rogers went over to meet Bernie and Malcolm and said we were willing to play for the councillors. They hadn't asked us. Trouble is McLaren rewrote history [by saying we would do the audition]. Whatever the managers were up to, we weren't part of. I wouldn't have done it."

"I would have done it," counters Brian. "I just like playing." No one auditioned. The next day, a show in Newcastle was cancelled.

The Damned did play Leeds after the first three aborted dates.[44] The next morning, McLaren sacked them from the tour. His press comment was that their having considered playing to the councillors in Derby meant, "We are not in sympathy with The Damned. We were disgusted by this and so they will have to get off the tour."

David commented, "Although we do not align ourselves with the Pistols' political position we sympathise, but we are going to do all the gigs we can and any others that come long."

McLaren responded, "We are disgusted by this statement and we feel that The Damned have no place on this tour."

How long The Damned would have remained on the tour without the Derby incident is moot, but now the post-Bill Grundy Sex Pistols were national news there was no commercial need for another band with a record out to play the tour. The Sex Pistols' name was enough. Although tickets would now be sold anyway, that was also rendered moot as only seven dates were played. As a promotional vehicle – albeit an unconventional one – the *Anarchy* tour outstripped anyone's expectations. It also set in stone the perception that punk rockers were a threat to society. Whether this was fostered by the press, overstated or plain wrong was irrelevant. Ironically, in the short term it did not help the Sex Pistols sell records. They parted company with EMI in January 1977 and never played a conventional live show in the UK again.

The Damned dusted themselves down and continued as they had. "Things fall to bits and you do the good old Hope & Anchor again," says Brian.

★ ★ ★

The *Anarchy* tour and its preceding rehearsal involved The Damned for a total of seven days: December 1 to the morning of December 7, when McLaren gave them the boot. That evening, there was no pause for breath and they actually did play the Hope & Anchor instead of the billed Clayson & The Argonauts. Cameras were there to make a promotional video for 'New Rose'.

The Sex Pistols became a major source of media curiosity in the ensuing months and overshadowed The Dammed. The focus on punk rock had shifted from the music press to also include the national press and was mostly concerned with the Sex Pistols' image as a threat to society. Other bands became ballast in the developing story. "We got eclipsed when the Pistols happened," says David. "To some of the critics, we didn't fulfil this political ideal they wanted."

The cleavage with McLaren, the Sex Pistols and, by proxy, The Clash on the *Anarchy* tour was nothing new. It continued what began at The Damned's first show when they did not pay McLaren for using the Sex Pistols' PA. Appearing at Mont-de-Marsan when the Sex Pistols had been blackballed and The Clash had pulled out further consolidated the divergence. The Sex Pistols' chum Sid Vicious throwing a glass at The Damned at the 100 Club was a further schism.

For The Damned, there was also the issue that they had close ties with passé pub rock. Joe Strummer had made himself over after leaving The 101ers and wore a shirt on which he'd painted the words "Chuck Berry is dead" so making a convincing case for himself as having abandoned pub rock. The Sex Pistols had played pub venue The Nashville. The Damned, however, were produced by an ex-member of Brinsley Schwarz and on a label run by the manager of Graham Parker & The Rumour and Dr. Feelgood's former tour manager who, in turn, became their manager. The single Stiff issued before 'New Rose' was by Lew Lewis, a former member of Eddie & The Hot Rods. The single issued after 'New Rose' was Richard Hell's 'Blank Generation' but after that it was 'Silver Shirt' by pub band Plummet Airlines. The Damned were thus surrounded by a pub rock infrastructure.

There was also the issue of stance. Mick Jones had complained to *Sniffin' Glue* in October that Brian said he "stands for enjoying himself". Jones, for his part, declared he stood "for creativity and change". In November, Brian had told Caroline Coon that, "I just like to get up and play". The Sex Pistols and The Clash projected a political attitude and did not shy away from peppering their interviews with polemic (in the case of the Pistols though, most of that came from Johnny Rotten: but no matter, as there was little interest in what the other three Pistols had to say).

The divisions between the two camps, The Damned on one side and the Sex Pistols and Clash on the other, was intensifying. The Damned's refusal to take on a political stance, their adoption of fun as a policy and their links with pub rock all meant they were uncool. They were outcasts. Tropes were being codified. Punk rock was now a trend, the word was spreading and the number of adherents was increasing.

New bands were appearing. Some, like Birmingham's Suburban Studs and Manchester's Slaughter & The Dogs were glam hangovers who had overhauled their look and sped up their music. The Vibrators, who got two singles out in November, had freshly shorn hair and punk-style clothes. Others were new, like Eater, Subway Sect and The Boys. The latter featured Matt Dangerfield, who had overseen the first Damned demo.

Other old faces were moving forward. Mick Jones and the Bernard Rhodes-managed Clash had attracted the attention of Polydor Records. Jones's London SS accomplice Tony James had joined Chelsea, who were managed by short-stay Damned manager John Krivine. Chelsea mark one hit the buffers after a show on November 21 but James, the band's guitarist Billy Idol and drummer John Towe next formed Generation X. The Damned's second manager Andrew Czezowski was managing Generation X[45] and put them on to open his punk-only Roxy Club on December 14. In September, Chrissie Hynde had been playing with Dave Batchelor and Colin Mills from Captain's old bands. The prospective trio was called The Unusuals, and Hynde rechristened Batchelor and Mills the Berk Brothers: Dave and Fred Berk.

The Damned had to move fast if they were to continue making waves in an increasingly crowded pond. Their look and identity helped. Once seen, no one was going to forget David Vanian. Captain Sensible and Rat Scabies were equally notable. In this context, Brian had no need to alter his look or radically change his name as he came readymade for punk. But still, The Damned had to confirm their status as first-generation pioneers.

Instead, the period immediately after the *Anarchy* tour had seen them play just the one show, at the Hope & Anchor. The date book for December was otherwise empty. Captain took time to rehearse with a newly configured Johnny Moped: he played guitar while Dave and Fred Berk were on drums and bass. The Damned's first show of the New Year, again at the Hope & Anchor on January 1, had Johnny Moped (with Captain in their line-up[46]) as support. The Damned had also finally signed a contract with Stiff.

When 'New Rose' was issued, Stiff had signed a distribution deal with United Artists to feed the demand. That, though, had been a one-off arrangement and the proposed Damned album required a backer to get it into the shops and fund the manufacturing costs. Stiff's last release had been the Plummet Airlines single. Following that, a shelved single by Motörhead.[47] Independence was fine, but financial support was needed.

Cash was tight for The Damned too. Instead of paying him back, The Damned played The Roxy in early 1977 for no fee to help Andrew Czezowski recoup his outstanding spend on the band in 1976.[48] After McLaren scotched the proposal that the Sex Pistols play there on January 1 with The Damned as support, The Damned played there three times in January and honed their stage personae.[49] Captain began wearing a nurse's dress on stage.[50] Rat had begun spraying his cymbals with lighter fuel and setting them alight. On the 13th, Led Zeppelin's Jimmy Page and Robert Plant turned up at The Roxy to see them.[51] Plant liked them so much he returned to the Covent Garden basement with Zeppelin drummer John Bonham on the 17th. Plant was not shy about sharing his enthusiasm and said, "I was impressed by them, thought they were really good, especially Rat Scabies, he's really got it. I was talking to Rat for a long time, and having a few drinks. He's alright, I like him, he's not like his name. Jimmy loved it, thought they were fantastic." Bonham clambered on stage after The Damned's set, telling the audience to get them back as "they're a fucking great band".[52]

The support of the world's biggest rock group was no help with Stiff and The Damned's first album. Negotiations had been taking place with Island Records and a two-year deal had been struck where Stiff retained its identity and mail-order sales, but the press and promotion aspects were handled by Island.[53] Excluding America and Finland, the deal was worldwide. Island's investment was £17,000. The Damned were set to face the market. The Sex Pistols, on other hand, had been let go by EMI a month earlier and entered their one-week relationship with A&M on March 9, 1977. Bernard Rhodes signed The Clash to CBS on January 26 and they were not yet ready to release anything. The Damned were the only one of the 1976 bands in a position to put punk rock into high street record shops.

A release date for their debut album was set. *Damned Damned Damned* was scheduled to hit the record racks on February 18, on Brian's 26th birthday, and the 'Neat Neat Neat' single a week later. With the support of Island Records, British punk rock had birthed its first album, the only one by any of the bands recorded in 1976.

★ ★ ★

In some quarters, *Damned Damned Damned* was an instant critical hit. "White light lives" raved Giovanni Dadomo in *Sounds*. "They'll be world-beaters...[the] musicianship is superb," said *NME*'s Tony Parsons. According to *Melody Maker*'s Chris Welch, the album had "ferocity, howling guitars and blazing vehemence" and was "a dynamic clatter that will encourage even the casual listener to minor acts of demolition." The more measured *Music Week* said, "Nick Lowe has captured a big loud sound and managed to give it the clarity that ultra-fast, super-loud rock needs. Brian James proves to be an angry songwriter who can touch all the right nerves. Big sales should not be beyond the capabilities of this surprisingly good album."

In others, reservations were aired. Parsons also asserted that "Rat Scabies should develop as a songwriter is necessary, in fact imperative, to the future of The Damned." In *Zigzag*, Mac Garry described them as "Jake Riviera's joke group" and fulminated "they can't sing or play, but there are enough cretins about to make this a viable release. The singer sounds like a ruptured seagull. It would be preposterous to treat The Damned as musicians. I've heard ice cream vans with a better sense of melody. You will be highly impressed with the music on this record. Especially if you happen to be a juvenile delinquent with a safety pin through your nipple and the brainpower of a haddock." Garry also assured readers that Lowe had said he recorded the backing tracks at 15 inches per second and then sped the tapes up for overdubbing the vocals: a mischievous contention borne out as a fabrication by aural evidence of the band playing live from around the time.[54] In *Sniffin' Glue*, after saying "The Damned have made a great album," Mark Perry concluded with the prescient payoff "The Damned will be successful, I wonder if they're pleased?"

Stiff, though, had much to be happy with. The label's first album –
advertised with the slogan "Play it at Your Sister" – was a chart hit, with
a five-week Top 50 run during which it peaked at 36 settling between
Showaddywaddy's *Greatest Hits* and Neil Diamond's *Love At The Greek*.
A week later, The Clash's debut single 'White Riot' began its short
foray in to the singles Top 50 run-down. 'Neat Neat Neat' had not
charted despite one of its B-side tracks not being drawn from the album:
Rat's 'Stab Yor Back' from *Damned Damned Damned* was paired with a
vocal-free version titled 'Singalongascabies'.

The front cover was a statement proclaiming for good that The
Damned's attitude to image ran counter to that of The Clash. The
picture sleeve of 'White Riot' showed the three core members facing a
wall, legs splayed with arms outstretched as if about to be searched by
the forces of repression. *Damned Damned Damned* featured a photo of
the quartet with their faces covered in what looked like cream and jam.
They appeared to have stepped off the set of a manic Marx Brothers
film.

"That was organised by this photographer called Peter Gravelle[55],"
recalls Brian. "Stiff had assigned him to do the thing. They thought it
was a jolly wheeze, little knowing that we would relish it, get into to it
and enjoy the whole experience."

"It was shaving foam and tomato ketchup," adds David.

On the sleeve's reverse, the first 2,000 copies of the Barney Bubbles-
designed package bore a picture of Eddie & The Hot Rods rather
than The Damned.[56] Jake Riviera was aware of the collector's market
and knew they would be snapped up, instantly recouping the costs of
album.[57] That this was an intended stunt was hidden, as early copies of
the Barney Bubbles-designed album bore a sticker declaring "Due to
Record Company error, a picture of Island recording artists Eddie &
The Hot Rods has been printed instead of The Damned. We apologise
for any inconvenience caused and the correct picture will be substituted
on future copies."[58] Subsequent versions had a shot of the band playing
The Roxy with Captain's back to the camera.

"Unfortunately, on the front cover I had more pie on my face than
any of the other buggers and on the back I had my back to the picture,"

says Captain. "So I went down a photo booth and got some pictures, cut one out and said 'put that on there' so I would have something to show my relatives, because I didn't think we'd be invited to make another album. This was going to be the one record I was on, so I wanted people to be able to see me." His face was stuck to one of the stage monitors in the live photo.

The single of 'Neat Neat Neat' had a cover image as playful and as strong as the album's: the band were seen with paper bags over their heads, challenging the idea that they had individual identities. "With most bands, one guy was the leader or they're a gang," says David. "The Damned were always a band that separately wouldn't be in the same room as each other. The common thread was the music. Instead of working against each other, we made it fit with the band."

Delineating the four individuals who made up The Damned had begun before 'New Rose' was released. Writing in late September 1976, Caroline Coon said Captain had "a front as mad as a village idiot's" and David "looks as if he's risen from Dracula's crypt". For her, the band were "all born performers without a shred of inhibition". A fortnight after the single was out, Tony Parsons wrote, "Captain cackles like the madman he is", that Brian resembled Johnny Thunders and had a "gaunt, white Keef lookalike face" while David was "shaded, small and sinister… and looks like a runaway from the Addams Family". As Parsons interviewed them, Captain and Rat followed spitting at each other with chucking dustbin lids at each other.

In the wake of *Damned Damned Damned*, their personae were further defined. Captain Sensible was "wonderfully lunatic", an "all-purpose loony", "virtually a show on his own" who said his favourite girls were "schoolgirls with navy blue knickers". David "tried very hard to look creepy", had "the appearance of a ghoul", "could have been designed by Fritz Lang…[was] a frail bundle of sinister energy, an amalgam of Nosferatu, Bela Lugosi and the toast of an SS gala night" and was "like a sexless spectre from an Isherwood nightmare who's fallen on hard times in pre-war Berlin". Brian had "this guitar-hero-as-the-crazed-rocker persona beautifully tied up", moved on stage with "rock and roll body language that goes back through Keith Richard and [Jeff] Beck, all the

way back to Eddie Cochran" and an "ominously aggressive personality…
[which] doesn't have the in-built safety valve of self-depressive humour
the others have, almost as though he takes himself seriously". Rat had a
"spike-haired extrovert energy" and said his hobby was "hanging dogs
upside down and whipping them with chains".

For their musical peers, a mention of The Dammed in 1977 invariably
provoked a robust response. According to Johnny Rotten, they were
"a very dirty version of The Bay City Rollers, Eddie & The Hot Rods
with make-up". The Stranglers' Hugh Cornwell thought they "feel a
bit lightweight. But they have a couple of really good numbers." For
Mick Jones they were "one of the wet fishes. It's just comedy horror
rock. The Damned are just not… essential." Joe Strummer, though, was
conflicted. After telling Caroline Coon, "I've changed my opinion of
The Damned. I've seen them a lot and I think they're fun to watch. They
play good. The only thing I have against them is that they can't play
as well as us," he revised his judgement and informed San Francisco's
Search & Destroy that The Damned were "wankers".

★ ★ ★

The band's multifaceted identity was displayed in front of the whole
of Britain on February 26 when they became the first punk band to
appear on a national, mainstream programme by miming to 'Neat
Neat Neat' on *Supersonic*, commercial TV's rival to the BBC's *Top
Of The Pops*.[59] Fellow guest Cliff Richard refused to introduce them
so the task passed to the American actor and country singer Dennis
Weaver. After soft-rockers Mr Big were done with lip-syncing
'Romeo', The Damned blasted through their slot with the surreal
movements of silent film being projected at the wrong speed. Captain
lurched, twisted and fell as if trying to put out invisible flames licking
at his torso. David stalked from side-to-side while Brian sporadically
stepped to centre stage. Shirtless on his drum stool, Rat grounded
this elemental manifestation. The nation's first chance to see one of
the new generation bands had not stopped traffic but was a critical
moment. There was no turning back. Potentially, now the cork was
out of the punk bottle, this music belonged to everyone.

Yet Brian's ambivalence about what punk was becoming and how The Damned were portrayed was beginning to surface. "I hate the word punk," he said at the end of February. "It conjures up visions of safety pins and dumb kids. No matter what a lot of people think, The Damned ain't out to change the world."

Damned Damned Damned

*D*amned Damned Damned was Brian's album. Beyond the cover of The Stooges' '1970' (retitled 'I Feel Alright') and Rat's 'Stab Yor Back', he wrote the songs[60] and decided what they sounded like. Fittingly, producer Nick Lowe's verité approach ensured The Damned's debut album sought to freeze-frame the live experience.

But what was a British punk rock album supposed to look like? Before *Damned Damned Damned* there were no visual precedents. Some singles had come out, a few of them in picture sleeves. Hardly any of these were punk, though. The first 3,000 copies of the Sex Pistols' 'Anarchy In The U.K.' came in a plain black sleeve. Issued on January 1977 on their own New Hormones label, Buzzcocks' *Spiral Scratch* EP set the band's name and the title in lower-case letters above and below a Polaroid shot of the band.

Beyond punk as such, The Stranglers' debut single, '(Get A) Grip (On Yourself)' – on United Artists, who had distributed 'New Rose' – featured a photo of the confrontational, quizzical-looking and facially hairy (and mature) band facing-off against the camera lens. The Vibrators had issued two singles in November 1976, both on pop mogul Mickie Most's RAK label and both in standard company sleeves. One was their R&B-ish 'We Vibrate' and the other the punk novelty 'Pogo Dancing', where they backed former Sex Pistols demo producer Chris Spedding. Most, his label and The Vibrators were uninterested in setting out any visual style.

Further breaching the boundaries of punk, there were a couple of albums as potential visual influences. Eddie & The Hot Rods' *Teenage Depression*, issued November 1976, bore a cover photograph of a young man seemingly about to commit suicide by shooting himself in the head: an image recycled from the sleeve of their second single, June 1976's 'Wooly Bully'. Generic stuff then. Looking back, Dr. Feelgood's first album, January 1975's *Down By The Jetty*, featured a photo – though taken outdoors – similar to that later used for fellow United Artists band The Stranglers' 'Grip': of a ready, rough, truculent and unvarnished quartet. A similar strategy was used in America for the sleeve of The Ramones' April 1976 eponymous debut album.[61]

If a focus group had been shown what was around and set the agenda, Britain's first punk album ought to have featured a photo of an unsmiling, dangerous-seeming foursome posing as if either they hated what they were doing or were about to lamp the photographer. It did neither.

Stiff Records had defined itself as quirky. This is what informed *Damned Damned Damned*'s front cover and the allegedly erroneous Eddie & The Hot Rods photo seen on early copies rather than notions of punkiness. Drollness was strewn across the label's releases. Its first single, Nick Lowe's 'So It Goes', said "Mono enhanced stereo, play loud" on the label. The fourth, The Tyla Gang's 'Styrofoam', came in a plain white bag stamped "Artistic breakthrough double 'B' side" and "This record certified gold on leaving the studio". On its label, 'New Rose' was shown to be one minute, 99 seconds long. Stiff grabbed attention with its madcap marketing, and so it was with *Damned Damned Damned*. The Damned, of course, had said they were here "to have a bit of fun" in their first interview. The nature of the custard-pie-in-face sleeve of *Damned Damned Damned* was no surprise. It also instantly subverted any snowballing views of Brit-punk as grounded in the doctrinal.

Yet what was heard on *Damned Damned Damned* bordered on the – and was frequently more than – dark. Its grooves had little room for sunshine. The title of 'Born To Kill' nodded to Iggy & The Stooges' 'Search And Destroy' but its lyrics painted a picture of a protagonist who could take anything and had "beat[en] a lot of crime away". He – it was a he – was inviting "honey" to "take a chance". For 'Fish' the narrator was "cold" and "need[ed] someone to hold". The feelings of disengagement peaked on 'Fan Club' and 'Feel The Pain' with the former's "one night stand", carried out "for my fan club" and resulting in wondering "why I'm sad?" "You send me pretty flowers while I'm slashing my wrists" it continued. The pay-off was "I'm the freak that's on display, so stand and stare". 'Feel The Pain' was more ambiguous but, with its references to the intravenous, dropping blues (amphetamines) and (again) the cold, alluded to the impact of drug abuse. Brian's lyrical connection with the edgy was exaggerated in Rat's only song on the album, 'Stab Yor Back': "I'm gonna stab yor back, you ain't nothing but a dead hag, now that you're 25, never gonna live 'til you're 29."

As an aural freeze-frame, the album's release allowed The Damned's lyrics to be examined for the first time. The ambivalent lyrical attitude towards women was tackled in an interview with San Francisco's *Search & Destroy* in which it was suggested that "the overall idea you guys project in your music and in the press and I guess in your life too, is a rather constant belittling of women... your attitude in demeaning [women]. In the midst of your new and vital music are these retrograde attitudes about women, like your song 'Fish'."

Brian riposted by saying it was a love song and David deflected the probing with "I don't know where you're getting this from."

After a little more pushing, Brian explained, "we're not talking about us, we're talking about situations". Earlier in the interview, Captain had declared "totally submissive women are the best. The sexiest. Troublemakers, they are. Women shouldn't be allowed to speak, they should have their voice boxes taken out." The two interrogators, Vermillion Sands and Annette Weatherman, were female. They set the misogyny aside and ploughed on.

Weatherman asked about 'Neat Neat Neat''s lyrics "ain't no crime if there ain't no law, ain't no cops to mess you around" and whether this was a statement of anarchy. Brian conceded "it could be read that way" but was actually "a statement of fact". Such scrutiny was rare. Beyond *NME*'s Mick Farren pulling David up about his SS lapel badge[62], no one else had asked The Damned to explain themselves in such searching terms.

In the end, *Damned Damned Damned*'s lyrics were not a subject of wholesale interest. As British punk's first album, promotion and reviews centred on what it captured: the "new and vital music", as Weatherman put it. And it was new and vital, and still is. Heard at any point from its release onwards, *Damned Damned Damned* remains extraordinary.

When it was fast, it was fast. *Zigzag* had thrown out that daft assertion that its backing tracks had been sped up but the live Damned – and their Peel sessions – showed this was not the case. On 'See Her Tonite', Brian's guitar playing seemed breakneck but was precise. Nothing was out of control. This was a guitarist of rare skill. Instead of coming off the rails, Captain's bass, as Brian had wanted from the beginning, held it all down. James Williamson, the *Search And Destroy*-period Stooges guitarist, was Brian's favourite but it was the Ron Asheton of The Stooges' preceding album *Funhouse* which Brian's playing most suggested: a similar space between the chords and individual notes, and a mutual tendency towards sudden fills and flurries. Which was where Brian drew from jazz.

When the tempo was held in check, it was atmospheric. Overall, 'Fan Club' defined brooding and was at one with the self-loathing of its lyrics. Imbued with menace on 'Feel The Pain', David's voice was more than up to the job of expressing impending doom. His instrument was malleable – actorly.

Though *Damned Damned Damned* had barely any room for daylight, it was defined by tonal shifts: from rapid to deliberate; from lyrics that were literal to allusive; a cover image in opposition to the nature of its contents. As a debut album, it was assured. However, as a basis for defining punk rock it was too varied, too complex. It also did not hide its debts to the past. Its uncompromising attitude aside, other albums would have to provide the building blocks for a musical style to typecast as punk.[63] Ironic, considering this was British punk's first album. The Damned's were in a field of one.

CHAPTER FIVE

Loud, Course, Rough
And Unrelenting

Cameras from the American television network NBC tracked The Damned in January 1977, catching them in the run-up to the release of 'Neat Neat Neat'. Securing coast-to-coast American exposure on the late-night news programme *Weekend* was a coup but more about documenting punk as a shock-horror trend than helping The Damned's career progression.

The New Elizabethans was a 25-minute report for *Weekend* opening with the voiceover: "This is punk rock and its purpose, one observer says, is to promote violence, sex and destruction in that order. Its other purpose is to make a great deal of money for the performers, agents, shop owners, record companies and fashion designers cashing in on the latest fad. That, of course, is not what its supporters say."

Malcolm McLaren and Mark Perry were interviewed, as were the Sex Pistols who were also seen live.[64] There was a brief snatch of a live Eddie & The Hot Rods. But the punks awarded most time by NBC were The Damned. Interviewed, Rat said, "I wanna get very rich, I want a big house, a car, loads of booze and loads of women."

Stiff's Jake Riviera had less aspirational thoughts. "The first rule in this business is that there are no rules," he told the camera. "Pop is meant to be throwaway. It's here today, gone tomorrow. If it turns out to be art later on, that's good and fine. People like Rat, they're pebbles on the beach. Musicians, there's a million more. If he drops dead, there's a million more where they came from."

Rat did not drop dead and in May, echoing what Jake Riviera had said, he told BBC radio that for punk rock, "the first rule is there are no rules. The second rule is you look after yourself." But becoming ill would not have been surprising. Stiff – his band's label and management – had him hard against the coalface. Between the time they were filmed for *The New Elizabethans* and when it hit America's TV screens on June 25, The Damned themselves had come and gone from America, completed two British tours and recorded a new single. The first set of dates was Britain's first real chance to see The Damned. In March, when they travelled the UK, it was not on an all-punk bill but as the guests of the pre-punk pop star Marc Bolan.

★ ★ ★

Damned Damned Damned needed promoting and, once again, the favoured marketing vehicle was touring. The collapse of the dates with The Flamin' Groovies and of the *Anarchy* tour were no obstacles to getting the band on the road. On March 10 they set out as the support band to Marc Bolan's current version of T.Rex. Stiff's comment the previous November that The Damned "are not interested in supporting or bailing out living legends" was forgotten.

After his positive comments about 'New Rose' in *Melody Maker*, Bolan was well aware of The Damned.[65] The paper's Allan Jones caught the tour's first date in Newcastle and concluded the billing was "shrewd. It's arguable that without The Damned, Bolan would be pulling no new faces to his concerts. One can feel The Damned already slipping into the embrace of the rockbiz, the smiles well practised, their anarchy carefully channelled. Good luck to them." *Record Mirror* was less reflective. After seeing the same show, it said The Damned "produced their usual tedious brand of badly played over loud songs".

"It worked so well," recalls Captain of touring with Bolan. "His crowd liked us and vice versa. He was such a great bloke, always giving us little pep talks in the bus. He took us in his own coach, really swanky. We were used to a Ford Transit van."

"I wouldn't say we won over every Marc Bolan fan," adds Rat. "But there weren't as many Damned fans as Marc Bolan fans. It wasn't like we were moving the world. It was Marc's tour, it was Marc's crowd. It wasn't like we were running him to ground for our fans."

Meeting a mainstream audience head-on in the largest venues they had played to date didn't become a problem. Neither were Bolan and his band. "I wasn't a big fan of T.Rex but I really liked Marc," says Brian. "The geezers he was playing with, they were worse than us. They had this fishing wire in the service stations to trip up the women collecting the plates." Then on a health kick, Bolan spent time at motorway service areas in a tracksuit jogging, rather than causing mayhem. His advice to The Damned included telling Rat how the melody of a song related to the notes of its chords and Captain that a producer should be treated as the band's fifth member.

The last date was Portsmouth on March 20 where The Damned joined T.Rex for a version of 'Get It On'. The short series of dates had built bridges between generations and also confirmed a punk band could tour the UK without incident. Still, though, there was a niggle. *NME*'s Mick Farren was with the band in Manchester and noticed the SS badge David wore on his lapel. The Damned's shunning of punk's fashions meant they were not tarred with flirting with fascism as the years went on. Nonetheless, Captain had sported a swastika on the rear of the 'Neat Neat Neat' picture sleeve. And the band's name was partly inspired by the film of the same name which had an ambivalent stance towards Nazi Germany.

Attitudes towards fascist posing and posturing were changing and The Damned were duly challenged by Farren. In January, he – Farren was a veteran observer of, commentator on and member of the British underground scene – had written about "the Nazi badges and arm bands [that] are turning up at clubs and a rock concerts as an essential part of street couture". He was concerned right-wing groups were sniffing around punk and that fashion victims were sleepwalking into giving fascism a platform. David's badge was bound to attract his attention.

It was a change from 1976 when *NME*'s coverage of the Sex Pistols' Screen on the Green show made no comment about the band's follower Siouxsie and her swastika armband. What attracted attention was that she had her "tits out" so was duly pictured with her breasts bared. Three weeks earlier, an interview with Alex Harvey was accompanied by a photo of him sat in front of a Nazi flag while wearing Third Reich regalia. Again, no comment. From David Bowie's apparent Nazi salute at London's Victoria Station and his comments that "I might have been a bloody good Hitler" and that he "strongly believed in fascism"[66] to Eric Clapton's anti-immigration outbursts at a Birmingham show, rock stars were flirting with fascism and racism in 1976. But whether it was words said in a quest for headlines, stupidity or empty-headed dressing up (as Rolling Stone Brian Jones had done in the Sixties and The Who's Keith Moon had in the Seventies), 1977 was the year when serious questioning of such idiocy began. The Rock Against Racism organisation had formed and there was greater scrutiny of how musicians comported themselves. David was in Farren's sights

When Farren asked David about the SS badge he was told, "it's just part of the show, anything you use to jolt people, to get them going, has to be worth it." Pushed on what would happen if their "Weimar pose" were to go wrong, the repost was, "Are you asking if the band should be responsible for what the audience does? No, that's their responsibility." With this, David was in tune with Rat when he had told NBC that, "The second rule [of punk] is you look after yourself."

★ ★ ★

The dates with Bolan helped sell *Damned Damned Damned*. The album's chart peak came the week after the tour had finished – sales increased while the band was on the road. Instead of consolidating the success with a headlining tour of their own, The Damned played odd one-off shows including their first headliners in Scotland. At Stirling University, a rain of beer cans forced them to leave the stage after 15 minutes. After another five minutes of trying, the show was abandoned.

Stiff then sent them to America. Jake Riviera had contacts on the east and west coasts through his time with Dr. Feelgood and he hoped to secure The Damned a contract with an American label. In the event, the first visit to America by a British punk band cemented the band's reputation as promoters of chaos, drew a line in the sand between the east and west coast's attitude towards punk and, unwittingly, altered the course of grassroots American music.

"Some of them in New York understood, the same as with London where they understood," recalls Captain. "But outside New York and Los Angeles, they didn't… like Macclesfield."

America's first opportunity to understand The Damned came on Thursday April 7 when they opened a four-day booking at CBGB, Manhattan's small but prime new-generation musical incubator. The band had arrived the previous afternoon. Over the run, they were set to play two sets each evening, regimentation they had never experienced before. They were co-billed with The Dead Boys, a Cleveland, Ohio band formed from the ashes of Rocket From The Tombs, which also spawned Pere Ubu. Stiv Bators, The Dead Boys' frontman, cast himself in the Iggy Pop mould and they had members called Johnny Blitz and Jimmy Zero. As friends of The Ramones, The Dead Boys – who had first played New York in July 1976 as long hairs in flares – were as close as America got to a self-professed post-Pistols, post-Ramones punk band at this point.

The Damned were warned about them. "I remember being in the Stiff office and someone saying there's this band called The Dead Boys, they're gonna kick your ass when you go over there," says Brian. "When we got there and met them, you couldn't have got a nicer bunch of geezers."

As the residency bedded in, The Dead Boys responded to The Damned's all-out drive and sped their own songs up in open acknowledgment the visitors were setting the agenda. The two bands joined forces on day three to run through 'Anarchy In The U.K.', with Rat joining Bators on vocals. The Ramones and Patti Smith came to the shows. Amongst the other curious onlookers were a contingent of British musicians in town, including Steve Gibbons, ex-Alan Bown and Bronco singer Jess Roden, Chris Squire of Yes and Mick Jagger.

Through their New York-based publicist, who felt it was a good idea to be associated with the new band, The Rolling Stones put their name to welcoming The Damned by ordering them seven meringue pies, two bottles of champagne, two-dozen carnations and three busty women. The pies were thrown at the audience. Rat also chucked a chair into the crowd as Captain fell off the stage. "You're so bad I love you" was yelled from the crowd. CBS and Sire were also there and said to be interested. Stiff had already tried to have its records released in America, but that was at arm's length and went nowhere.[67]

America's show business bible *Variety* caught the first night, thought The Damned "loud, coarse, rough and unrelenting" and concluded "success may grow in cult terms only. The Damned hardly seems capable of reaching a wide audience. But that's not what they're aiming for." *The New York Times'* John Rockwell said they were an "outré avant-garde experience [that had its] definite charms".

CBGB's proprietor Hilly Kristal said he put The Damned on as he had "heard all about the scene in England and about how all the groups were better than the American groups". He found them initially unconcerned with appearing at their best as they "didn't tune up and they screwed around a lot, and the first night when all the reviewers came was pretty bad. They improved on the second day, and the third day was much, much better, but they were careless, and you can't be careless on an important gig. They're nice people, and by the end of their run they were better than they'd been written up as being. But they didn't have their sound together at all." Offers from CBS and Sire were not forthcoming after all.[68] The latter, though, did sign the Hilly Kristal-managed Dead Boys.

The final day at CBGB became a problem. It was Easter Sunday and Patti Smith had been booked to play what was tagged "La Resurrection", a comeback show following a period of inaction forced by a neck injury. Her return to the stage meant The Damned and The Dead Boys were relegated to matinee slots. Smith was introduced by William Burroughs and attracted attention by pulling off a neck brace during her set, but there was friction with The Damned as she barred them from the venue's dressing room after their set.

Initially, the visit to America was meant to be CBGB only but Riviera secured dates in Boston and Los Angeles, the latter as support to New York's Television. Once on the west coast, San Francisco was also added.

On Easter Monday, The Damned travelled to Boston for the first of two nights at The Rathskeller – The Rat – which, like CBGB, seated its audience at tables. Boston had many no-frills, up and coming bands: a scene celebrated on the 1976 double album *Live At The Rat*. Like The Dead Boys' hometown Cleveland, the city had been one the few receptive to New York's pioneering musical disruptors The Velvet Underground. The Ramones were also well liked there. It ought to have been right for The Damned.

For the first night, 28 people turned up, sat at their tables and gave no sign of any interest in The Damned. "It was one of those 'what's this shit' reactions," recalls Captain. "So we had tables and chairs put up on the stage the next night and we sat there and ordered pizza. In between songs we'd have a discussion amongst ourselves. After about four or five songs the audience suddenly got it, that we were having a go back at them." The band lay down on cushions they'd placed in the stage.

"They started chucking pizza," says Brian of the audience.

"There was an antagonism by the end of the set which was quite good," offers Captain.

The Boston let down was followed by another. They arrived on the west coast to learn that Television – who had shared many bills with The Patti Smith Group: their leader Tom Verlaine had played on her records – had removed them from the bill of their Thursday April 14 Whisky a Go Go show. "Tom Verlaine didn't fancy working with us," says Captain. "Obviously the word had got to him that we were a bit, um, ha ha. It was pretty mad at times. Maybe he was right. If you want an easy life, I wouldn't work with The Damned."

"Jake told us that Tom Verlaine wouldn't do it because we were a punk band," says Rat. "We liked Television, we thought they were a very cool band. We had heard 'Little Johnny Jewel'. We were rejected for not being artistic enough."

Despite not being allowed to take the stage, The Damned went along to see Television anyway. David saw them twice and said, "The second time they were very boring. They did a dreadful version of 'Satisfaction'." Iggy Pop and The Runaways' Joan Jett were also there. Rat, *Record Mirror* said, "fancied his chances [with her at the Television show], became annoyed and had a tussle with Iggy".

Being pulled from the Television bill meant there was no money for hotels so they stayed with the band The Screamers, who had yet to play live. Jake Riviera and Brian were also taken in by Marina Muhlfriedel aka Marina Del Rey of the band Backstage Pass, as was Rat who then moved in with their bassist Joanna Dean, who he called Mistress Spock as she liked science fiction. On the Saturday afternoon, the band made an in-store appearance at the record shop run by Greg Shaw's Bomp Records. Everyone attracted by punk was there: members of LA's first punk band The Weirdos and new band The Germs, who hustled the relative veterans into letting them make their stage debut at their show that night. Scenesters Pleasant Gehman and Hellin Killer were at the shop too. The Damned being in town provided a focal point for the emerging LA punk scene and they were integral to it coalescing.

At a loose end that evening, the band – minus Rat – and Riviera turned up with The Screamers and DJ Rodney Bingenheimer to see The Weirdos play the Orpheum Theatre. Captain jammed with them on a version of The Seeds' garage-punk nugget 'Pushin' Too Hard'. Also on the bill were the pushy Germs, playing their first live show.

The next day, Sunday April 17, Los Angeles punk magazine *Slash* interviewed The Damned for their first issue. David said nothing but Rat declared, "We're just morons. I have never sat there and thought I'll smash my drums up tonight. If it happens, it happens." As to which members of The Damned said they were in America for the purpose of "fuckin' as many women as possible", "I'd like to stick my cock in Margaret Thatcher's mouth" and that *Zigzag* was the worst of the British music papers, *Slash* printed the quotes but did not attribute them. In the evening, the band did a two-band, double-header appearance with Blondie on Bingenheimer's radio show. It descended into chaos when the two bassists, Captain Sensible and Gary Valentine, took an instant and vocal dislike to each other.

Then, they got to play. On the Monday, the first of two hastily arranged shows at LA's prime punk venue The Starwood metaphorically breached the dam. Anything went. With money in short supply, Jake Riviera was at the venue's door making sure no one got in free. An appeal to the audience for funds to get home led to coins being thrown at the stage. David swung a lit roadside flare as the band played. Captain took his clothes off. It was inspirational: The Dickies formed after seeing them. Joan Jett was there, and her presence became of interest to Britain's music press. After the show the band and their new fans – including future X bassist John Doe – went to Canter's delicatessen where a food fight ensued. The *Los Angeles Times* hailed The Damned as "The Ambassadors of Punk Rock".

San Francisco was next. On the Wednesday, the first of two nights at North Beach venue Mabuhay Gardens had the same effect as the Starwood shows on the local scene. The Dils, whose members were in the audience, trimmed their songs and sped their playing up. The Damned were back in the UK by the weekend. Jake Riviera, though, stayed on in Los Angeles. His focus was on getting a US deal for recent Stiff signee Elvis Costello, whom he also managed. However, no contract with an American label for The Damned had been secured.

The American jaunt was first characterised for British fans in an interview for *Zigzag* undertaken on June 29 when the band played Dunstable. The interviewer's lack of fondness for The Damned was already a matter of record. Mac Garry had panned *Damned Damned Damned* in the magazine and was also, according to that review, a friend of Jake Riviera. Garry quoted Rat as saying America "was just an endless cycle of taking drugs, playing, drinking, fucking and travelling. We fucked our way through America. The only time I got out of bed was to do the gig or to have some photos taken. I tested the women all over America and I must say that the ones in Boston are not so good. New York and Frisco were very good, but the ones from LA were the best of all. There was one chick in the dressing room of the Starwood who gave nine of us blow jobs. One after the other. And we stuck the head of a Fender bass up her. She was on her knees giving one guy a blow job and there were eight others all round her shouting 'me next, me next'."[69]

Asked about this, Rat says, "This was Jake [speaking], I was there [for the interview] but this is all Jake. Jake did all the talking and it's credited to me. Why not? *Zigzag* wasn't a big paper, it would come out and there was no longevity to it, certainly not [enough] to come up 40 years later. You don't expect it to come back and bite you on the arse." Which is what the article – whether reliable or not – did as 1977 continued.

While The Damned were in America and after their return, as he remained there, Riviera was working hard for fellow Stiff artist and his other management charge Elvis Costello. A year earlier, Costello's was the first demo tape received by Stiff. On March 25, 1977, they issued his debut single 'Less Than Zero'; the next Stiff seven-inch after 'Neat Neat Neat'. The prize of American contract may not have come for Costello while Riviera was still there, but it did arrive in October 1977 when he signed with the Columbia label. The Damned got no such reward after their trip to America.

The Sunday after playing San Francisco, with their manager still in California, The Damned headlined their biggest London show to date at Camden's Roundhouse, topping the bill over Motörhead and recent Stiff signees The Adverts. They played before a banner saying "Tax Exiles Return. Hurray For The Captain's Birthday!"[70] In celebration, Captain wore a ballet tu-tu. He began by throwing cream cakes at the audience and David, and ended by taking his clothes off.

"I had mixed feelings," says Brian about Captain taking his clothes off. "I thought it was good he was expressing himself, living out fantasies or whatever he was doing. I don't care about being naked on stage, The Pink Fairies used to do that, so did Iggy. But I didn't like the way it was turning into a joke for some people."

Reviewing the Roundhouse show in *Sounds*, Jon Savage said they were "impressive – they've merged into a powerful and coherent force which can now accommodate such antics [as Captain's stripping]… without too much loss of power or sound." Savage also saw The Damned in traditional terms – as a form of showbusiness – and said "tonight is a *show*". *Record Mirror*'s Barry Cain concurred and concluded that "the key word is show, 'coz that's what The Damned are all about".

By the middle of the week following the Roundhouse date, The Damned were off again, to continental Europe on their first tour. One Thursday: they were on a San Francisco stage. The next: one in Paris. Between: one in Camden. No band could keep this up.

"The touring was very intense," notes Captain. "There was a lot of drinking as well. We were drinking a fantastic amount. I don't know how we managed."

"Very good speed," says Brian. "One thing The Damned was never into was heroin. We were probably most sober on stage."

★ ★ ★

By early May, when The Damned returned from Belgium, France and Denmark, The Clash had already set off on their month-long *White Riot-'77* tour, which began the first weekend of the month. The headliners were joined by Buzzcocks, The Slits, Subway Sect and (initially) The Jam. As a punk package tour, it gave the whole of the UK a chance to see what the new music was about in one handy chunk. The Clash's eponymous debut album had been issued on April 8. It was generally hailed as an instant classic in reviews and became a strong seller.

The Sex Pistols had not stood still either. After being ditched by EMI in January and then spending less than a week with A&M in March, they signed with Virgin on May 12. 'God Save The Queen', their belated second single, was being readied for release.

With *White Riot-'77* and the Sex Pistols signing, May 1977 was not quite when punk broke but it was the month access to the prime motivators increased. Voguish but less palpably punk bands were advancing too. The Vibrators had signed with CBS imprint Epic and issued 'Baby Baby', their first single for the label on May 20. The Stranglers consolidated the success of their debut album with the 'Peaches' single, issued earlier in the month. On April 29, The Jam's 'In The City' had hit shops and they became the first of the new bands to appear on *Top Of The Pops*. On Stiff and on the same day, the fine and recognisably punk Adverts had issued 'One Chord Wonders', their sole single for the label.

As the punk platform became ever-more crowded, The Damned recorded their second session for John Peel on May 10. Two new songs featured: 'Sick Of Being Sick' and 'Stretcher Case Baby'. Both were written by Brian, but Rat contributed lyrics to the latter. They also taped a BBC live *In Concert* on May 19. But recording something new for release was the priority.

'Sick Of Being Sick' and 'Stretcher Case Baby' were chosen for the next single. They had to be, as they were the only new songs. Instead of sticking with Nick Lowe as their producer[71], they chose the legendary Shel Talmy, known for his work during the Sixties with The Bachelors, The Creation, Manfred Mann and Pentangle and, more pertinently, The Kinks and The Who. Although not in line with the pervading Clash-driven ethos of "no Elvis, Beatles or The Rolling Stones", it made sense. The Clash's '1977', the B-side of their debut single, borrowed a Kinks riff. Their album track and subsequent single 'Remote Control' had shades of the early Who as well as The Kinks. In 1976, The Clash had recorded demos with Guy Stevens who, before he was a producer, was a prime mover in defining the soundtrack to the mod era. The Sex Pistols had covered songs by the Talmy-produced bands The Creation and The Who, and the repertoire of another mod band, Small Faces. Coming face-to-face with a figure from the past was a bold move but it was not surprising. Little digging was necessary to disinter British punk's mod-era roots.

"Shel was one the heroes, having done all the great Who stuff and The Kinks," says Brian. "It was an idea to do something different. It's a logical thing after the first album."

"Brian suggested Shel Talmy," recalls Rat. "I thought that was a good idea. His work with The Kinks, The Who and The Creation: we liked that sound. It was that Sixties drums and guitar sound, what we had grown up with." Camden's Roundhouse Studio was booked for the sessions.

Talmy had not seen the band live. "I was not surprised," says Talmy of being asked to work with The Damned. "Lots of people got in touch and many of them were asking me to do projects that would have been much stranger than asking me to record The Damned. I didn't think much of punk rock as most of the bands in that genre couldn't play their instruments, sing on key or write commercial songs. For many of them, commercial was a dirty word. I thought The Damned were the best of the bunch and thought it fair that I didn't condemn the entire genre out of hand without experiencing it personally, so I agreed to do the two sides."

"The sound didn't seem right," says Rat of the session. "We didn't take very long on the drums and I didn't like the sound he was getting. He hadn't caught what we wanted. I don't think there is enough going on with the melody."

Brian's take is different: "It was an experiment that worked, we had total respect." Yet The Damned and Shel Talmy did not work together again.

Looking back, Talmy says, "I was only asked to do two tracks as it was certainly an experiment on both sides and considering that they and I came from pretty widely separated ideas about music, I thought it turned out well. Punk is not really my cup of tea, it was fun to do it once and I don't think it would have benefited either of us to do more."

There was no time to do any more. On May 13, The Damned began a month-and-a-half British tour with their friends and labelmates The Adverts[72], whose bassist Gaye Advert often joined them on their encore. Stiff trailed the dates as "The Damned Can Now Play Three Chords, The Adverts Can Play One, Hear All Four Of Them." As well as 'Sick Of Being Sick' and 'Stretcher Case Baby', two other recent songs were aired on the tour: 'You Take My Money' and 'Politics'. The lyrics of the latter, Brian's reaction to how punk was being portrayed, took aim at The Clash and the Sex Pistols: "I don't need no politics to make me dance, No rules no laws no regulations... My politics don't sell clothes, And riots don't sell my soul... Give me fun not anarchy."

Brian had seen The Clash at the Rainbow on May 9, where sections of the audience destroyed the venue's stalls seats. The experience encapsulated his misgivings about what punk had become. "It was on their *White Riot* tour," he recalls. "The place was packed and it could have been a Bay City Rollers gig. Everyone was dressed in their Clash uniform. I thought 'What's this all about, where's the expression? It's missing the point.'"

On their own tour, The Damned experienced how punk-sensitive venues were reacting to the new-style audiences and bands which meant they may not get to play, even up to the last minute. At Stafford, the third date, staff did not open the doors so no one was let in and the show was abandoned. The next day, Southampton University's bar staff and porters refused to work. The show went ahead without drink. In Newcastle-under-Lyme, the venue's owner Mecca refused to let the band play. West Runton Pavilion was cancelled. That Saturday, St Albans City Hall was cancelled due to fears about public order after Hertfordshire police refused to attend. Only seven of the tour's first 12 dates went ahead. Cheltenham Town Hall on June 16 was pulled too, as was Southend Kursaal on June 18 when the local council stepped in to stop the punks.

An A. J. Milne of Grimsby caught the tour and was moved to write to *Melody Maker*, saying, "I have just seen The Damned and The Adverts. It was the most appalling rock concert I have ever witnessed. It is disgusting that groups so devoid of talent can get so much publicity when there are a thousand bands all over the country who deserve far more than these." Brian told Wigan's *Post and Chronicle*: "We give the audience a great time. We swear and blaspheme like anyone else and throw things like cake and pizzas at the audience. We hate conforming to society. We've freaked out."[73]

There was more to contend with than venues cancelling and the odd disgusted letter writer. At Lincoln, on June 14 (already a problem as the originally scheduled date for June 7 had been cancelled), 30 to 40 skinheads stormed the Drill Hall venue with bricks and pieces of wood, broke windows and the toilets, and then hung around to beat up the audience after the show. The Adverts and The Damned left their dressing room to find the tyres of their van had been let down and that the skinheads were waiting for them at the end of the alley in which it was parked. Its windows were smashed and there was no alternative but to call the police. At Penzance on June 23, heavies broke in to the dressing room, attacked David and left him with a dislocated shoulder. Four days later, at Lancaster, The Damned's roadie was dragged off stage and beaten up by four men.

Despite the violence and pulled dates, the tour was extended by four days to July 1, to accommodate shows booked to make up for the cancellations. Two days later, the band began what was supposed to be a four-day residency at London's Marquee to celebrate their first anniversary. Copies of the Shel Talmy-produced single had been pressed as a give-away for handing out to ticket holders. Jake Riviera allotted a specific amount of the 5,000 pressed for each evening, equivalent to the venue's capacity and tickets sold. The singles ran out on each of the first two nights, so Riviera knew The Marquee had oversold the shows and pulled the second pair of dates. The Marquee, which booked each August's Reading Festival, had already objected to the band's on-stage banner obscuring the venue's logo and removed The Damned from the proposed 1977 bill.

On a business level – as well as the lost revenue from the cancelled Marquee shows – there were other problems. The 'Stretcher Case Baby'/'Sick Of Being Sick' single had, like any record, cost money to record and manufacture. Giving it away recovered nothing. Members of Stiff's *Damned Disciples* fan club were sent copies, as were 250 readers of *NME* who entered a competition to win copies. The goodwill gesture was not a money spinner.[74] It was a money loser.

★ ★ ★

The pandemonium surrounding The Damned went further than live shows and the generous but ill-judged free single. There was friction between Stiff and its backer. In late May, finally back from America, Jake Riviera said he had "torn up the contract with Island". During the first week of June, Island ceased distribution and promotion of Stiff's records and barred its staff from their offices. They wanted their unrecouped £17,000 investment back. Even though *Damned Damned Damned* had charted, they had not seen a return. Furthermore, they wanted the same sum on top to cover their costs in setting up the internal organisation to deal with Stiff. The relationship was patched up and Stiff's records returned to shops, but there was little certainty about Jake Riviera, Stiff, Island, the future and the relationship between all four.

Brian was also under pressure. "We were touring and touring and touring and the record company were saying, where's the new album?" he recalls. "Put that in perspective. You haven't got a lot of time to write."

The answer, Brain thought, was to bring a second guitarist into the band, to take the pressure off him and refresh the sound. It was to "make it more exciting," he says. "It was my idea. I thought we had said it all on the first album. I thought that would be the easiest thing, like the MC5 twin-attack thing. I like change."

CHAPTER SIX

Rat Abandons Sinking Ship (Temporarily)

By July 1977, a wary music business was actively swatting punk aside to make way for something more digestible which was going to be given a new label. New wave had arrived.

Melody Maker had already said of *Damned Damned Damned* that "the new wave is making its biggest splash with The Damned". In July, the paper described a budding band called Advertising as "up-and-coming new wavers" who professed to set themselves apart from "the whole punk thing". But in the same issue, punk and new wave were also interchangeable. A letter from a reader in Edinburgh was headed "cut out the violence, punks" but actually mentioned "new wave concerts" and "new wave bands" – the word punk did not appear in the letter. This new wave was a slippery tag. Elvis Costello was to be its exemplar and his debut album *My Aim Is True* was reviewed in the same issue. The creator of Stiff's second album proper[75] was declared a "refreshing young performer" who it was hoped would be on the charts. The label had taken out a double-page ad for the album.

Costello's labelmates The Damned figured – albeit covertly – in that week's small ads. The same issue, July 23, included a musicians wanted notice seeking an:

INTERESTING GUITARIST into
Stooges, Damned, MC5, wanted
for name high energy band –
229 7146

The phone number was Stiff's. The Damned were looking for that second guitarist. Captain says he "had no part in the decision. I was never asked. We were on tour most of the time. At the time I thought Brian was – and I still do – one of the greatest guitarists this country has ever produced. I didn't think we needed another one." Nonetheless, potential applicants calling found Captain or Rat on the other end of the phone.

"Brian wanted another guitarist in the band," recalls Rat. "Beats the fuck out of me why. Not much point in having Brian. He would never let Captain play the guitar at the same time as him, as it would make him foolish. Brian would never entertain the idea as Captain, in Brian's words, was a buffoon. It was to do with egos, nothing to do with music. There was too much ego in the band members to ever allow anyone else more of a glory spot than what they already had. At the same time, I was aware that Brian was beginning to get stagnant and not have new material. He did obviously need something. He said the MC5 had two guitarists and it would be good if we could have something he could feed off."

For Brian, beyond giving him support, the arrival of an additional guitarist wasn't going to change things that much. "The Damned's sound was me, Captain, Rat and Dave singing," he says. "It seemed silly to fuck with that. It didn't really occur to me that Captain would do it, or want to do it. Dave and Captain were a bit bemused about me wanting another guitar player."

★ ★ ★

The auditions were held at the band's Putney rehearsal studio. "Mad, insane," says Captain of the try-outs. "Every quarter of an hour a new person came in. After a while it got really boring, most of them were muso tosspots, twiddly-diddly merchants. There was a lot of it about at the time, techno-flash guitar players going up their own bum. So we would stand there with our trousers round our ankles and see what they thought of that. We'd be waving our plonkers at them. There were not many people that could take it and he could: his name was Robert. We called him Lu, short for lunatic. 'Get that lunatic back' the cry went out."

Robert Edmonds had not been in a band before. At the time of the *Melody Maker* ad, he worked for two building contractors. For one, he demolished concrete structures and mixed mortar for brick layers at Hendon Aerodrome. For the other, he prepared concrete as well as mortar. The money earned was saved and spent on buying guitars. His elder brother exposed him to free jazz and his parents to musicals and records by American satirist Tom Lehrer, but his tastes veered towards blues, soul, British Sixties pop and psychedelia. His favourite guitarist was The Sensational Alex Harvey Band's Zal Cleminson. Keen on Dr. Feelgood, he also thought punk was worth paying attention to. After failing to form his own band, a couple of earlier auditions had come to nothing. He owned no records by The Damned, but liked the idea of them and knew Rat set fire to his cymbals.

He describes the audition as "like going into the dentist, a queue of sweaty hopefuls on a very hot day. I laughed a lot, it was all very nervy but amazing to see them. They were very wild and excited." On the floor and on his back, he made feedback-infused noise, was called back and asked to join.

David's initial reaction to Edmonds' arrival was positive. "I thought this is great, they could be duelling on stage," he says of how he imagined the new arrival and Brian would sound together. "Instead, Brian played less and Lu played what Brian played."

Although Edmonds arrived in The Damned when their individual personas were well-known and set, he quickly realised the band was "mainly split between Rat and Captain, and Brian and Dave: the hooligans versus the serious ones. Brian was the leader, the eldest. Everyone else was a cartoon character, living in an alternate reality – pushing themselves towards that. By the time I met them, they had all become larger than life and fractious. The dynamic varied depending on the intake of beer and maybe drugs. In all, Dave was very self-contained, Brian was the broad-minded aesthete, the experimenter – French films and hot curry – while Rat and Captain were intent on mayhem." No time was wasted further introducing Edmonds to the havoc. His first show with the band was on Friday August 5, 1977, a week-and-a-half on from when he was gently invited into the band.

Following the 1976 effort, Mont-de-Marsan was hosting its second and final punk rock festival. Time had moved on and the bill embraced punk as such. No coaches this time round: the Brit contingent flew into France. Friday kicked off at 4 p.m. with a packed arena seeing the French bands Strychnine, 1984, Asphalt Jungle and The Lous, who were followed by The Maniacs, The Police, The Boys, The Damned and The Clash. Saturday's bill was a repeat of 1976's pre-punk pub rock billing, albeit with a first-time-round headliner: The Tyla Gang, Little Bob Story, Bijou (a French trio which pre-dated punk but were spiritually of the moment), Eddie & The Hot Rods and, on last, Dr. Feelgood. Little in The Damned's set suggested the addition of a second guitarist had immediately changed the band's approach or sound. Instead of a new, added element to the sound Brian and Lu played with each other – effectively, in unison. More power, but no radical change.

"Nobody explained anything to me," recalls Lu, reflecting on whether he was given any guidance. "The MC5 had two guitarists, and maybe Brian wanted to emulate that – get a thicker sound to allow himself to fly off out more. The Damned already had two guitarists with Captain and Brian, so they got three. I think I probably could have been better off as the bass player had Brian and Captain ever agreed to play together. But they didn't and couldn't. Brian skids, careens and is 100-per-cent rock'n'roll. A leader-type guitarist. Maybe I'm a bit more structural, hold arrangements and perhaps have more acute timing."

At Mont-de-Marsan, Captain disrupted headliners The Clash after they played their cover of Junior Murvin's 'Police And Thieves'. Joe Strummer told the audience, "The Damned just came on stage and put some stink bombs up here because they're fucking jealous. They can just fuck right off. And another thing, we all ain't got a sense of smell." For his actions, Captain was thrown off the stage by the festival's security and ended up landing with the stage-front barrier between his legs. He seemed comatose and an ambulance was called. As it pulled away from the arena, he roused and scrabbled over the roofs of parked trucks to get back to the festival. The next day, a meeting was held between The Clash and The Damned. Rat said, "The war between The Clash and The Damned is over." Of Captain, Strummer said, "I like the geezer. I accept that he's got a few screws loose and I like him."

On the festival's second day, in addition to making peace with The Clash, Rat was talking to *NME*'s Tony Parsons, who brought up the Los Angeles debauchery. Rat apparently declared: "The interview we did with *Zigzag* was well over the top because America is like that. And I didn't stick a Fender bass up a girl's arse. I was well pleased when I got pulled by a Runaway. But she was a very lousy lay. And I only threw her out of the dressing room when she started smashing everything up." As for the backstage blowjobs, he was "off to one side, wanking". The further account of the behaviour in California generated a hand-written letter from Jett to *NME*, who said, "I did not fuck Rat Scabies... I don't get all hot and bothered over two-and-a-quarter inch erections anyway."

The Thursday after Mont-de-Marsan, The Damned joined The Clash to play Belgium's Bilzen Festival. Elvis Costello & The Attractions were also on the bill, the first and only time The Damned played with them. Edmonds' second live outing took place behind a 10-foot barbed-wire fence the festival's organisers had set in front of its two side-by-side stages to keep the audience at bay. Bilzen was a four-day jazz festival which had added punk to its usual smattering of folk and rock acts, and was taking no chances with the sort of audience that it might attract. Costello went on after a trio featuring Flemish chanson singer Johan Verminnen, Belgian skiffle and blues pioneer Roland Van Campenhout and guitarist-singer Big Bill Krakkebaas. The Damned hit the stage after Costello. The Clash were to close the day.

Costello's set was without incident. The Damned played to a hail of beer cans but were called back for an encore by an enthusiastic minority of the crowd. The Clash, though, had it worse. Paul Simonon was hit by a brick. A five-inch steel bolt was thrown. So were rocks. There was a fight between Joe Strummer and security men. Afterwards, the stress caused Mick Jones to vomit. The next day, on the coach home, Captain Sensible tied the shoelaces of a sleeping Elvis Costello together, stuffed cigarette butts into his mouth and then set fire to his shoes.

Lu says, "By the time I joined, they were all a bit exhausted and shot – from touring, instant fame syndrome, the slow realisation of that the money was in songwriting[76] and a collapse in support from Stiff. It was made clear that I should participate in all forms of excessive behaviour, which is in some ways more controlling than being told what to play, and I was just 19. Jake hated the whinging and misbehaviour."

Britain got its first chance to see the new, five-piece Damned over two nights of the next week at The Sundown, a large Charing Cross Road disco[77] which had short-lived ambitions to be London's leading punk venue. The audience dropped beer cans on the band from an open balcony above the central stage area.

★ ★ ★

Considering the lack of time between the release of *Damned Damned Damned* and beginning a new album, Brian says, "A lot of people, especially people at Stiff, thought this thing's not going to last, let's milk it. They didn't realise the longevity of it, even the bands that came up in our wake." The Jam and The Stranglers each released two albums in 1977. As did The Damned.

By the Sundown shows and after the release of *Damned Damned Damned*, The Damned had only six new songs: 'Don't Cry Wolf', 'Politics', 'Problem Child', 'Sick Of Being Sick', 'Stretcher Case Baby' and 'You Take My Money'. 'Problem Child' was already earmarked as their next single and, like 'Stretcher Case Baby', had lyrics by Rat. Otherwise, they were all Brian's.

"We didn't know what to do, we knew that we didn't have any material," recalls Rat. "We were very short of songs. The old 'lifetime to write the first album and three months to write the second'. Brian had refused to let anyone write a song. There was a fight to get 'Stab Yor Back' on the first album. Everyone called him the fuehrer. He was the policy maker. That's all well and good as long as he keeps coming up with the goods. But when he stopped, it was 'you guys had better write a song'. He did this turn-around."

"We were on tour and it was like 'who's got any ideas?'" confirms Brian. "We encouraged Rat because he did 'Stab Yor Back'."

"Apart from 'Stab Yor Back' me and Captain had never written a song in our lives," says Rat. "Suddenly, we had to have songs for an album. Being my usual optimistic self I said, 'We can do this, it's easy.' It was the first time I looked at a guitar neck with Captain and said, 'It's on there somewhere, all you have to do is move your fingers around.'"

While the band got used to having a second guitarist and figured out how to counter their deficit of new material, Stiff pushed them to get in the studio. This time, though, Nick Lowe was not going to be their producer. He had said, "I'll not be producing any more Damned records. The first time I encountered them [The Damned] I was totally turned off. I mean, who are these obnoxious mouthy geezers blabbering on about Iggy Pop...who the fuck is Iggy Pop? I'd never heard of the New York Dolls or MC5, but there was still something there, a kind of arrogance that I admired, that I latched on to. I used them. I worked with them because I wanted to and it was great. We'll never do anything together again though. There'd be absolutely no point. I've exhausted all that."

The dalliance with Shel Talmy was in the past, too. Their starry new producer came through their publisher, The Rock Music Co., who also had pub rockers Kokomo and The Kursaal Flyers on their books. Progressive folk outfit Gryphon and country rockers Unicorn were other clients, as were Hawkwind. Rock Music's star client, though, was Pink Floyd, whose drummer Nick Mason had a gap in his diary following the completion of the worldwide tour to promote their *Animals* album. Pink Floyd also had their own a studio, on Britannia Row in Islington, a 25-minute walk from Pathway where 'New Rose' and *Damned Damned Damned* had been recorded. Mason was approached to produce The Damned's second album. It was potentially controversial to cosy up to Pink Floyd: they were dinosaurs. Johnny Rotten had worn an "I hate Pink Floyd" T-shirt on stage.

"It's a difficult thing to say you like Pink Floyd because of what they became," says Captain. "Two totally different bands, they became a bucket of shit when Gilmore stopped copying Syd. Syd Barrett was inspired."

Pink Floyd's original guiding light and songwriter Barrett had been sacked from the band in 1968, after which he had made two other-worldly solo albums and then retreated from the music business. Public appearances were rare. The 1975 Pink Floyd song 'Shine On You Crazy Diamond' was a tribute to him. As much as they wanted him, the likelihood of Barrett producing The Damned – or any band – was nil. Instead of Barrett, The Damned were given another founder member of Pink Floyd as their producer in early August. The Mason pill was sweetened by the band saying they had tried to get Barrett to produce them rather than Pink Floyd's drummer.

"We didn't know who was going to produce the second album," says Brian. "It was a joke: 'No chance of getting Syd to do it?' Really, it was because it all fitted perfectly. Pink Floyd's studio was free, Nick Mason fancied doing something."

"Never," says Rat of the perception that Barrett was to produce The Damned. "We knew that, Syd is a much better story."

Practically, the more pressing issue was what was going to be on the album. 'Alone', which they had played at their earliest shows in 1976, was resurrected. Brian suggested they record The Who's 'Circles', which they had covered early on. That was vetoed by the rest of the band, however.

Even more change came with the appearance of saxophonist Lol Coxhill on the grinding, intense 'You Know', The Damned's most extreme recorded moment. Although an overt nod to Steve Mackay's contributions to The Stooges' *Funhouse*, further inspiration came from a knowledge of British edginess and who Coxhill had played with in the past, "To a large degree it was inspired by *Funhouse*," acknowledges Brian. "As a lover of jazz, it drew from that but it was also inspired by Kevin Ayers and [his band] the Whole World [which Coxhill had played with]. Captain liked it."

Coxhill played with Ayers in his band the Whole World and had been a questing figure on the British jazz scene since the mid-Fifties.

Coxhill's music touched on the African, blues and soul. Free jazz and improvisation were as familiar as structured music. An avowed alternative figure, he played without being paid and busked. After encountering him at a petrol station on London's North Circular Road, The Damned had jammed with him in Dunstable. Getting Coxhill on the new album drew a direct line from themselves to the British avant-garde. "Lol Coxhill may have been one of the old guys, but he didn't like voting, the police," recalls Rat. "He was part of the intelligentsia, Henry Cow, Soft Machine, all of that left field music thing. Captain was into it." Unwittingly, the collaboration echoed the contributions of Xerxes to Captain's pre-Damned adventures with Johnny Moped. At the album sessions, the unconventional Coxhill was accompanied by a knitted child on roller skates which he called Darren.

As for Mason, Brian says, "He didn't really contribute at all. To be fair to him, he didn't detract a lot, he just didn't really do anything. The only time he got a bit more animated was when we got Lol Coxhill, he liked that."

"He could enthuse for hours about his motor bikes and racing cars," says Captain of their producer. "But when it came to music, I don't know if he was that interested."

"I never noticed what Nick Mason was doing," says Rat. "I used to hit him up for equipment. He had this warehouse with flight cases full of drum stuff. He took me around. He gave me a foot pedal as I'd broken mine. It went to Ian Dury who was drumming for Wreckless Eric. From Pink Floyd to Wreckless Eric."

No time was wasted between the completion of the album sessions and offering the first evidence of the band's liaison with Mason. The 'Problem Child' single was issued on September 16, less than a month after the band had been at Britannia Row and days after David's September 7 marriage.

None of the reviews of 'Problem Child' addressed the incongruity of working with a member of Pink Floyd – the record's producer and the addition of second guitarist were not mentioned. *Sounds* noted "chunky Who-style staccato riffing", "cleaner production" and said it was "certainly catchy enough to get airplay".

Melody Maker chose Elvis Costello's 'Watching The Detectives' as the week's lead single and directed readers to "buy 20 copies". Of 'Problem Child', in the same column, The Who were again mentioned with the pay-off "you can do better than this, lads". In *NME*, Charles Shaar Murray said it had "no chewn", immediately below saying in the column that the Sex Pistols' 'Holidays In The Sun' was a "a shapeless rant rather than song". *Record Mirror* went further, talked of a "lack of motivation, direction, power" and of The Damned that "the whole concept was brick-wall transient. This record merely highlights the wane." Interest was lacking and good will was in short supply.

★ ★ ★

The response to 'Problem Child' did not matter when it was issued because, as usual, The Damned were out on the road. A couple of British live shows in the last week of September were followed by a tour of Switzerland, France, the Netherlands and Germany booked for most of October.

Although Stiff had the album they wanted from The Damned and concrete evidence that Elvis Costello was on the up and up, the label's major concern was the promotion of a package tour branded "Stiffs Greatest Stiffs Live" that was being promoted from early September. It would feature Costello, Ian Dury & The Blockheads, Nick Lowe, Larry Wallis, Wreckless Eric and special non-Stiff guest Dave Edmunds. Implicitly and explicitly, their label did not consider The Damned one of their greatest. With The Adverts gone and now with the Anchor label who issued their chart hit 'Gary Gilmore's Eyes', none of Stiff's other acts had roots in the punk boom of 1976. Instead, most had ties with the pub rock boom that preceded it: as Julie Burchill and Tony Parsons put it in 1978, Dury and Costello "were pub-rockers seeking a second bite at the banana by pushing a contrived calculated image".[78]

The Damned, though, had generated interest from EMI, whose A&R manager Nick Mobbs wrote to Jake Riviera with a firm offer to sign the band. The terms he suggested on September 7 were a worldwide one-year deal, with options on two subsequent years. The Damned were to be with EMI for three years: an advance of £50,000 was proposed for year one, with £60,000 and £70,000 each for the next two years. The band were expected to release one album and two singles a year, and EMI were to retain the rights in perpetuity. Mobbs asked to negotiate directly with Riviera as both the band's manager and as a director of Stiff. The offer was not followed up as Riviera's relationship with Stiff was falling apart and EMI shifted their attention to ex-Sex Pistol Glen Matlock's Rich Kids.

Riviera had a massive argument with Dave Robinson on September 24. The man who managed The Damned and brought them to Stiff was, at this point, on the road with the "Stiffs Greatest Stiffs Live" tour as Costello and Lowe's manager but was no longer a part of the label. After the bust up, Riviera left, took Lowe and Costello with him and signed them to his new Radar label in 1978. The partnership he had with Dave Robinson for Stiff and the related management company Advancedale Artists was arranged that if one of them left, all deals had to be renegotiated. In the fall out, Dave Robinson became The Damned's manager.

"Jake just walked out," recalls Brian, "He went off with Elvis Costello. We didn't even know he had gone. Dave Robinson said, 'Jake's fucked off, I'm managing you now.' It was, 'We ain't signed to you, we signed to him.' Without Jake there, it wasn't the same for us. And that was it. To me, Jake will always be a wanker."

"I felt betrayed," says Captain. "I'll never forgive him."

Then, their old producer Nick Lowe was interviewed by *Melody Maker*[79] and said, as he had in July, that he "didn't really want to get involved" with The Damned's new album. He had heard the as-yet unreleased tracks and made his opinions plain: "The new album I think is a bit dodgy. It took Brian James something like five years to get all the songs together for the first album. And they were good songs. So the songs aren't up to it. And he wasn't man enough to admit it. I suggested that since they didn't have the songs they should have recorded a 'Damned play the old wave album'. Can you imagine The Damned playing all Deep Purple and Black Sabbath songs. It'd be an absolute gas, man. And it'd be straight up the chart. They didn't have the bottle for it though. Nick Mason's done the new album and it's so clear you can hear every instrument. And The Damned just aren't up to that kind of scrutiny. I'm not sure about The Damned at the moment."

Dave Robinson, The Damned's new manager, was fully occupied with his label's concurrent "Stiffs Greatest Stiffs Live" tour. Their new album wasn't out, Lowe had already panned it in the press, Costello was on the up and Ian Dury was about to become Stiff's next critical success and big seller. As Brian puts it, "It was back to their good old pub boys." Nonetheless, continental Europe beckoned.

No one had a close eye on The Damned. Rat had already proposed leaving the band and it was not a concern. "I'd already told Jake I didn't want to do the tour and wanted to leave," recalls Rat. "Jake talked me into doing the second album. I realised on an artistic level it was over, we shouldn't be making another album. I felt I couldn't have done the tour and remained sane. What was bad for me was the band."

Rat's misgivings were compounded by tensions arising from his and Captain's dislike of David bringing his new wife on the tour. Brian was also accompanied, as he had been on previous road trips, by his girlfriend, the photographer Erica Echenberg. "She was snapping at me and Captain and Lu every time we opened a beer," says Rat. "'Hey you guys, get off that.'"

Still, though, the band did make it to France and Brian was getting a feeling for who Lu was. "He was the sort of guy you couldn't get to know that well," says Brian. "Very nice, serious. You could imagine Lu hatching a plot, like Guy Fawkes, or a college activist. An agitator who looked for conspiracies."

Lu recalls that "Captain and Rat didn't like that I was living quite close to Brian, who they resented for his publishing score. I always got on OK with Dave, who I liked a lot. All of them though were likeable and they made me laugh a lot. I was the youngest and least street wise."

In France, Rat only played two dates. The first, in Nancy, was brought to a close after ten minutes by members of the French right-wing party Le Front National smashing the venue up. Captain was so drunk he lay behind his amplifier. The second date, in Colmar on September 29, was Rat's last of the tour. He told someone in the audience that it was his birthday – it wasn't – and was given a handful of pills, which he took. As the band played, a glass headed through the air towards him. Coming out from behind his drums, Rat ran towards the man he thought had thrown it, grabbed him by the hair and threw him out. He headed back to the Hôtel Colbert. "That was the night I got beaten up," he recalls. "I was drifting."

The hotel's basement housed a nightclub, Le Toucan. He wasn't allowed in the lift as the manager thought he was gatecrashing an event there, rather than staying in the establishment. Annoyed, he threw some cushions around the lobby and was then pulled out into the street. "I was outside fighting this guy," continues Rat. "Two guys were walking past, he said something to them in French and they joined in. As I'm being punched and kicked I looked up and the band were standing there watching. The only one who got me out was the one I hated, the hippy tour manager."

Back in the hotel Rat was, he says, "for the rest of the night, very delusional". He tried to climb out his room's window to get into Brian's to find money to pay for a getaway.

"My memory of it is different to Rat's," says Brian. "My memory is he had drunk a couple of bottles of brandy, which should have knocked him out and was building a camp fire in the middle of his room. All right, if he wants to do that, let him do it but don't burn the hotel down. In my mind, Rat was suffering some form of nervous breakdown. He was trying to jump out of the window. We were pulling him back and it was like, 'Rat go home.' And that was it, he went off."

The next morning, Rat was given enough money by the band's tour manager to get to Paris. He found Mont-de-Marsan organiser Marc Zermati, stayed the night with him and was given enough to get back to London. "This was the dream come true, this was my life and I just wanted to get out," he recalls of how he felt. "Suddenly, it was I'm not going do this anymore." Rat Scabies had left The Damned.

★ ★ ★

News travelled fast. *NME* and *Sounds* reported the incident as a suicide attempt. Speaking to *Sounds*, he denied that. He was, he said, "fed up with the John Wayne syndrome – people poking you in bars trying to prove how hard they are."

"There was no attempted suicide, no breakdown," he says. "I just wanted to get out." A week after arriving back in London, he had a rehearsal with The Heartbreakers, whose drummer Jerry Nolan had left. Rat's playing wasn't a good fit and he did not join The Heartbreakers. Instead, his first public appearance after leaving The Damned was on Monday October 17 at punk venue The Vortex with Johnny Moped. Paul Gray of Eddie & The Hot Rods was on bass while Rat's old Tor bandmate Slimey Toad was on guitar. It was a bizarre job swap: Johnny Moped's drummer Fred Berk had replaced him in The Damned and was playing Amsterdam that evening.

After a day's rehearsal with Berk in a French barn, The Damned ploughed on with their substitute drummer. Lu Edmonds says there was "a sense of relief all round," about Rat leaving. "Dave Berk came in. Captain was *very* happy with that and we all had a good time. Rat by that point had become very overbearing and dark and tried unsuccessfully to take it out on me, and there were physical incidents."

In Holland at Amsterdam's Melkweg, five days after David's 21st birthday, The Police were one of the resumed tour's support bands. "Brian chased Sting out the dressing room," recalls Captain. "He said, 'Can I have a bottle of your wine, we haven't got any.' Brian said, 'No, you're the support band, you can fuck off, when you're top of the bill you can have as much as you want.' Sting had to give the bottle back."

The band's drummer Stewart Copeland suggested he join The Damned. "We could have changed the course of history there and then," recalls Brian. "Stewart, who was a friend of mine anyway, came over and said, 'Are you looking for a drummer, how about me?' But I didn't want an American drummer. I have no idea why I wanted to keep it British."

After their return to London, the new album was about to be released and there was supposed to be a national tour with The Dead Boys as support. Dave Berk wasn't staying, so early dates were cancelled while they auditioned a replacement for Rat. *NME* reported that the band had met with Rat and wouldn't be using him. Instead, 50 drummers were auditioned after an ad had been placed in *Melody Maker* saying:

THE DAMNED
REQUIRE A GREAT DRUMMER
FAST

Only people who feel they can handle the job straight away
need apply.
We want the best. Time wasters will be dealt with.
**Phone 01 408 1788, Wednesday, Thursday,
Friday, between 4pm and 6pm only.**

It came down to two candidates: Canada's Jim Walker, who was later in Public Image Ltd, and Jon Moss from cash-in punk band London.[80] Moss got the job as he was, indeed, British.

"Dave Berk, unfairly in my opinion, was discounted for not looking right," recalls Edmonds. "Jon got the job for looking right. Jon is a good drummer but his forte is a genius business brain. His drumming is basically like what it would be later with Culture Club: he keeps time nicely and organises everything. Rat is by far and away the right drummer for The Damned and plays with blazing rockets over everything, huge dynamics, exuberance and brilliance in his rolls, great shuffles in his patterns. He is in many ways a jazz drummer, but with a Keith Moon attitude."

Music For Pleasure, the second album Nick Lowe thought "a bit dodgy", was issued on November 18. "It was an experiment that didn't work," says Brian. "At the time, punk was about change, and it was trying to be different from the rest of the punk stuff and the first album. I don't think we pulled it off in any way at all, but no one can blame us for trying."

"It was supposed to be psychedelic," adds Rat. "I think it was pretty dreadful. A lot of people don't agree."

"It would be so easy to repeat yourself," notes Captain. "I didn't like the album so much though. Reviews went along with what I thought anyway. But it's not as bad as I thought then."

Sounds was generally positive and noted that *Music For Pleasure* "extended on the Wall of Sound of first album". In *NME*, a considered Nick Kent pointed to a "sheer lack of substance". He went further by bemoaning the relentless coverage of The Damned and suggested the band tried to live up to it. "I recall seeing Sensible at a reception at the height of it all in his usual madcap attire – a leather jacket and ballerina's tou-tou. He was encircled by a bunch of cretin-sycophants willing him on to pursue further heights of self-demeaning idiocy for their own kicks. At one point, I saw his face that night looking so horribly vulnerable, so completely confused and bleak that it somehow mirrored just what that side of The Damned's image and the whole gobbing headbanger slant had turned into."

★ ★ ★

Not everything was going downhill. Stiff recorded the band at The Roundhouse for a prospective live album. Their three tour dates there were sell-outs. *Music For Pleasure* came in an amazing Barney Bubbles sleeve. 'One Way Love'/'Don't Cry Wolf', from the album, was issued on December 14 as a single in a hopefully sales-generating magenta vinyl edition.[81] But the crumbs were few. The Boomtown Rats' Bob Geldof reviewed the single and concluded "it used to be neat neat neat. Now, sorry lads, it's awful awful awful."

At the second of The Roundhouse shows, Rat turned up but wasn't allowed into the band's dressing room. Backstage, Captain told *Sounds'* Pete Silverton, "The Damned are in the dumpers. Everyone knows that. No one wants to know us." It also looked as if the band members didn't want to know each other. On the tour during which The Roundhouse was played, *Melody Maker*'s Allan Jones witnessed Captain and Lu wrestling on the bus and throwing lighted cigarettes. Having enough of it, Brian grabbed Lu by his hair, dragged him into the aisle and then bit him on the ear.

A week after the tour finished and five days before Christmas, Stiff's seasonal gift for the band was to drop them. In the new year, Dave Robinson said the move was "part of a clear-cut policy to make way for new talent. This is a record company not a museum." The official statement continued, "Stiff is entering a new phase and The Damned does not come into our category."

Brian's response was bold. "The band and us have come to a joint decision that they should develop and go off on their own," he said.

"[With Jake Riviera gone] there is no longer any connection with the company. We're a new band and Stiff's a bit like an old pub rock label. We are negotiating as it were with various companies. The laying off period is proving quite useful, giving us time to write some new stuff. It makes it more exciting for us."

"Stiff stiffed us," says Captain.

There were more bad tidings. On New Year's Eve, Jon Moss was in a car crash and went through the windscreen. Seriously injured with a broken nose, he required 100 stitches to his face and was kept in North London's Royal Free Hospital for a week. Following his discharge, he returned to the drum stool for a Croydon show on January 15. A week earlier, *NME* ran an article by Charles Shaar Murray which echoed the concerns Nick Kent had expressed when reviewing *Music For Pleasure*. He had met the band ten days before Christmas and was troubled by Captain. "There is a steadily increasing desperation quotient in the Captain's determined assaults on the consciousness of everybody who passes through the portals of Stiff Records and proportional increments of desperation are being displayed by his audience," he wrote. "This afternoon, the Captain's dementia is turned strictly against himself, as – ultimately – it always has been. His throat is caked with something that looks like blood. No one cares enough to ask him whether it is. I didn't either. Sensible doesn't seem to be having a good time, but he's putting himself on the line for absolutely nothing at all."

Shaar Murray pointedly suggested they were in an "ongoing blowing-it non-achievement situation", bemoaned "Scabies making a total idiot of himself over the redoubtable Joan Jett, and of backstage bully-boy nastiness. (Heard the one about the New York groupie and the Fender bass? If you laughed, you're an asshole)[82]" and concluded, "The Damned are still slugging on regardless. Keeping on playing to whoever wants to see them, carrying on in whatever direction takes their fancy, fuelled principally by their unshakeable belief that The Damned are the greatest rock'n'roll band on the surface of the earth. Pretty much the way they started out, in fact."

At the beginning of February they picked up publicist Alan Edwards as their new manager and it was duly announced that any internal problems were settled, new material was being worked on and that, implausibly, Frank Zappa had been approached to produce a new LP. Lu had been writing with Moss and, separately, Captain had recorded demos with Lu.

Any impressions of movement were a façade. Zappa was unaware he was in the frame to enter the studio with The Damned. A couple of live dates in late January and early February were followed by Brian resolving to split the band. Following a rehearsal on February 22, he told them of his decision.

"It had really stopped halfway through the European tour after we had recorded the second LP," says Brian. "Rat left, we finally settled on Jon Moss as his replacement. Good drummer but if Rat hadn't left, we might not have split. Then we did a tour with The Dead Boys and I thought, this isn't the same band, I'm not enjoying it. The energy isn't here anymore. Our manager Jake Riviera had left, gone off with Elvis Costello. He didn't even say goodbye. Jake had been like a member of the band. There was a feeling of apathy, it got like flogging a dead horse. I wouldn't say we were any more out of control than we had been before. I said I want to split the band up."

There were the customary official statements: "Musical differences of opinion between James and the other members of the band had become increasingly apparent, and a break was the only obvious solution." Brian was said to be worried about the band's "clown image". Captain was quoted as saying that he and Lu Edmonds had written songs together which the rest of the band didn't like. He had 15 songs of his own that were "like a cross between Soft Machine and ABBA, with a bit of The Damned thrown in". They were jazz influenced and allowed room for improvisation.[83] Brian commented: "There was no point in continuing. I was writing one kind of thing and Lu in particular was doing something different – it was very good, but it wasn't the direction I wanted the band to go. The Damned's image was always one of fun and now I want to get more serious. I didn't want us to be stamped with that horrible punk thing forever."

David said Lu Edmonds' arrival had set the band's demise in train. "Getting in another guitarist gave Brian someone to identify with, but it turned out that the other members of the band plus guitarist caused too much friction. It worked out as two bands, or three bands in one separate band. It just didn't work out."

"I was pretty shocked," says Captain of Brian's decision. "I couldn't see it coming, maybe I should have done. I quite liked the thing, jumping around on stage, getting paid to have beer and having a laugh. I didn't know what I was going to do with my life. I got very, very drunk and ended up at a launch for an XTC album. They had this cake in the shape of XTC, which went all over the place. I was chucking it everywhere."

On the rebound, Captain claimed to *Melody Maker* that he was going to form a band with Johnny Rotten, and that The Clash were about to split as Mick Jones and Joe Strummer hated each other. There were spurious reports he was joining Paul Cook and Steve Jones in a new-look Sex Pistols as a replacement for Sid Vicious. In truth, he had no idea what he was going to do and was numbed by what had happened. Immediately after Brian saying he was splitting the band, Captain had gone on his own to a screening of *ABBA, The Movie*.

★ ★ ★

Of British punk's first trio of bands to hit stages, one remained standing. The Sex Pistols had split while on tour in America during January. The Clash – whatever Captain said – were knuckling down to getting their second album off the starting blocks in the wake of the release of February 1978's 'Clash City Rockers' single.

At Stiff Records, Ian Dury was proving a financial saviour. Eight months after it was issued, his album *New Boots And Panties!!* lodged itself in the charts from April 1978. At the same time, the 'What A Waste' single was a bona-fide pop hit. Dave Robinson said The Damned had not kept the label afloat. Though *Damned Damned Damned* had sold 45,000 copies, the profits were, he said, swallowed up by bills for damage at venues and hotels. With sales of 20,000, *Music For Pleasure* had not been a money spinner either. The "Stiffs Greatest Stiffs" tour had lost £11,000. Stiff itself could have been stiffed. Dury became the label's cash lifeline.

Beyond Dury, the other long-term certainty to emerge from Stiff's first year-and-a-half was Elvis Costello, who Jake Riviera had taken to his new Warner Brothers-backed Radar label. His first releases for the imprint came in March 1978 with single '(I Don't Want To Go To) Chelsea' and second album *This Year's Model*.[84] As a jumping-off point, Stiff was no longer necessary to Costello or his manager.

The Damned had given Stiff its profile. Without The Damned and British punk's first single, the label had to wait until Elvis Costello recorded anything which resonated more widely than a series of eye-catching slogans and one-off singles by warmed-over pub rockers and oddballs like Wreckless Eric. Without The Damned, Stiff may have achieved traction but not so early, so quickly and with such a high profile.

As to whether a cleavage between Stiff and The Damned was inevitable, the band was moving so fast and was so unstable there were no certainties. The only certainty was that there was no certainty. Which was confirmed within months of the band's split.

Music For Pleasure

Writing in 2001, Creation Records co-founder and former Jesus & Mary Chain producer Joe Foster said, "Some albums are pushed to the margins by critical fashion, some are pushed right under the floorboards. Indeed, there are some works that seem to be deliberately denied any hope of redemption."

In making the case for *Music For Pleasure*[85], Foster spoke to Captain who told him, "It was a load of bollocks. Absolute crap. Don't be afraid of saying it. It was rubbish." Foster went on to argue that "*Music For Pleasure* was by no means as coherent as its predecessor, but neither was it the disastrous faux pas of legend. The sound of a band over-reaching and being punished for it? Maybe. Place *Music For Pleasure* next to the hundreds of 'punk' albums that have appeared since '77 and it sounds like a full-blown masterpiece."

The process of condemning The Damned's second album had begun before it was even released. Nick Lowe, who did not produce it, was quoted as pronouncing it "a bit dodgy", with "songs [that] aren't up to it" and "production [that] isn't right for them" four weeks in advance of it reaching shops. And, as the years have gone by, advance publicity like that prevented *Music For Pleasure* from gaining friends. Commercially, in its afterlife, it does not appear a winner: *Damned Damned Damned* is reissued endlessly; *Music For Pleasure* is not.

Nonetheless, despite all the complications, it looked as if Stiff Records were still behind the band. They hired Pink Floyd's studio to record the album and Barney Bubbles painted a superlative sleeve based on Vasily Kandinsky's 1923 artwork *Komposition 8*. Hidden within Bubbles' imagery were the faces of all five members of The Damned. Bubbles also created a series of arresting ads for the album, in which the band members' faces were as distorted as the creatures created by H. G. Wells' Doctor Moreau – branding the album "uneasy listening". Unlike *Damned Damned Damned*, a printed inner sleeve was authorised.[86] One side bore a photo of the band which, if red- and green-tinted glasses were put on, was in 3D. On the other, a blurred shot caught the band moving during a long exposure: Rat appeared to be dissolving – apt, as he had left by the time the album was out. Further evidence of trouble taken came with a comparison of September's 'Problem Child' single and the album version: remixing had subsequently taken place, and the *Music For Pleasure* rendering was more dense, more punchy.

The support, though, was almost exhausted. Jake Riviera left Stiff in September. The Damned and the label were firmly in his past. Days before Christmas and four weeks after the album was issued, Dave Robinson discharged The Damned from the label's roster. The turmoil of 1977 and how the music business closest to The Damned behaved towards them has fed into notions of how *Music For Pleasure* is seen. The album's subsequent reputation was already being written.

However, none of this is surprising. *Music For Pleasure* was released when it had no context. Whatever The Damned did would never fit in. They actually were damned if they did (try to develop) or damned if they didn't (remain the same). For some, punk was now a sonic template to adopt. Two weeks before *Music For Pleasure*, Eater had released *The Album*. It was as prototypically reductive as expected but the record which most defined the received sound of punk was September 1977's *I Don't Wanna* EP, Sham 69's opening shot: the terrace chant choruses of The Clash married to block-chord, Ramones-speed riffs ('Ulster Boy' excepted) and guttersnipe vocals.

What could The Damned do? Making *Damned Damned Damned* part two would have been a declaration of bankruptcy, as would adopting any of the now-customary punk tropes. Equally, trying something new was also risky.

Knowledge of its genesis also impacts on reactions to the album. *Damned Damned Damned* featured songs Brian drew from his creative bank. This was now close to tapped-out. Apart from the churning, *Fun House*-esque 'Alone', originally titled 'Comfort' and played live early on but swiftly dropped, everything was written after the band had taken off. Where Rat had pushed to get his 'Stab Yor Back' on *Damned Damned Damned*, Brian solicited material from all band members. This led to some new writing credits: 'Idiot Box' was by Sensible/Scabies; 'Your Eyes' by Vanian/James and 'Problem Child' by Scabies/James. Circumstances — Stiff's push for a second album — forced The Damned to become a songwriting collective.

Opening with 'Problem Child', the album's chunky trailer single, suggested the album's direction. Not a chance. 'Don't Cry Wolf', up next with its hiccupping riff and a handclapping lift from the New York Dolls' 'Jet Boy' was another hefty rocker and sat well with the opener. The next track, 'One Way Love', was different to anything The Damned had done before. It featured Brian playing slide guitar (as per The Flamin' Groovies' 'Slow Death') and a metronomic stop-start rhythm. The song anticipated post-punk, but in a 1977 context.

Music For Pleasure really only has three low points. Despite its jittery anti-Clash, anti-Sex Pistols lyrics, 'Politics' was unmemorable and the remake of 'Stretcher Case' inferior to the version recorded with Shel Talmy. The unformed 'Your Eyes' was weak melodically, lacked power and was the album's nadir.

'Idiot Box' though was outstanding. A takedown of Television, it was written in reaction to being booted from playing with them in Los Angeles. Each member of the band was mentioned, beginning with "Tom Verlaine you may be art, but you sure ain't rock'n'roll." Of their Fred Smith, David sang "hope he gets a lot of shocks, from his Fender bass". The vitriol was tempered by taking on Television's sound with nods to their 'Marquee Moon' and 'Prove It'. The Damned did art rock when they wished to.

They also did dense and intense. Album closer 'You Know', which featured Lol Coxhill, was relentless, Stooges-indebted and the single-most concentrated dose of the Brian James Damned as the musical equivalent of a bulldozer shifting a seemingly immovable object.

On most of 'You Know', the two guitars united as a single entity but elsewhere the just-joined Lu Edmonds laid foundations allowing Brian to develop his penchant for squalls of notes, giving the performances an added edge. The differences between each guitarist were highlighted by Nick Mason's production, which was clean, not a sonic blur and had a marked separation between instruments[87] and voice. Edmonds was chunky; Brian's playing formed a lattice. Brian has expressed a wish to revisit the multi-track tapes and mix the album afresh, but they have not been found.

As to whether *Music For Pleasure* was "bollocks", "crap" and "rubbish"? No. It was recorded by a band under pressure and, with their choice of its producer[88], making a brave attempt to connect with the psychedelic era. At its most jagged, the album suggests where The Damned may have gone next: an irregular musical world with no antecedents and, in 1977, no peers. But The Damned were never going to be seen as progressing and the growth heard on *Music For Pleasure*'s best tracks was irrelevant. Instead of developing further, The Damned publically disintegrated as their second album was tossed on the scrapheap of musical fashion.

CHAPTER SEVEN

Farewell And Comeback

The Damned played a farewell show at London's Rainbow on April 8, 1978. Since the idea was floated in early March, booking a valedictory concert had been a struggle. The Roundhouse, the band's first choice, had a full schedule. The Lyceum Ballroom would not allow them through its doors as it was owned by the Mecca chain whose banned band list was The Adverts, the Sex Pistols, The Stranglers and The Damned.

While Captain wore a white shirt, jacket, tie and a swastika armband, the Rainbow concert was otherwise notable as the main support were the Robyn Hitchcock-led Cambridge psychedelic oddities The Soft Boys, a band which – like Captain – drew inspiration from Syd Barrett. Two drum kits were on stage and for the encore, Rat joined the band to play in unison with Jon Moss after gobbing on him. Lol Coxhill contributed to an extended 'You Know'. After 'I Feel Aright', that was it, The Damned had said goodbye. Two years after he first brought Brian, Captain and Rat together in a band, Nick Kent said it was "the best I've seen them". *Sounds'* Pete Silverton wondered whether "it [was] a wake or a funeral? And is there any real difference anyway – both serve the same function of helping the living to come to terms with the loss." After the show, Captain told him, "I'm glad it's all over. That's all I can say."

Brian says he "felt terrible afterwards. I jumped in a cab thinking 'uh, I've just said goodbye to what's been my family'."

He returned to the stage in June with Tanz Der Youth, his new band, whose name drew from the film *Dance Of The Vampires*. He consciously wanted to leave punk behind "and to get up punk's noses". Drummer Alan Powell was a former member of Hawkwind. Brian looked into the possibility of a psychedelic-style, black-and-white light show. Seeing their debut show at The Nashville Rooms, *NME*'s Ian Penman drew a comparison with Howard Devoto's post-Buzzcocks outfit Magazine. Brian was openly talking of the "transmagical" and said the band were "very much a sound of the Eighties". Taking time out from an ill-considered and swiftly curtailed tour supporting Black Sabbath, they played The Roundhouse on a bill tagged as the "Bohemian Love-in".[89] After a single on Radar and a Peel session, Tanz Der Youth split in September. Subsequently, Brian's erratic course took in solo releases, a vehicle called Brian James & The Brains and live work with Iggy Pop. In early 1982 he found his feet with Lords Of The New Church, which he formed with former Dead Boy Stiv Bators.[90]

The other members of The Damned also grappled with what to do next. Lu Edmonds and Jon Moss formed The Edge. Moss later found global fame with Culture Club and Edmonds ultimately joined John Lydon's Public Image Ltd. In both cases, it was a testament to the soundness of the choice made by The Damned when each was picked from amongst 1977's auditionees. Rat, Captain and David were on their own though.

★ ★ ★

After he left the previous October, Rat's try-out with The Heartbreakers and show with Johnny Moped were followed by attempts to form a new band. In early December, he hooked up with guitarist Denise Mercedes, who he had met in New York when she saw The Damned at CBGB. A fixture on the bohemian scene which grew from the beatnik era, she knew Allen Ginsberg (recording with him and Bob Dylan in 1971), had appeared on stage in Bob Dylan's *Rolling Thunder Revue* in 1975 and was close to Ginsberg's partner, the poet and sometime actor Peter Orlovsky. She was also seen in Dylan's 1978 film *Renaldo And Clara*.

For its second show, the initially nameless band they formed was billed as Rat Scabies & The Runners. The singer was Kelvin Colney (also known as Kelvin Blacklock) an old friend of Mick Jones who had passed through The London SS and fronted Jones's earlier bands The Delinquents and Little Queenie. Most recently, after singing with Ian Hunter, he was living in New York and fronting Tuff Darts. The bassist was the unstoried Steve Turner. This unlikely New York-London band with its pre-punk members played just two shows.

With Mercedes out of the picture[91], Rat next formed Drunk & Disorderly, who also played just two shows, each supporting The Clash at The Rainbow. Colney and Turner stayed on for the new band which also featured short-stay early Clash guitarist Keith Levene and Patti Smith's keyboard player Richard Sohl. Next up was a proposed four-piece called Teenage Dream with Colney, former Chelsea and Rage guitarist Eddie Cox and Turner on bass. Rat said they would be like "Richard Hell doing a poppy 'My Generation'". In the new year, this unit was renamed The Whitecats (sic) and started from scratch. Rat said that "I imagine we will be tagged as power pop" and thought that perhaps they were "easy listening". Two Peel sessions were recorded in April and August 1978.

Captain's post-Damned trajectory was as haphazard. Two weeks before The Damned's farewell show, Johnny Moped had issued the *Cycledelic* album on Chiswick. Captain played on it, co-wrote 'Groovy Ruby' and 'Hell Razor', and played guitar with the band at the album's launch show at The Roundhouse. But Moped himself was erratic and nothing with him was sustainable. Captain had to look elsewhere if he was to build a future. In March, Captain was asked to come to Amsterdam by The Damned's former roadie Michael "Big Mick" Smith, who lived there and played guitar with the trio The Softies. Bedding down on the barge of the band's drummer Joe Thumper, Captain joined The Softies as their second guitarist and played The Netherlands and Germany. In early April, he checked in with *Melody Maker* to say he had made a jazz-rock single with The Softies. That never emerged.

123

Instead, an English-language version of Plastic Bertrand's Belgian punk novelty 'Ça Plane Pour Moi' was released. It followed the template of the similarly Anglophone Elton Motello version, which had already been released under that pseudonym by the song's co-writer Alan Ward. Coincidentally, and unknown to Captain, Ward had been in Bastard with Brian James.

Playing with The Softies was a stopgap. In July, Captain was back in London and had formed his own band, King, made up of the Mopeds' Dave Berk on drums, former Chelsea and Wreckless Eric bassist Henry Badowski (who had first met Captain in Amsterdam when the Wreckless Eric band played there) on joint lead vocals, keyboards and saxophone, and Kym Bradshaw on bass (who had just left the Australian band The Saints). King had a manager in Rick Rogers[92] and they immediately recorded a Peel session and got off to a flying start. Captain thought Badowski was a pop genius because of his ability to come up with memorable but quirky songs in the Syd Barrett tradition. A run of dates were played at Paris's Club Gibus in June, and shows were announced for New York's Hurrah along with a full British tour in September.

David Vanian's post-Damned progress was more succinct than that of Captain and Rat's. When it was announced that The Damned were splitting, it was also reported that David had joined the Doctors Of Madness. While with The Damned he had made no secret of his liking of the Kid Strange-fronted pre-punk but punk-anticipating art-rockers. He had sung with them on encores in November 1976 and March 1977. Strange was the best man at his wedding and David had been photographed wearing a Doctors Of Madness badge. A man down as violinist Urban Blitz had left in January 1978, the band were operating as a trio. Strange was the singer, so David's role was ambiguous. Nonetheless, Strange said, "Dave was really wasted in The Damned as he was singing 12 versions of 'Neat Neat Neat' in a set. There's no hard and fast answers about what it will be like. We're just doing it because it seems like a fairly exciting idea for both parties."

In practice, although the union completed a studio recording of 'Don't Panic England' (planned as a single but never released), this meant David joined the Doctors towards the end of their live set as an adjunct. In May, Strange said "the experiment with Dave had run its course". Once again, David was without a band.

Soon, it was the same for Captain and Rat. Despite the promised live shows, King had fallen apart by early August. The Whitecats had not generated any interest from record companies and their singer had a single out under the name K. K. Black in June 1978 while still with the band. The version of The Rivieras' 1964 single 'California Sun'[93] (also covered by The Ramones) went nowhere but it confirmed Colney was hedging his bets. The Whitecats broke up in September. Where his former band had released nothing, on November 17 Kelvin Blacklock issued a second solo single on EMI.

Looking back, Rat says, "I realised The Whitecats weren't going to do anything and that my songwriting wasn't strong enough to carry a band. I liked the guys in the band, but they just weren't Captain and Dave." Captain, David and Rat had tried to build their individual futures but nothing had gained traction.

★ ★ ★

On August 15, 1978, Captain and Rat were seen in public together for the first time since the Rainbow show. Rat was drumming for the Vicious White Kids at Camden's Electric Ballroom. The one-off band had been put together by ex-Sex Pistol Glen Matlock as a send-off for Sid Vicious before he left for America. The name reflected those of its frontman, The Whitecats and Matlock's post-Pistols band The Rich Kids[94], whose guitarist Steve New also featured in the temporary band. Vicious's girlfriend Nancy Spungen tried to sing backing vocals but her microphone was deliberately not plugged in.

Before the show, the various contributors assembled at the Halfway House pub across the road from the *Rock On* record shop. Captain and his German girlfriend Christiane Kistner, aka Cursty, turned up bearing placards saying "*Bunty* is unfair to its readers" which they then took into The Electric Ballroom. The protest was about the girls' weekly comic's recent axing of the *Melody-Lee – A Dancer She'll Be* series, first printed in October 1977. The story breathed its last in June after 38 instalments telling the tale of the girl abandoned as a baby who wanted, against enormous odds, to become a ballet dancer. While begging on the street to pay for her dance lessons, she was spotted by the ballerina Alla Lanova who helped her achieve her ambition. For Captain, the disappearance of *Melody Lee* was an issue worth taking up to disrupt Sid Vicious's final moments of glory on British soil.

Three weeks later, on September 5, a band initially billed as Les Punks played The Electric Ballroom. It was the first hint that The Damned were back. "I spoke to Captain on the phone," recalls Rat of the idea's genesis. "The exact conversation was, 'How's it going with King?' 'Not so good. How's it going with The Whitecats?' 'Not so good, why don't we get back together?'"

The conversation resulted in Captain agreeing to play guitar rather than bass, and making contact with David and Motörhead's Lemmy, who agreed to be the bassist for what was seen as a one-off. "It just happened, really," says Captain of the switch to guitar. "I played guitar with the Mopeds. I think a lot of people must have thought I'd been the guitarist [in The Damned] and Brian was the bass player."

A mix-and-match set featured familiar Damned material which Captain learned on guitar: 'Born To Kill', 'Help', 'I Feel Alright', 'Neat Neat Neat', 'New Rose', 'Problem Child', 'Stab Yor Back' and 'Stretcher Case Baby'. 'Jet Boy Jet Girl' was tackled, as was 'Anti-Pope' from King's repertoire and The Whitecats' 'Second Time Around'. Lemmy was left with his old band Hawkwind's 'Silver Machine' and The Pink Fairies' 'City Kids', which Motörhead had recorded. The MC5's 'Looking At You' was also covered. The only new song in Les Punks' set was Rat's Kinks-via-The Heavy Metal Kids' vaudeville oddity 'Burglar'.[95] During the show, David missed the last verse of 'Looking At You'. 'City Kids' was abandoned halfway through. If this was a new beginning, the heavy debts to the past didn't wholeheartedly make a case that moving forward was easy.

Of the motivation, Captain says "we were desperate for cash. Everyone was absolutely broke. Rat was quite good at putting together money-making schemes. Rat was staying in a place with cockroaches in Portobello Road. He was sleeping in the bed and I was on the floor. So I would wake up with the cockroaches crawling across my face, which wasn't an awful lot of fun."

Repurposing the temporary as something stable began immediately. Lemmy was a non-starter as a full-time bassist, so King's Henry Badowski was brought into the line-up. Likewise, their manager Rick Rogers came in to handle the business side. David was induced to come on board after being erroneously informed that American dates were in the offing. In the last week of September, it was announced that "three-quarters of the original Damned" had become a full time unit. A record deal was being negotiated. Like the supposed US shows, this was a fantasy. *Sounds* reported it as The Damned reforming, but the band was dubbed The Doomed. "It didn't feel like reforming," says David. "I've always had this dark desire the band would make it, sheer bloody-mindedness."[96]

Asked what he thought of the return, Brian says, "I was intrigued. There was no reason I was bothered, it was my decision not to do that anymore."

Following the split, the rest of the band had not been in contact with Brian. He says, "I didn't own the name The Damned. I had just thought of it." The lack of communication ensured that whatever Brian thought, the reanimated band didn't play as The Damned due to a perception he owned the name. Of what they were called, Brian says "no one asked me".

Badowski was inducted into the band while practising at Rat's parents' Redhill house. After one rehearsal and following dinner, the three other members pursued him along the surrounding country lanes. It came to a stop when Captain brought him down and Rat pissed on his head. Once he had learned what he was dealing with, Badowski slogged around Britain with The Doomed from the end of September to late October. Shorn of the Lemmy-related songs, the set was much the same as at The Electric Ballroom with the addition of a cover version of The Sweet's 'Ballroom Blitz'. Although playing live addressed the money problem, revisiting Brian James-era material offered little sign this was a band with its own musical identity. The band had also been to see Stiff's Dave Robinson to ask for financial support. He, Captain said, "sat there and laughed. Looked at us and laughed... then he told us to fuck off."

As well as funds, there was a problem with Badowski. His ability to regurgitate at will the beer he had just drunk was impressive but he was being needled by Rat who wasn't shy about declaring that he had wanted Eddie & The Hot Rods' bassist Paul Gray in the band and began taking it out physically on Badowksi, punching and kicking him in the band's van. The abuse meted out culminated in a full-on fight which spilled out onto the hard shoulder. A shaky peace was restored and the dates continued.

After the British dates, at the end of October, Badowski was out of the band. His replacement was Alisdair Ward, a Croydon native universally known as Algy who had known Captain for years and had just left The Saints, the band that King's bassist Kym Bradshaw had come from. Algy lasted longer than Badowksi's six weeks with The Doomed.

"I heard Henry was getting a bit flaky," says Algy. "I saw them with him and thought, 'What's he doing drinking a couple of pints and deliberately throwing them up?' I used to bump into the Captain and we hung out when I was in The Saints. It was, 'Fancy giving it a shot old boy?' Simple as that. There was a rehearsal in the basement of one of Steve Strange's shops in Covent Garden and that was that that. We went to France."

Then 19, Algy had been in Croydon band Trackway, which he describes as "jazzy tinged rock with vocals". Through his brother Ian, who was their road manager, he joined The Saints in August 1977 after their bassist Kym Bradshaw had left. When they fell apart in summer 1978, the connections between them meant Algy's entry into Captain's band was predictable. He had worked at a clerical office at The Fairfield Halls and knew Captain, though they hadn't worked there at the same time. At 13 and 14, he had moved gear for bands playing the venue, and had seen Rat's old band Tor. Trackway's PA had been used by the early Johnny Moped band. Algy drank with Captain at the Railway and Telegraph pubs. The pair used to catch the night train back from central London together: Captain got off at Selhurst, while Algy did so one stop down the line at East Croydon. Now, they were in the same band and on their way to Paris.

On arriving in the French capital, Algy was given a makeover. His mop of curly hair was cut by Rat. The six-person entourage was meant to have three twin rooms but as the first two hotels threw them out, they ended up in a dormitory. A chair was thrown through the window onto to the room's balcony as David swung from the curtains. After Paris's Le Bataclan, the next show was Le Havre's cattle market.

Again, curtains suffered. "The gig was dreadful," says Algy. "We were supposed to play an afternoon show. Scabies shat in [support act] Auntie Pus's[97] priceless acoustic Gibson. All sorts of mayhem carried on. We trashed the hotel, vodka, some of the backstage rider, duty free and cider, bottles thrown out the window, curtains set on fire, riot police were called, went in nick, released, band sent home, that was it. You never realised in those days, in 1978 with anarchists, we could have been [like the then-active Italian revolutionary organisation] the Red Brigade."

Rat and Algy were arrested for exploding a Molotov cocktail in the street outside their hotel. Improvised from a coke bottle, lighter fuel and strips of cloth ripped from a curtain, Rat says, "I was just showing the lads how to make a petrol bomb."

As to why, he says, "Drink. Everyone thought it was witty and charming. I lit it, threw it out into what I thought was an empty street and, as I threw it, the rag came out and set fire to the curtains. I threw them out the window."

Rogers made a deal with the local police that he would pay the hotel for the damage in return for freeing Rat from jail. The equivalent of £2,000 demanded was more than the band's total earnings from the French shows. On returning to Britain with a hole in their finances, The Doomed played Ireland, Belfast, Scotland and the north of England. David missed the Scottish dates and his place was taken by The Heavy Metal Kids' Gary Holton[98] who, after getting lyrics wrong, was pissed on by Captain on stage in return for doing the band the favour of filling in for their absent singer. "Vanian had had enough," says Rat. "We were offered some dates in Scotland and the money was good. But I always got the feeling that Dave thought we didn't take the band seriously enough." They got away with the change in singer by announcing on stage that David had died and that the shows were a memorial.

Even so, David returned from the dead and it looked as though The Doomed were picking up creatively. The new songs 'Love Song' and 'Melody Lee' were being played. 'Love Song' and 'Burglar' were recorded for a single which was given away at a pre-Christmas show at The Electric Ballroom and sold at the *Rock On* shop. Although it was a self-pressed white label, a sticker on one side said "Dodgy Demo Co. The Damned."

The Camden show was the last time they played as The Doomed, under which name they recorded a John Peel session on December 20. The Dodgy Demo single was hard to find so the radio session, broadcast January 8, 1979, became the first time the new Damned was widely heard. Along with 'Looking At You', all the new songs were taped: 'Burglar' (with Rat declaring he was going to steal Peel's record collection), the *Bunty*-inspired 'Melody Lee' and 'Love Song'. The latter pair were melodic: kinetic pop, suggesting the prospect of reaching new ears. That possibility became closer when, with the help of Rat's accountant father John Millar, they secured the right to use the name The Damned. Rat Scabies, Captain Sensible, David Vanian and Algy Ward were scheduled to play their first show as The Damned at Croydon's Greyhound on January 7, 1979.[99]

The music press announced "The Doomed are now the Damned" and that "the reformation is permanent". It was less than a year since the Rainbow farewell show. Captain's band King had come and gone. So had Rat's Whitecats. David's short liaison with The Doctors Of Madness was history. Now, all three were back where they belonged.

CHAPTER EIGHT

Boycott For Pope

That The Damned were back was more than apparent on Thursday May 10, 1979 when they appeared on *Top Of The Pops* for the first time, opening the broadcast. Their new Chiswick single 'Love Song' was in the charts. In a beret which quickly flew off and his furry okapi suit – a lime green top and pink trousers with added tassels – Captain lurched as if on springs while Algy stood relatively still in his biker jacket-Motörhead T-shirt combo. Rat seemed to be about to destroy his kit while an all-black-clad and gloved David prowled side-to-side. Elkie Brooks followed them with the glutinous 'The Runaway' to restore a calm that was reinforced as The Shadows plucked their way through the sedate 'Theme From The Deer Hunter (Cavatina)'.

Two weeks later, the single was still rising up the charts and *Top Of The Pops* issued a return invitation. This time, the plan was for Captain to wear a wedding dress and, in keeping with the song's title, appear as David's bride. As the promo for David Bowie's 'Boys Keep Swinging' was being broadcast in the show, the producers wouldn't allow the fake nuptials as they could be interpreted as mocking the drag worn by Bowie in the video. Captain only got to wear his dress for the rehearsal.

In the year up to May 1979, bands associated with the early and formative days of punk had, to varying degrees, scored hits. There were Buzzcocks' 'Everybody's Happy Nowadays', Generation X's 'King Rocker', Wire's 'Outdoor Miner', The Jam's 'Strange Town', The Lurkers' 'Just Thirteen', Siouxsie & The Banshees' 'The Staircase (Mystery)', The Skids' 'Into The Valley' and X-Ray Spex's 'Highly Inflammable' amongst them. There were others who had used punk as a springboard, a milieu in which to adapt or as a means not to compromise: Elvis Costello's 'Oliver's Army', Dr. Feelgood's 'Milk & Alcohol', Nick Lowe's 'Crackin' Up', Motörhead's 'Overkill', The Police's 'Roxanne' and Squeeze's 'Cool For Cats'. A Johnny Rotten-free Sex Pistols had 'Something Else' and 'Silly Thing'. Chrissie Hynde had finally found her natural home with The Pretenders and the Kinks cover 'Stop Your Sobbing'. All had chosen a course and followed it. The Damned had not and were a wild card.

For both *Top Of The Pops* appearances, The Damned slotted into shows balancing the new arrivals on the pop scene with the venerable. On the second, The Skids mimed 'Masquerade'. Elvis Costello & The Attractions ('Accidents Will Happen'), Dollar ('Who Were You With In The Moonlight') and Tubeway Army ('Are "Friends" Electric?') also attempted to look as though they were performing for real. On the first, The Shadows and Brooks were joined by Strawbs offshoot The Monks, whose 'Nice Legs (Shame About Her Face)' attempted to be a bit punky while succeeding in being overtly sexist and wholly rubbish.

The Damned had not intended to become a *Top Of The Pops* band. It just happened. They were popular live and had a strong following. 'Love Song' was a fantastic, melodic single. They now had the support of Chiswick, a label which knew their history, what they were and appreciated their unpredictability. If there was a moment when they could break barriers, this was it. But, as Captain concedes about having a hit, it was "bizarre. I like the sound of loud guitar married to a tune, that's a winning combination for me. There's something beautiful about that. It was a catchy tune."

★ ★ ★

Otherwise, no fanfares had welcomed The Damned's return. As 1979 began, the music press were more interested in the first live shows by

John Lydon's Public Image Ltd, which had taken place on Christmas Day and Boxing Day 1978. The Clash were beginning a new UK tour. Elvis Costello's third album *Armed Forces* was just out. Ian Dury was still hot as his *New Boots & Panties!!* had been confirmed as the 14th best-selling album of 1978. Costello knock-off Joe Jackson was being promoted and new band The Ruts were playing "excellent basic punk". Los Angeles' Dickies, who had formed after seeing The Damned in 1977, were featured in *NME*. A broad church of electronic music from Throbbing Gristle and Kraftwerk to David Bowie and beyond was being embraced. The return of The Damned was confined to brief entries in the music weekly's news pages.

The British one-nighters The Damned played over January and February 1979 were of little concern to a music press either in thrall to the next big thing or propagating the sure-fire. However, the shows were sell-outs. A couple of early March London pub dates were also played under the name The School Bullies. Although a draw, they existed apart from the music business's order of the day.

Then again, there was national press coverage of sorts after Captain and his girlfriend Cursty went to Heathrow Airport to greet the English cricket team's return from Australia, where they had won the Ashes. Former Yorkshire Captain Geoff Boycott had called for the sacking of the England Captain Mike Brearley. Resonant of his protest about *Bunty*, Captain and his accomplices were armed with placards saying "Boycott for Pope" and "Brearley must go". He told newspapers, "Geoff is the hero of punks across the country" and "that punks are the only true cricket fans". Boycott was offered a free ticket to see The Damned. A week later, Rat got in on the act media-wise by posing amongst the heaps of rubbish dumped at Leicester Square while bin-men were on strike during Britain's Winter Of Discontent.[100] He could "hardly wait to get to grips with the mounds of smelly garbage in London's Leicester Square" and hadn't "had so much fun since he accidentally fell down a rubbish chute when he was five".

Publicity stunts were no answer to the pressing question of how The Damned were to re-establish themselves as a band with a future. While they had reformed to solve their money problems, and had secured a manager, there was no plan as such. Although the self-pressed Dodgy Demo single was rough, 'Love Song' was a gem suggesting itself as a wider-reaching musical calling card. It also had memorable, witty lyrics, epitomised by the first verse: "I'll be the ticket if you're my collector, I've got the fare if you're my inspector, I'll be the luggage if you'll be the porter, I'll be the parcel if you'll be my sorter". Chiswick Records was independent and took up the challenge.

"Our manager Rick Rogers was saying that Chiswick were convinced they could make 'Love Song' a hit," recalls Rat. "Nobody in the industry wanted us. It was probably because we were at the absolute height of our mayhem and chaos. We were too much of a handful for the majors to take on. So Chiswick's Roger Armstrong said 'really, Chiswick are the only people interested'." The band signed a one-off deal for a single.

There was an inevitability about landing with Chiswick. The label had paid for the recording of the first, pre-Stiff, Damned demos in 1976. Rogers – who had tour managed them on the *Anarchy* tour – worked for them after he left Stiff and handled Chiswick's press promotion. Looking back with ambivalence on the new relationship, Captain says, "When you're broke and someone offers you some money it's hard to see that if you hang on, it might be in your better interest and get something proper."

"I didn't think they were going to get to a major label," says Armstrong. "As far as the majors were concerned, punk rock was thankfully dead. The Pistols were gone, The Clash had moved into the rock band thing whereas The Damned were regarded as punk. I didn't think they would have been seen as viable. There was their reputation too. In a sense, they should have burned bright and died young but it's their intelligence [which kept them going]. Rat is a great drummer, Captain is a great guitarist and brilliant writer, and Dave is a great performer. The Damned really weren't part of the [punk rock] three chords [style]."

"Chiswick were a very interesting label," says David. "They absolutely loved music and could see something in us and genuinely liked us. That was important. We weren't treated like a piece of toothpaste."[101]

From shortly after it was launched in late 1975, Chiswick was as much about the present as the past. Their first record was an EP by hard-hitting pub rockers The Count Bishops. In 1976, they reissued Vince Taylor's 1959 Brit-rocker 'Brand New Cadillac' within weeks of the only single by Joe Strummer's 101ers.[102] The Clash would later cover it. The label's Ted Carroll and Roger Armstrong DJ-ed at early punk shows, knew Malcolm McLaren and every other mover on the scene. Initially, they had sold second-hand records to collectors and had a keen sense of what was good and sought-after. They kept rock-history inclined members of the new generation like Brian James, Joe Strummer and Paul Weller fed with vinyl. The Jam had almost signed with Chiswick, but their few overtly punk releases by The Radiators From Space and The Rings were complemented by many more from by uncategorisable, wayward bands like The Gorillas, Motörhead and The Radio Stars. Indeed, Johnny Moped had found a home on Chiswick. But the only Chiswick band which had charted by the end of 1978 were Fifties revivalists Rocky Sharpe & The Replays. Their success was helped by Chiswick having a distribution and pressing deal with EMI.[103] The Damned came on board as that association had been shown to be a success.

Chiswick booked The Damned into Utopia Studios on March 17 with Eddie & The Hot Rods' producer Ed Hollis. Armstrong felt the results too rough for radio play, so booked Camden's Chalk Farm studio on April 2 to record a new vocal track. David's voice was captured by a Neumann valve microphone, the type Frank Sinatra favoured for its ability to attain a warm sound. Following a remix undertaken the next day, The Damned's comeback single was ready for release.

The deal with EMI meant comprehensive marketing was possible. The first pressings of 'Love Song' came in four different pictures sleeves: one for each member of the band. "The four sleeves were to get it onto the charts," admits Roger. "There were fewer Algys. We knew about the fan base, we knew about fan bases – we sold records, our experience was behind the counter. We knew we would sell four times as many records. Then we followed it quickly with the red vinyl."

According to press reports the first-week sales of 'Love Song' matched that of a band like Paul McCartney's Wings. EMI's pressing plant apparently couldn't keep up with demand for The Damned's single and 24,000 copies were sold four days after the April 27 release.[104] A week later, 50,000 had been sold. That all may have been hype, but the single was a strong seller. "I wasn't expecting a hit," says Rat. "I didn't think it would ever be an acceptable pop record. I thought it was too fast, uncommercial."

★ ★ ★

The success of 'Love Song' meant Chiswick signed The Damned to a three-year contract. The single was initially conceived as a one-off but its paperwork included an option to pick the band up for a long-term deal. Another trigger was a sold-out show at London's Lyceum on April 8. On the bottom of the bill were Coventry's The Specials, another band on the books of The Damned's manager, Rick Rogers.

At the sell-out show, at which the PA cut out, older material like 'Born To Kill', 'Help', 'I Feel Alright', 'Neat Neat Neat', 'New Rose', 'Problem Child', 'So Messed Up', 'Stab Yor Back' and 'Stretcher Case Baby' filled out the bulk of the set alongside 'Jet Boy Jet Girl', The Whitecats' 'Teenage Dream' and covers of 'Ballroom Blitz'[105] and 'Looking At You'. The only new, post-reformation songs played were 'Love Song', 'Melody Lee' and 'Suicide'. New material was needed.

Chiswick had signed a band they knew were a potential problem. This wasn't just to do with the lack of fresh songs. "They were very difficult to deal with," avers Roger. "They were a handful. They could be real wind-up merchants. Sometimes it was funny, sometimes it was not funny. There was a bluntness about the way they dealt with the world which could flip over into being slightly brutal."

In Nottingham at the end of the month, *Sounds'* Sandy Robertson learned a degree of braveness was needed when edging close to The Damned. The firecrackers they threw at him burnt his trousers. They also tried to set their tour van alight. Rat told the writer that he and Captain used to compete to "pull the ugliest dodgy boilers".[106] At a local radio interview, Captain laid out the band's mission statement: "We just make a noise and that's it. Have a few beers. We've got no politics, no nothing." That evening, their show included manglings of Rod Stewart's 'D'Ya Think I'm Sexy', John Travolta and Olivia Newton John's 'Summer Nights' as well 'Great Big Tits', a renamed 'Ballroom Blitz'. Two weeks later, when Robertson's article appeared, 'Love Song' was in the shops and the headline declared "Pop Stardom at last for The Damned".

Their label's prompt response to 'Love Song' entering the charts was to organise a joint recording session with Motörhead, for a single to be billed as by Motordamn: all members from each band were to be heard. Motörhead's planned side was 'Over The Top', The Damned's was 'Ballroom Blitz'. Two days at the Old Kent Road's Workhouse Studio were booked. Only one run through of 'Over The Top' was attempted as Motörhead's drummer Phil Taylor was so drunk, he was incapable of more. Their guitarist Eddie Clarke lost patience as Captain roamed the studio with the chords to 'Ballroom Blitz' on a placard. With only Lemmy left from Motörhead, a rough version of The Sweet song was completed but the results were not useable.

As well as a shelved single and the standard studio costs, Chiswick received an additional bill for £100 which covered a broken pair of Beyer headphones, the damage incurred by beer tipped into a Neumann microphone, a damaged TV, a broken window in the studio's toilet, paint sprayed along a corridor and onto a window, and sundry damage to crockery, furniture and a pool table. Three-quarters of the bill was met by Motörhead's management as their crew was found to have done most of the damage. Chiswick's joint Damned and Motörhead single got no further. 'Love Song' would have to be followed up some other way.

A week later, The Damned began recording for real. This time, they knuckled down. Four studios were booked for between two and three days each over the final week-and-half of May: Camden's Sound Suite, south London's Workhouse and SGS, owned by the father of former Pink Fairy Larry Wallis. Nine tracks were taped: 'Anti-Pope', 'I Just Can't Be Happy Today', 'Looking At You', 'Machine Gun Etiquette', 'Melody Lee', 'Plan 9 Channel 7', and

Parts 1 and 4 of 'Smash It Up', an ambitious song conceived as a blend of four discrete sections. While 'Anti-Pope' had been played by King[107], 'Machine Gun Etiquette' was the retitled Whitecats song 'Second Time Around', and 'Looking At You' was a cover version. Despite the repurposed material, this was an astonishing outcome. Under pressure, The Damned had written new songs. With 'Love Song' added in, they had the basis of a new album.

Up to this point, the reanimated Damned had played one-nighters and short strings of dates. A full tour was booked from the end of May into June. Their new status as pop stars did little to change the minds of those who still saw them as a menacing punk rock band whose audience was disagreeable. They were banned from Edinburgh's Odeon, Guildford's Civic Hall, Leicester's De Montfort Hall and Purley's Tiffany's. The replacement Edinburgh venue, Tiffanys, also rejected them.

In Newcastle, the ban on The Damned came directly from the formidable Arthur Stabler, city councillor and chair of the local authority's recreation committee. He said, "They'll not get here while I have any say in the matter. They were here a year ago when they used foul language from the stage and tried to incite the audience. If we allowed them back, things could get out of hand, people could get hurt." Stabler was a World War II veteran, worked at the Vickers Armstrong Engineering Works and became Lord Mayor of Newcastle-upon-Tyne in 1983. He had a rigid anti-punk track record and had prevented the Sex Pistols' *Anarchy* tour from reaching Newcastle in 1976, when he said, "It was decided to cancel the concert in the interests of protecting the children. We can control what happens at the City Hall but not what happens on the stage." In August 1977, he had appeared on national TV in the BBC's *Brass Tacks* current affairs programme on the punk rock phenomenon to outline his concerns. Local reader Norman Brown wrote to the Newcastle *Sunday Sun* in support of Stabler's views on The Damned, saying, "He is neither narrow-minded nor Victorian. Carry on councillor, throw out the punk junk." Despite the paper being told by their booking agent that The Damned "are obviously a bit zany, but they play pop music, not what is generally called punk" they did not play Newcastle.

Zany was probably as good an adjective as any. Captain usually wore either a Hawaiian shirt and beret or his furry okapi suit, so named after a game the band played on tour when they worked their way through the alphabet naming obscure animals.[108] Often, he finished the set naked. A version of the Sex Pistols' 'Pretty Vacant' crept into their set. David began wearing a bald wig and pointed false ears as a tribute to actor Max Schreck's Count Orlok in the 1922 FW Murnau film *Nosferatu, eine Symphonie des Grauens*.[109] Within the band, he had acquired a new nickname: Creature.

Each night, the first band on the tour bill was selected from those who had written to The Damned suggesting they play – the music press had printed an appeal inviting hopefuls to send a postcard saying what type of band they were and where they were from. They were advertised as "Local Heroes". Amongst the successful applicants were Stoke-on-Trent punks Discharge, Blackburn's quirky new wavers I.Q. Zero and the Sheffield post-punk band Artery. In Hemel Hempstead, The Nips found themselves on the bill. Their singer was early punk and future Pogues frontman Shane MacGowan. Their bassist was Shanne Bradley, the booker of The Damned's second show in 1976. Bringing a new generation of bands in front of an audience was a principled gesture.

The main support act was The Ruts, who Rat had known since April 1979 when he found out their bassist John "Segs" Jennings and drummer Dave Ruffy lived on the same Forest Hill street as him. Rat used to visit them at home. Consequently, The Ruts had played a few dates with The Damned in April. "The music was good," says Rat. "But we loved them as people." Auntie Pus rounded out the bill, ensuring The Damned had friends with them on the road. On the tour, Algy, Captain and Rat began the day with scotch and coke, and lines of speed. There was also a boost from John Peel, who repeated The Damned's most recent session and aired The Ruts' new single 'Babylon's Burning' on his May 28 show. During its chart run, 'Love Song' peaked at 20 in the week of May 26.

A regular feature of the dates was a joint Damned-Ruts encore featuring each other's songs (typically 'Love Song' and 'In a Rut') and a romp through 'Blue Suede Shoes'. Captain was often naked for the encore. During The Damned's set, Ruffy took the drum stool to allow Rat to head stage-front to bark-out 'Burglar'. In Whitley Bay, Captain attempted to distract attention from The Ruts as they played by sitting at the back of the auditorium reading a newspaper. The next night, at West Runton Pavilion, Captain and Rat walked across the stage during their support band's set eating fish and chips. At Leicester, on June 16, The Ruts had got hold of a sack of pig's manure which was brought on as a bag of swag during 'Burglar' (Captain was on drums). First, Rat threw some of the excrement at Segs. Then Algy threw more at Ruts singer Malcolm Owen. Their guitarist Paul Fox chucked some in the audience. As more flew, Segs was pulled off the stage. The tour ended the next day.

A week later 'Babylon's Burning' entered the Top 40. It hit number seven in the second week of July. In September, the release of The Ruts' debut album *The Crack* acknowledged the bond between the two bands: its cover painting featured Captain and Rat and luminaries like Jimi Hendrix, Keith Richard, Charlie Watts, astronomer Patrick Moore and the comedians/actors Peter Cook and Dudley Moore as well as The Ruts and their dogs. While The Ruts were penetrating the British singles chart, North America got its first chance to see the new Damned. Although they had no records out there, over June and early July they were booked into high-profile venues like Boston's Paradise, New York's Hurrah, San Francisco's Old Waldorf and Toronto's El Mocambo. In Los Angeles, they headlined the Whisky a Go Go where, in April 1977, Television's Tom Verlaine had vetoed them as his support band.

Of The Damned's 1979 return to America, Rat says, "After a week we'd had so much trouble. I'd take anything that was given to me, it didn't matter who it was, or what it was. The others were brighter than that. Rick Rogers would see the promoter and say, 'Do you know what you've got tonight, what will happen?' We had to warn everyone."

Algy says that on the tour, "Scabies was being a tosser, overuse of powders. I think Creature didn't want to go. I used to room with him and it was let's not talk, just don't talk about it, let's get on with it."

Over the whole of the tour, Captain's grievances about America amounted to it being a country which stank. As *Slash* magazine summarised it, he did not like "its cars, its finances, its audiences, its lack of reality". The writer pointed out that the latter was a bit rich coming from a man in a furry suit. For the tour, the band were each on a daily allowance of $20. Still, the gripes about America and Americans did not prevent Captain and Rat having sex with local women they dubbed "boilers". In New York, Rat developed a chat up line in which he was an alien whose only form of communication was via his penis. Speaking with him was only possible when his organ was in a mouth.

The first date was Dover, New Jersey's Showplace where Algy put a hole in the stage with his bass guitar. In New York, a couple of days later, photographs of the band were taken while out and about in the city. They heard gunshots while posing on a street-corner pile of demolition rubble. At Hurrah, Algy broke a full-length, shop-front sized mirror as the culmination of their opening show at the venue. They were booked to play two nights, so forfeited their $1,000 guarantee for the second show to pay for the damage. During night one, Captain traded words with the Manhattan audience after someone shouted, "We want punk." "You don't know fuck all about punk," he retorted. "It's just a fashion to you. If Ted Nugent had short hair, you'd think he was a punk. It's people like you that split us up." The show descended into disarray with Rat trying to play 'Pretty Vacant', Captain behind the drums in his underpants, the guitar going flying and the demolition of the drums and Algy's bass.

It was a conscious decision to make each tour date as impactful as possible. "We knew the same audience went to everyone who came through," recalls Rat. "Next week it would be Buzzcocks, The Clash, 999, who played it like the record. We didn't do that, we wanted it to be different to the record, give them something to remember."

Their June 28 Boston show at the Paradise was a highlight as they went out drinking with Blondie (Deborah Harry bowed out and went back to her hotel), also on tour and in town that day. In Buffalo, on July 1, the post-show entertainment was Captain setting off all their hotel's fire alarms. In Los Angeles, they were booked to play two nights at the Whisky a Go Go, with two sets a night. For the first's second set, Algy played while sat cross-legged. David spent a lot of the set singing from the audience. Rat began playing guitar and then hit a kid in the audience in the face with it. As the crowd yelled at Rat, Captain vented his opinions about America. Algy walked off and Rat destroyed the drum kit.

On stage at the Whisky, Algy said of the crowd, "I'm fuckin' annoyed. All those fuckin' people get in a car, come up to this gig, drive halfway down the street, you change into your fucking punk clothes, and you walk up here scared shitless of being beat before you get here. That ain't no fucking punk rock." Rat added, "I love America and LA, it's just the fucking audiences are so fucking lazy with their fucking Cadillacs and their fucking cheeseburgers." *Slash* printed a pen portrait of them on stage: "Captain Sensible was resplendent, sporting an unbelievable fluorescent shag-rug outfit that made him look like an overgrown shooting-gallery prize. Vanian had the legendary Transylvania gear, the pallid face, the oily haircut, the burning eyes. Rat looked like a slob and Alistair like a tourist." Excepting David, on the day following the show they spoke to *Slash* which said of each of them that, during the interview, "Rat Scabies ([was] overweight and pasty), Alistair (chubby and pasty), and Captain Sensible (pasty with a band aid on his eyebrow)."

At San Francisco's Old Waldorf there were, says Algy, "great amphetamines, bad equipment". Their early evening set went fine, but the second was even more confrontational than the opening at Hurrah. As the set turned to free-form chaos, in a matted, long-hair wig, Captain told the crowd they were "stinking American arsehole shit-cunts", then dispensed with the okapi suit's trousers and pissed over the edge of the stage as 'Neat Neat Neat' was attempted with Rat hammering away as he chewed his jaw off due to the drugs consumed. Now naked, without the wig and with his guitar obscuring his genitals, Captain led the band through a surprisingly coherent version of The Stooges' 'No Fun' after which a metal chair thrown from the audience hit him on the back of the head. He was taken to hospital for stitches.[110]

"That's what Captain used to do," says Algy. "He used to go off, come back naked and start pissing. Scabies would go in the crowd and hit somebody. Dave would go off and I was 'fuck this' and do a bass solo. It all depended how long it took and then I'd fuck off."

Of his on-stage condition, Rat says "no, not really" of whether he was lucid and aware of what was going on. "There was lot of serious drinking and drug taking at the time. Cocaine. We'd be doing lines before breakfast. I couldn't hear anything so I'd follow the vocals."

"We were animals," is Rat's summing-up of the behaviour of three-quarters of The Damned on the US tour. "I was incredibly bad with success. Of all the people that handled it badly it was me. There was a feeling of power, but you weren't sure what you had a power over. There was nothing there. I didn't have a power over them three. I didn't have a power over the roadies."

On their return to Britain on July 11, Rick Rogers resigned as The Damned's manager and devoted his time to The Specials, whose first single 'Gangsters' entered the Top 40 exactly a month later.

★ ★ ★

Chiswick's Roger Armstrong promptly became the band's caretaker manager. The success of 'Love Song' needed building on and he booked them into Sound Suite studios the week they returned from America to continue working on the album. As well as being one of the directors of their label, he was also producing their forthcoming album. "I was doing too much for them," he admits. "I was organising too much for them and it was creating a conflict with my role at the record company." For now though, the goal was getting them to record.

At Sound Suite, they worked on overdubbing the nine tracks recorded in May and taped a new version of 'Noise, Noise, Noise', one of 'Love Song's two B-side tracks. Then, in August, they were booked into Highbury's Wessex Studio to complete the album. The Clash were also there working on what became the *London Calling* double album. Although The Damned did some tracking in the larger Studio 1 which was The Clash's base, they mostly worked in the smaller Studio 2.

The two bands got on well. There was none of friction of 1977 and mucking about together included Rat entertaining all with a pub-style piano version of 'Knees Up Mother Brown'. With his mandolin, Captain and a spoons-playing Rat also tackled 'New Rose'. Joe Strummer joined in as it turned into 'White Riot'. Rat's dog Pup contributed barking. An impromptu band of Clash producer Guy Stevens on vocals, Strummer on piano, Captain on drums, Mick Jones and Paul Simonon on their usual instruments and Clash drummer Topper Headon on guitar also tackled an endless 12-bar jam. Headon and Strummer formed part of the chorus on The Damned's final, released version of 'Noise, Noise, Noise'.

There was rivalry though. Armstrong remembers, "Mick Jones, bless him, trying to play a line in 'London Calling' and he wasn't getting it. Lots of takes. I was making tea outside Studio 1 and Captain was there. He was standing there playing it right. I said, 'Fuck off Captain, stop that.'"

Of The Clash, Algy says, "They were off their fucking tits, smoking dope and on brown. I couldn't handle all that stuff, that's why I stopped going in to Wessex. I just thought I didn't want to be part of it. When The Clash weren't there, we did some work." The Damned's time at the studio racked up a bill for recovering its pool table, two broken cues, the replacement of six halogen parabolic reflector bulbs and the recharge of fire extinguisher which had been let off.

A more pressing issue for Armstrong was Algy's approach to recording. "He brought this huge Marshall stack and turned it up full, way past 11. It couldn't be recorded as there was no mic you put in front of it, it bled into everything. He was playing with so much aggression it was bouncing the strings and clicking on the pick-ups." It resulted in Captain overdubbing the bass parts.

According to Rat, "Algy played very little bass on that album. Most of the bass you hear is Captain. Algy would come in absolutely legless. It would only take an hour or so for Algy to go off the rails. He would only drink neat whisky."

Armstrong says, "Algy's on 'Liar'. The bass intro on 'Love Song' is Algy, but pretty much everything else [on *Machine Gun Etiquette*] is Captain. Captain playing bass changed the album as his bass was certainly more lyrical. Algy was a bit of heavy metal player." 'Liar' was a new song recorded at Wessex, as were 'Smash It Up (Part 2)' and 'These Hands'.

The Damned had now completed their new album, their third. They also had another new manager: Doug Smith, who also handled Motörhead[111], had signed on at the beginning of September. At the end of the month, the music press announced that what was to be called *New World Symphony* was scheduled for release on November 2. A major tour was scheduled for most of the month.

★ ★ ★

The tour did not begin during the first week of November as planned. Even though the album had been completed, it was announced that The Damned were remixing what they had recorded and they hit road two weeks later. The album was issued on November 9 and titled *Machine Gun Etiquette* after a phrase Algy and Rat heard on the BBC's World Service, rather than *New World Symphony*.

'Smash It Up' was chosen as the next single and issued on October 5, three weeks shy of six months on from 'Love Song'.[112] Reviews were generally positive. *Sounds'* Garry Bushell said it "assures them of their biggest hit to date" while *Melody Maker's* Ian Birch declared "they're becoming a good pop band, independent of prevailing fashions. A deserved hit." *NME's* Paul Rambali said it was "a half-way competent pop single".[113] Although 'Smash It Up' charted, it only reached 35. The BBC felt the lyrics were an incitement to violence and limited airplay.[114] There was no *Top Of The Pops* appearance.

Chiswick was primed to repeat the success of 'Love Song' and had paid for a promotional video, made on October 4. As the band mimed along with 'Smash It Up', tempers flared. "I spilt some Jack Daniels and Coke on Scabies' jacket," recalls Algy. "He was off his tits on the powders, it escalated and then I had the drum roadie holding me while Rat beat me. Then we carried on filming." Despite the bust up, a promo for the album's 'Plan 9 Channel 7' was filmed the next day in the garden of Rat's parents' house.

"Algy was a fucking great bass player, he really had it," says Rat. "Captain really wanted him in the band. Algy was very straight-ahead, wasn't a big personality. If you need to compete with three people who have got those personalities, you have to stay afloat just to stay on the same page. Algy's way of coping with it was to drink constantly." Despite Algy having sound reasons to leave The Damned and his having earned Rat's antipathy, he did not.

Melody Maker's Paolo Hewitt was sniffy about the album, saying that The Damned were "a tasteless joke" and that he "doubt[ed] whether their particular brand of punk and heavy metal, mixed with a limited pop sensibility will see them through". *NME*'s Deanne Pearson pointed to "heavy metal guitar riffs in every song" while *Sounds*' Pete Silverton awarded four stars out of five, saying the album was a "bewildering mix of genius, garbage, taste, idiocy and noise." It peaked at 31 on the album charts.

Initially, it was planned that early copies of *Machine Gun Etiquette* would be accompanied by a four-track seven-inch EP of cover versions: one chosen by each member of the band. David's was The Walker Brothers' 'The Sun Ain't Gonna Shine Any More'. The other tracks were to be The Who's 'I Can't Explain' (Algy), 'Let There Be Rats' (Rat: a retitled version of Sandy Nelson's 'Let There Be Drums') and Pink Floyd's 'Arnold Layne' (Captain). Recordings of all except 'The Sun Ain't Gonna Shine Any More' were attempted but not completed. The Pink Fairies' 'The Snake' and The Who's 'Happy Jack' (as 'Happy Rat') were also taped. Cream's 'I'm So Glad' was trashed as 'I'm So Bored'. David had also suggested Jefferson Airplane's 'White Rabbit'. What was in the frame for the abandoned album bonus reveals the wide-ranging musical inspirations in the band at the time. As *Melody Maker* had recently said, The Damned were independent of prevailing fashions. They also still did not care about reining in their behaviour.

★ ★ ★

Three days before the release of *Machine Gun Etiquette*, The Damned were seen on *The Old Grey Whistle Test*, the BBC's serious music programme. They played live. 'Smash It Up' and their next single 'I Just

Can't Be Happy Today' were performed, with Captain barking "we're The Damned, we're a punk band" before the latter. By the end of their five minutes 53 seconds, Captain had wrenched his keyboard from its stand after its amplifier ceased working. Rat destroyed his drums as Algy kept playing. Presenter Annie Nightingale said, "You must bear in mind these studios are haunted by The Who."

As always with the programme, the segment had been taped the day before as a safety mechanism in case there were glitches during a live broadcast. After a day at the studio, filming finally started at 9.30 p.m. after the band had been drinking whisky and Coke. At 9.20 they warmed up by running through Cream's 'Sunshine Of Your Love', 'Summer Nights' and Motörhead's 'Overkill'. David was so drunk his hand was gaffer-taped to the microphone to prevent him dropping it. After Rat announced, "This is the first time we've played the *Whistle Test*, I'm going to make fucking sure it's the last", the filming began and they launched into their own songs. Instead of canning the footage, the BBC broadcast it as caught on camera.

"You know what the BBC are like," recalls Algy of the appearance. "You turn up and have to wait for hours. We did the soundcheck in the afternoon and had to hang around all day in the bar. Scabies went out to score some powders to keep us all going. He counted 'Smash It Up' in and it was too fast. Captain was all over the place."

Two weeks later, they set off on the rescheduled tour, which was briefly interrupted by an appearance on the December 6 *Top Of The Pops* to mime the aptly titled 'I Just Can't Be Happy Today' single.[115] By this point, Algy and the rest of the band were not speaking. On the tour's first night, the American band The Misfits played support – they had paid their own way to the UK and turned up outside David's Islington flat where they lobbied to play with The Damned.[116] It became their only show, as friction between them and Rat culminated in their bailing out after the second date's soundcheck. The other band on the bill, Ireland's Victim[117], continued as the tour made its way around the UK. The highest profile show was London's Rainbow where members of the audience threw some of the stalls' seats at the band. Although Captain admonished them by saying The Damned would have to pay for the damage, he threw some of their equipment into the crowd. He was naked.

As the tour began, they recorded a session for BBC Radio 1's Mike Read which featured the new song 'Drinking About My Baby', which was largely Rat's. Algy says, "It was a pile of old shit compared to what we had done before."

After the tour finished, the year culminated with a one-off date on December 22 at Camden's Electric Ballroom. At home, on New Year's Day 1980, Algy got a call from the band's manager Doug Smith. "I got sacked," he recalls. "I don't know why. I wasn't happy, at the time it was a surprise. But I wasn't happy with the direction, I didn't want to play 'White Rabbit' or anything like that – I'm not into hippy shit. I also didn't like a lot of the new material like 'Drinking About My Baby'."

"Algy was on self-destruct," says Rat of what led to the firing. "I was just the one who turned round and said [to the others and Doug Smith] it's time for this to end."

The Damned had reformed in September 1978. They now needed another new bass player, their third since getting back together. They had experienced their most successful year ever: 1979 had seen three chart singles and a chart album. As well as playing America, they completed two high-profile British tours. Although they had a strong fan base, the music business had not welcomed the reconfigured band with open arms. They were on the independent Chiswick, a label with a history roughly paralleling that of their first, Stiff. Yet things had changed. Despite the antics – from the appalling, like pissing on an audience or abusing their bass players, to the mild, like disrupting a Ruts set – The Damned had shown they were contenders. As they entered 1980 without a bass player, there was a lot to build on.

Machine Gun Etiquette

Henry Rollins usually begins his regular Friday night listening session at home with *Machine Gun Etiquette*. He is, as he says, a "Bowie-fixated, Zeppelin-worshiping Stooges freak" but The Damned's third album sets the bar for what follows, issuing a challenge to all his other favourites. Rollins' view is shared by the Oxford University Press which, in its *Encyclopedia of Popular Music*'s entry on The Damned, describes their third album as "one of the finest documents of the punk generation".

Machine Gun Etiquette wasn't made with the goal of securing retrospective assessments and, as ever, there were never any plans. The album took shape in a piecemeal fashion from May to August 1979 at three different studios. 'Love Song', the reanimated Damned's opening shot, had been recorded in March and April and became track one, side one.

The image of the rowdy band on the back of the sleeve was part of the overall picture: one which actually had elements of deliberation. Towering over a photo of Chiswick's home base – Camden's *Rock On* record shop – designer Phil Smee's 3D montage had London landmarks toppling or in flames.[118] On stage, in front of the collapsing cityscape, Rat pulled his drum kit apart as Captain lay down with his guitar. In his

Nosferatu get-up, David was prone. Only Algy was doing what a band member normally did. On the front cover, the band were caught on New York's streets in a shot taken in June.

Machine Gun Etiquette's inner sleeve bore more normal portrait shots and a logo with the words "Three Years Of Anarchy Chaos & Destruction". Two words – "Bye Rick" – marked the departure of manager Rick Rogers. On the other side, a cartoon by Captain instructed buyers how to play 'Smash It Up'. The character hosting the lesson was "Mr God Awful Ugly", a pig rustler. After running though the chords, Mr Ugly instructed readers to "write a concept album about a fat peg-leg mongol called Tummy".

It wasn't wholly apparent at the time to the world at large but the band lacked new songs when they signed with Chiswick Records. Recycling and repurposing was necessary. Or, from another point of view, digging into material already out there but not yet fully realised. 'Looking At You' was an MC5 song which initially surfaced at the first Electric Ballroom show where Lemmy played bass. Seen in the context of the songs considered for the abandoned cover versions EP proposed to accompany *Machine Gun Etiquette*, it stands apart. What had been there to bolster a possibly one-off live appearance was co-opted into the band's repertoire and recorded for the album. 'Anti-Pope' was by Captain's brother Phil and had been played by his band The Cowards; 'Machine Gun Etiquette' was a retitling of The Whitecats' 'Second Time Around'; the keyboard solo in 'I Just Can't Be Happy Today' drew from that of King's 'Baby Sign Here With Me' (King had also played 'Anti-Pope').

There were outside helpers too: music writer Giovanni Dadomo[119] helped with the lyrics of 'I Just Can't Be Happy Today', as did Rat's then girlfriend Jennet Ward (no relation to Algy) with 'Noise, Noise, Noise'. In a sideways fashion, Captain's favourite comic *Bunty* was another helper as 'Melody Lee' drew so much from one of its strips. Though less overt, The Who's 'Happy Jack' was referenced in 'Melody Lee's' closing shout of "I saw you". Yet each original song on the album, with the necessary additional credits to Phil Burns, Giovanni Dadomo and Jennet Ward, was annotated as by "Scabies/Sensible/Vanian/Ward".

For songwriting purposes – whatever each song's history – the band were a unit and shared equally in any publishing income. It was no longer as it was with *Damned Damned Damned*, where one member – Brian James – was the main writer and, as such, received more money than other band members.

Beyond re-establishing The Damned as a going concern, no single concept underpinned *Machine Gun Etiquette*. Whatever its source, apart from 'Smash It Up (Parts 1 and 2)', each song was an entity in its own right which nonetheless sat comfortably with the remainder of the album. Overall unity was reinforced by opening with *Coronation Street*'s Albert Tatlock[120] greeting listeners with the words "ladies and gentlemen. how do" and the overture introducing 'Love Song'. The album closed with a locked groove of another spoken voice endlessly saying "nibbled to death by an okapi".[121]

Despite the mutual songwriting credits, individual songs were from individual band members no matter how they were transformed into conduits for the band. 'Machine Gun Etiquette' was Rat's and 'Liar' was Algy's. David's 'Plan 9 Channel 7' told the story of a fabled relationship between actress-model-TV host Vampira[122] and James Dean. 'These Hands', also David's, was, says Rat, from "an old Marty Feldman sketch. That's where the lyrics come from: 'these are the hands of a demented circus clown'. It was a running gag in the back of the van about musicians and their precious hands. Then Dave turned up with this tune." 'Love Song' was a joint Captain-Rat composition with the balance towards Captain, but the greatest songwriting input into the album was Captain's.

With *Machine Gun Etiquette,* even though the album was born from turmoil, the whole of The Dammed stepped up the plate to make a coherent statement summing up who they were. There was no filler – 'Looking At You' slotted in without breaking the flow – and no flab. Whatever the humour and abundant pop-cultural references – from *Bunty* to *Coronation Street*; from *The Hitchhiker's Guide to the Galaxy* to The Who – they were serious about setting a stall and making a mark. Regardless of punk or even who it was by, it was and remains a terrific pop-art album, one that remains as fresh as it was in 1979.

CHAPTER NINE

Not Related To The Beatles In Any Way

No announcement was made that Algy Ward was no longer in The Damned. Instead, on March 5, 1980, over two months after his dismissal, a short news item in *NME* said "Algie Wood (sic), former Damned bassist, has formed his own three-piece metal band called Tank. They've already recorded a single for rush release by Chiswick." In the event, Tank's debut single – produced by Motörhead's Eddie Clark – became the first release on the Kamaflage label in 1981. As for The Damned, there was no news.

Their manager Doug Smith, who also had Motörhead on his books, had spent January pulling together a tour of continental Europe over April and May despite the lack of a bass player. Dates were planned for Italy, Switzerland, Spain, France, Germany and the Netherlands. With no British shows since December 1979, The Damned looked as if they had given up on promoting the previous month's *Machine Gun Etiquette*. As 1980 began, momentum had stalled. But punk and what it had sown was moving on.

Machine Gun Etiquette was released a month before The Clash's similarly musically wide-ranging double album *London Calling*. Between

152

the two, John Lydon's Public Image Ltd had issued the unambiguously challenging *Metal Box*, which first came as three 45rpm discs in a metal box and was then released as a double album. All three bands symbolised ground-zero for British punk rock and each was distinct from what punk had become. In early March, according to *Sounds*, The Cockney Rejects' gap-toothed, grimacing, two-fingers-up frontman Stinky Turner was "the new face of punk".

This new punk – a punk of slab-like, block-chord guitar and terrace-chant style songs – surfaced in 1979, a year defined by new trends, the hunt for them and youth culture factionalism. The mod revival was counterbalanced by Two-Tone. Heavy metal was back. *The Face* magazine and *i-D* (initially a fanzine) were launched in 1980[123] – each were more about style than the music to which it was pegged. As a consequence, punk was one among many trends. Furthermore, the new-brand punk remained at the margins rather than breaking through with a sustained presence in the mainstream.

For The Damned, who had registered strongly in the non-punk world, none of this was an issue. However they were tarred, and whoever they played with, they ignored trends, and had no time for pleasing critics and spoon-feeding the media. But after reforming, they had their most successful year to date and were primed to build on what they had achieved in 1979. Instead, they side-stepped the public eye as Captain and Rat began recording demos in South Norwood's small RMS Studios over 12 days in January 1980. About 330 yards from Captain's primary school Whitehorse Manor, the studio was only six streets north-east of his parents' house, where he then lived.

★ ★ ★

At this time, the band was dispersed around London. Chiswick's Roger Armstrong says, "They lived in different places and worked together. They didn't socialise, they weren't that kind of band." While Captain was at his family home, David was living in north London, in Islington. Rat was out in west London, in Chiswick.

Recording in Croydon brought Captain the security of the familiar. Armstrong recalls "seeing Captain in Croydon at his mum and dad's.

A small sitting room, his mother was sitting in front of the television, his dad was in a corner by a table and I was at the other end of the table. Then Captain switched the telly off, his mother switched it back on and before she sat down he put a whoopee cushion under her. It was a strange, clown-like atmosphere. Both his parents were quite quiet. He seemed like a completely different person to them: big, very demonstrative and hyperactive. I met Phil, his brother, and he was quite quiet too."

Choosing to work in Croydon fostered productivity. However, in February, time was booked at Wessex to record new tracks. On his own, David had also come up with songs. They now needed a bass player and as it had been with finding Henry Badowski and Algy Ward, they looked for someone in their orbit. The small ads answered by Lu Edmonds and Jon Moss were not used again.

Rat wanted Eddie & The Hot Rods' Paul Gray in the band and had said as much when they reformed as The Doomed in 1978. His past history with The Damned went back to 1976. Gray saw them before the Hot Rods were billed with them at the Mont-de-Marsan punk festival. His band were pictured on the sleeve of early copies of *Damned Damned Damned*. He had played with Rat in an ad-hoc line up of Johnny Moped in October 1977. Despite his pub rock background, there was an obviousness about Gray joining the band. He got the call in March.

"We were very lucky to get Paul," says Captain. "He was probably the best bassist in Britain at the time. Well, now that I'd switched to guitar anyway. He could certainly rock out and once said to me that if he was paid by the amount of notes he played he'd be a millionaire. He also did subtle, which was handy as we were heading into moody atmospheric territories. Paul and myself also shared a passion for real ale and used to have these plastic jugs filled with draught Bass every day in preparation for the evening's session."

At Wessex and with Gray on board, the band recorded early try-outs of 'Dave's Song (Grip Or Something)' (later retitled 'Curtain Call'), 'Dr. Jekyll And Mr. Hyde', 'Rabid (Over You)', 'Seagulls', 'Theme108' (later retitled 'History Of The World Part 1') and the New York Dolls-esque 'White Cats' (later retitled 'Sick Of This And That'). Then, it was back to RMS for 13 days to tape more demos and polish what had been captured at Wessex. It was the lengthiest continuous series of sessions The Damned had ever undertaken. While the work went on in South Norwood, David signed up with vocal coach Glynne Jones for two lessons a week over the whole of March. She had worked with Shirley Bassey, Tom Jones and Scott Walker and her future clients would include Annie Lennox and The Spice Girls. Jones's technique was to help singers focus on pitching while strengthening their voice and breathing without losing their identity.

Things were going so well that Captain and Rat wanted to welcome Gray into the band properly. He also needed to learn the repertoire in advance of the continental European dates set for April and May. Chiswick footed the bill for hiring a boat for a week, just as they had underwritten David's singing tutorials. In the first week of April, Anglo-Welsh Narrow Boats provided the boat Napton for what was on their books as a week's holiday cruise.

Captain and Rat didn't bring any instruments. They had no intention of rehearsing. Gray met them on the second day of the jaunt, at Didcot in Oxfordshire. He had his bass with him and was told it wasn't necessary. They made their way to Kennet & Avon Canal. All that had been brought on board the narrow boat was an air rifle and beer. The main driver for the outing was to visit as many waterside pubs as possible. Gray woke the next morning to see his boots floating past – doused in lighter fuel, they had been set on fire and thrown overboard. The crockery that came with the hire was used for target practice. While in locks, washing-up liquid was dumped into the water, coating it with foam. Any remonstrating boat owners were targeted with the air rifle. On the sixth day, Napton was abandoned. Chiswick received a letter from Anglo-Welsh Narrow Boats saying their staff had found the boat to be in "a filthy state" with "damage to the inside of the boat far in excess of the £20 deposit which we are retaining in full". They would not be hiring out a boat in future.

On their return from Britain's waterways, the band were booked into west London's Shepherds Bush Studios to rehearse. David did not turn up. In the nine hours they were there on April 9, the ceiling tiles and coving were burnt and broken. Chiswick was billed for "damages caused deliberately to the studio by the band".

After further work on demos and another visit to Wessex, the tour began in the Netherlands and continued to Italy and France. By this point, Doug Smith was co-managing the band with their long-term tour manager Tommy Crossan. The band wanted a coach, but Smith had booked a mini bus. Shortly after leaving London, its seats were set on fire and an attempt made to rip its roof off. Once gaffer-taped back together, the compromised vehicle continued on its journey as Smith would not hire anything else. In Turin, the first Italian date, the band arrived after their road crew and equipment truck.

Without their or their managers' knowledge, The Damned's tour had been hijacked as a front for smuggling drugs from the Netherlands into Italy. "Here's what I saw," says Rat, explaining what happened. "We were late for the first show, the first show in Italy. The crew are travelling in their own van, we're in our van and we have a truck with the PA and backline. The band and everyone else are there before the truck. I'm standing there with the promoter and Doug Smith's guy is saying nothing comes off the van until you pay Motörhead what they're owed [from a recent show]. The next day, while the crew are having lunch, someone took their van away, smashed it up and then parked it back outside the restaurant. They freak out, head for the border, drive into Switzerland. We turn up a bit later, 'Where's the equipment?' We were the only ones there."

"At the hotel," continues Rat, "I get a phone call from the crew saying, 'Get out, you're dealing with the mafia.' Then there were meetings with men in suits and the promoter in the hotel bar. Viv, later my wife, was there, she speaks Italian but they didn't know. She said, 'They were saying they knew it's not the band's fault, but they're not going to let you go until what was picked up in Amsterdam is delivered'. It came on with the equipment, it came on with the PA and the backline. We were mules." The show went ahead but the end of the tour marked the cessation of Doug Smith and Tommy Crossan's tour of service with The Damned.

Despite the studio sessions in January, February, March and April, no new or unreleased songs were played on the road. Leaning heavily on

Machine Gun Etiquette, the sets usually climaxed with 'Help', 'Stab Yor Back', 'Neat Neat Neat' and 'New Rose'. There was no announcement that Gray was in the band and, beyond a couple of one-off shows, there hadn't been a sequence of British dates since late 1979. For six months, little suggested to the outside world that there was life in the newly manager-less The Damned.

★ ★ ★

A new single had been scheduled for a May release. It was to be a three-cut, seven-inch of tracks recently recorded at Wessex. Initially, 'Rabid Over You' was favoured as the top side but a version of Jefferson Airplane's 'White Rabbit' won out. 'Seagulls' was the second track on the B-side. Test pressings were manufactured. Two stuffed flying gulls and a pair of stuffed white rabbits were hired as the stars of the photo session for the sleeve.

Captain was happy with what had been recorded. "We were all into garage psychedelia," he says. "The Seeds, Electric Prunes, Chocolate Watch Band, and 'White Rabbit' was one of our faves. That was the highest I ever heard Dave sing. He could have joined The Bee Gees after that."

Yet the single was released in France and Germany only as, late in the day, Chiswick decided that a cover version was not right as a Damned single. Nonetheless, import copies made it to the UK.[124] It was another four months before the band's next single proper was released.

Abandoning 'White Rabbit' at such a last-minute stage didn't mean Chiswick had called off their commitment to The Damned. They were booked into Rockfield Studios in Wales from May 25 to June 14 to work on their new album. "There was a good vibe in the band," says Captain. "We were confident that we could make a great album and were certainly prepared to experiment, and push ourselves to the limit of our capabilities to achieve this. Dave Vanian's writing was particularly good by then, and I enjoyed working with him on the wonderfully dark material he was coming up with."

"We were filled with optimism," confirms David. "We were very close. We felt very confident and focused. We felt nothing could stand

157

in our way, we were strong enough and united enough as a band to break down barriers."

Of their approach to music at this point, Rat explains, "Every time we went to make an album we'd always ask what our critics were saying and do the opposite."

Rockfield was a new experience for The Damned. This was the first time they had recorded outside London. A residential studio located north-east of Cardiff in south Wales, its rural setting contrasted starkly with Britannia Row, Pathway and Wessex where they had previously recorded. These studios were off main roads in the north London borough of Islington and from the outside resembled light industrial buildings. Rockfield was surrounded by fields – the name did not relate to music, but was taken from the nearest village. Charles and Kingsley Ward had opened the studio in 1963 after converting farm buildings. With producer Dave Edmunds, The Damned's 1976 short-term tour headliners The Flamin' Groovies had recorded there. Dr. Feelgood, Graham Parker & The Rumour and Motörhead had been there too. So had Queen, whose 'Bohemian Rhapsody' became one of the studio's most successful recordings. This was also a first for Chiswick. The label had not previously committed to such a major studio booking for one of its bands.[125]

The label planned to team The Damned with Alvin Clark in the producer's chair. He had worked with the band at his Camden studio Sound Suite and also at Wessex. "I decided I wasn't going to produce the next album," recalls Roger Armstrong. "I thought Alvin could do it. I sent him down to Rockfield and he lasted about half an hour."

"I fired the producer," says David. "We were more than up to the job to produce it ourselves, even though the record company thought we were doing the wrong thing. We were given free rein, grudgingly." On arriving at Rockfield, Clark had said he wanted to give the band a nice poppy drum sound. The album ended up being self-produced, with the band working closely with engineer Hugh Jones.

"We were such a bunch of egomaniacs," adds Rat, on the reasons for the self-production. "We'd desperately been waiting for the chance to get in there, be experimental: backwards cymbals, backwards echo. But it got honed down by the time we'd finished."

"Poor old Huge [sic: Hugh] Jones had his work cut out," continues David. "Rat and Paul seemed to work best in the day and myself and Captain till very late at night. The more creative stuff was usually done after dinner which was served at seven. Nothing to do with the copious amounts of wine that got quaffed."

"The night shift was when the crazy ideas would come into play," says Captain. "Playing the piano strings with drum sticks, cutting chunks of the two-inch tape out and splicing it in again backwards, stuff like that."

There were distractions. "The Wards, a great rock'n'roll family, thankfully turned a blind eye to most of our jolly japes," continues Captain. "Smashed windows – I tried to blame it on the studio mutt. Redecorating the kitchen with three-dozen eggs and blasting grapefruits amongst other stuff with the shotgun they lent us." Captain found his inner cowboy and took to wearing spaghetti western-style clothing.

They were at their most creative. The demos recorded earlier in the year ensured 'Dr. Jekyll And Mr. Hyde', 'Sick Of This And That' and 'History Of The World (Part 1)' were swiftly completed. 'Curtain Call' was more labour intensive. What had begun as four minutes of David with the harmonium in his Islington flat grew. Ultimately, two separate recordings were stitched together with what the band dubbed the "horror chord" to become a 17-minute piece. As a consequence of completing 'Curtain Call', it was realised this was more than a traditional two-side album. But three sides were not a double album. A fourth side of live recordings was the solution.

A run of live shows was booked for July and culminated in one recorded for the new album. At this point, it was belatedly announced Paul Gray had joined the band. There were mixed messages about his status. *Record Mirror* reported, "Whether he'll be joining the band permanently isn't yet known." *NME* said, "Paul Gray is not confirmed as permanent." *Sounds* disclosed the problem: "No one is prepared to make him officially a member of the band as there are still various management complications to be resolved." It was also announced that 'History Of The World (Part 1)' was their new single, with a late July release date; a tour was duly booked.

The tour's first date was July 17. The band's friends The Ruts had decided to part from their singer Malcolm Owen as his escalating heroin use had made him so unreliable that they couldn't see a future with him. To help him, Owen was asked by The Damned to come out on the road with them and play support in some way. It was hoped that being on the bill would help him focus and perhaps get straight. Owen was found dead of an overdose on July 14. Inevitably, the mood was miserable. On stage, on the second date, there was friction between Captain and David during 'Dr. Jekyll And Mr. Hyde'. Captain played keyboards whilst prone. David tried to throw the organ off the stage. Rat thought the band was over.

Looking back at the period, Rat says, "I've never recovered from when Malcolm died. The Ruts had split and Malcolm wanted to clean up so we offered to take him and his girlfriend out on the road. I knew people in Redhill who had died, knew what it was about before I met The Ruts, before Sid Vicious. My heroin stories way pre-date that by a long way. I knew what the going rate up the Dilly was, that you went to Chinatown to score. I rejected it with The Heartbreakers. The Heartbreakers turned up [in 1976] with their heroin and suddenly people were jacking up in the toilets. I've always been anti heroin." In the spirit in which they extended a hand to Owen, The Damned asked the three members of The Ruts to join the tour. Confusion and grief ensured emotions ran high. Coincidentally, the dates had been tagged as "The End Of The Human Race As We Now Know It Tour (Part 1)".

A stage at Shepperton film studio was booked for recording the live part of the new album. The Ruts played too. "We were playing the older material so well with Paul," says Captain. "Side four did need to be filled with something. We invited The Damned's fan club: the Flashman Society, named after those hilarious books by George MacDonald Fraser which I'd recommend to anyone. We kinda identified with Flash's approach to life."

"There were lots of fights at Shepperton," recalls Rat. "There were free drinks and coach loads turned up." 'Neat Neat Neat' was interrupted and had to be reprised. Although they were not released, the encores included 'Burglar', a joint Damned–Ruts version of 'In A

Rut' and Splodgenessabounds' 'Two Pints Of Lager And A Packet Of Crisps Please' with that band's vocalist Max Splodge.

Two days after the live taping, they were back at Rockfield for a week to continue with the album. It was going to be a double, with three studio sides and a live side. 'History Of The World (Part 1)' was still earmarked as the next single. But whether it was possible to pick up from where things had been left commercially at the end of 1979 was an open question.

★ ★ ★

Chiswick Records were determined that 'History Of The World (Part 1)' was going to make a splash. It was issued in late September, rather than July as originally planned. In the intervening period, the original recording from Rockfield was overhauled by Hans Zimmer, who added synthesiser and was credited as its co-producer. Although he went on to compose the scores for *The Dark Knight*, *Gladiator*, *Inception* and *The Lion King*, Zimmer was then little known outside the music business but had attracted some attention in 1979 for being involved in Buggles. For Chiswick, he had produced the 'Stranger Than Fiction' single by The Radiators. The label tapped him to bring some gloss to The Damned.

For *Melody Maker*, the single was The Damned's "finest moment since 'New Rose'". *Sounds* said it was "a cute and hilariously medium-paced giggle containing the odd gorgeous touch of bad taste". *Record Mirror* felt they had gone "all psychedelic" and that "it doesn't really suit them" while the pop glossy *Smash Hits* detected "overtures to the mainstream" now they had been "outflanked by The Cockney Rejects and UK Subs in the punk slapstick stakes". 'History Of The World (Part 1)' stalled at 51, failing to break into the UK's Top 50.

Any questions about what actually suited The Damned were not asked. Similarly, *Smash Hits*' idea the band would make "overtures to the mainstream" due to be being pushed aside by the reductive template punk of The Cockney Rejects or UK Subs was threadbare reasoning. As ever, The Damned's music bore no relation to received notions of what it should be. The album which followed 'History Of The World (Part 1)' into the shops – *The Black Album* – could not be pigeonholed.

"I remember someone somewhere saying to me that the more interesting of the punk groups were the ones that didn't necessarily listen to punk music," explains Captain. He says the influences on *The Black Album* were "garage bands from the Sixties and I wanted to get some organ on the record. I had worn out several copies of *Befour* by Britain's greatest-ever Hammond player Brian Auger and luckily they had a Hammond B3 organ in the studio. Also, we had just discovered classical music – Messian, Rachmaninov and of course Rimsky-Korsakov who had a great influence on one particular portion of *The Black Album*. The great thing about having four writers in the band was that they all brought different influences with them. Rat was pretty keen on Gong for example."

"The band were getting more into Sixties American garage bands," agrees David. "Cap and Rat were into prog rock but we were all listening to The Doors, Seeds, Shadows Of Knight. The *Pebbles* albums had just come out and we thought it was amazing you could get so much great music on one album.[126] Also, I was always more into film music, including incidental music, and I was bringing that into the band."

"Things were changing musically," says Rat. "I was listening to the *Hitchhiker's Guide To The Galaxy* on the radio, Terry Riley. We'd been through the Hendrix stage and were just hitting The Doors. *Nuggets* and *Pebbles* were around. More haunting music was beginning to emerge."

As the music took shape at Rockfield, stories were drip fed to the music press. Jimmy Page had apparently been in the frame as the producer. The band were said to be unable to confirm that Page was their producer. In July, photos of Rat's dog Pup with her paws on the studio mixing desk were issued to the music press. The new album was apparently going to be titled *Atom Heart Mugger* and was, musically, a "radical departure".

One digression no one heard was Captain, Rat and Paul Gray's piss-taking vocals added to a version of David's 'Dr. Jekyll and Mr. Hyde'. His reaction to their funny voices and raspberries was to fire the studio's shotgun from his room over the heads of Captain and Rat. He had, though, emptied the shot from the cartridges before taking aim.

After three final days at Rockfield in September, the album was scheduled for release on November 3, 1980. 'History Of The World

(Part 1)' had not charted high, so work was needed to help The Damned return to the public eye. Chiswick engaged veteran music business publicist Keith Altham to help promote *The Black Album*. The band now had former Whitecats manager Peter Scarborough handling their affairs and tour dates were planned from November into the New Year.

Speaking to *Melody Maker* at the end of September, Captain acknowledged that the band would look favourably on a change in their circumstances. "We always said we wanted to be rich," he said. "I was always angry because I never had nothing in my life, I still haven't got anything." "I've only ever had one royalty cheque," added Rat. "There's a vast amount of money going through the bank account, but the bills are big and so are the expenses. We get £80 a week. My old lady earns more than I do."

The Damned was not the only thing on Rat's mind. He had produced singles by former support bands The Satellites and Victim as well as Anti-Establishment and The Bouncing Flowers (who featured his former Tart bandmate Mark Sullivan). In September, he spent a week at RMS Studios working on a proposed solo album, a project that was rapidly abandoned. Instead of that, a single credited to The Rat & The Whale was issued in October: the version of Brian Auger & The Trinity's 1968 take on Bob Dylan's 'This Wheel's On Fire' featured Vivian Mason, Rat's girlfriend and future wife on vocals.

But laying the ground for the forthcoming album continued. Two BBC radio sessions featuring versions of seven of the new songs were recorded in the first week of October: one for John Peel's show, the other for Mike Read's. On November 17, they appeared on national television, on the Cardiff-filmed youth magazine programme *Something Else* running through 'Drinking About My Baby', 'Dr. Jekyll & Mr. Hyde' and a special cover version of Eddie Cochran's 'Something Else'. *The Black Album* had been released that day, rather than the planned November 3.

Press reactions were favourable but measured. *NME* noted David was shaping the band's direction, pointed to the Terry Riley influence on 'Curtain Call' but said it was "fun in the way a knees-up in a cardboard crypt would be". *Sounds* pointed to "evidence of their melodic maturity", nods to Syd Barrett and Beach Boys on 'Silly Kids Games', said 'Curtain

Call' was self-indulgent and awarded four-and-a-half stars out of five. *Melody Maker* said they were "striving too hard for versatility" and that it was a "brave try". The radio plugging company Multi Media were working the album hard and, on the BBC, tracks were played by John Peel, Mike Read, Richard Skinner and Tommy Vance. On the London commercial station Capital Radio, Nicky Horne aired 'Silly Kids Games'. As much as possible was being done to promote The Damned's new album.

"That title seemed appropriate," says Captain. "Some of the material had a dark, melancholy feel. We weren't the biggest Beatles fans around though. I preferred The Kinks and The Groundhogs."

David says, "It was said that The Beatles had their *White Album*, we had our *Black Album*. The sleeve isn't related to The Beatles in any way. I thought it was great, the best thing we'd ever done, truly a mix of everything we were really good at. It had everything, pop songs, anthemic songs, filmic songs."

Although a double, *The Black Album* sold for the price of a single album.[127] This was a contrast to the 12-inch edition of 'History Of The World (Part 1)' which was priced more than its seven-inch counterpart. Rat said, "Just as we are trying to hammer home a value for money policy, the record company comes up with a scalper." He declared that the band would sign copies bought to make up for being out of pocket. A week after the album's release the band's Christmas single, 'There Ain't No Sanity Clause' was issued on seven-inch.[128] Though *The Black Album* peaked at 29, the new, stand-alone single did not chart.

A date at London's Hammersmith Odeon was the high-profile focus of the tour promoting the album.[129] Captain told the audience they were "the ugliest I've ever seen" and asked "are there any punks out there?" in what national newspaper *The Guardian* described as "a ritual exchange of insults between the audience and the band". While ignoring *Music For Pleasure*, the set ranged over the other three albums. A second encore featured The Ruts and a broom-wielding Lemmy on 'Ballroom Blitz' and 'Noise, Noise, Noise'. *Sounds* said the show found "The Damned fluttering perilously close to perfection." After the tour's next six dates, they discovered their manager had vanished with the takings. "It was a bad decision on my part," says Rat of engaging Peter Scarborough as their manager. "I let him convince me. I never realised the contract was with a limited company and after the shows they folded the company, [there was] nothing you can do about it."

Over Christmas, Captain was penniless. Rat and his accountant father John Millar took control of business. The band's seasonal card sent to fans was signed by Captain, David and Rat but not Paul Gray.

★ ★ ★

'History Of The World (Part 1)' had not sold as well as the three *Machine Gun Etiquette*-related singles. 'There Ain't No Sanity Clause' had been and gone. With its two-for-the-price-of-one cost, sales of *The Black Album* were not going to quickly recoup all that had been spent on demoing and recording it during 1980. The money from the tour promoting the album had vanished. The Damned's equity was profoundly negative. They had made their most ambitious album, but had weaker foundations than a new band yet to make a record.

Chiswick's Roger Armstrong was acutely aware that, "We were struggling. Captain said to me, 'Why won't people take me seriously as a musician?' I said, 'Probably because you end up bollock naked on stage most nights.' We couldn't keep the success up. *The Black Album* was not a hit, we were getting financially into the hole. It was a case of chasing good money after bad. We knew our EMI deal was winding down, we weren't getting success there."

The label had nothing else on their books with the sales potential of The Damned. 'Driver's Seat' by Sniff 'n' The Tears had been a fluke hit in June 1979 and Rocky Sharpe & The Replays were not a long-term bet. Chiswick's future ultimately drew from the past. In 1979, Chiswick had begun a strategy of securing licensing deals with American labels to reissue their back catalogue. The first were with Los Angeles' Modern Records and Texas' Glad Music. The Ace imprint, dedicated to catalogue reissues, ran side-by-side with Chiswick. In parallel, records by bands like Diz & The Doormen and Red Beans & Rice, grounded in the music of the Fifties, were also issued by Ace. The keen sense of music's history ensured Chiswick's long-term outlook.

As 1981 began, The Damned, the label's biggest contemporary band, appeared to be at an impasse. Despite their arrangement with EMI, who pressed, distributed and marketed the records, Chiswick was an independent and unable to write debts off like a major, and then have the sums vanish amongst the business' overall budget. Cross collateralisation was also not possible – there was hardly anywhere else from where to draw cash.

Nonetheless, as Roger recalls, "John, Rat's dad, stared writing us letters about lack of accounting which was nonsense. Breach of contract, blah, blah. It was a manoeuvre to get them out of the contract. John was the oddest character. Later, in 1986, they played Finsbury Park and I was in the back area, and he had long hair, a velvet jacket and the mysterious one hand missing, and he was discussing the search for the Holy Grail with his wife. He had driven to France and the clouds had turned into the number 666. She interjected, and said, 'John can handle his acid.' A very strange man. He was quite well off. The house in Redhill was a big pile. It was always said, 'He knows the tax man'. His job seemed to be to usher people into the system."

John Millar spent three weeks checking the books and found nothing amiss. The inspection of Chiswick's finances was not going to improve the band's relationship with their label as a bond of trust had been broken. The audit also forced the label into being unable to finance anything to do with The Damned as their account was frozen. The band's sole source of ready income had to come from live dates. Yet apart from a fan-club show at London's Hammersmith Palais on March 3, 1981, the new year did not begin with a tour. Odd dates at pubs and small venues around London like Canning Town's Bridge House, Croydon's Star, Fulham's Greyhound and Hammersmith's Clarendon were not going to bring home anyone's bacon.

And, as The Damned were contracted to Chiswick, negotiations with other labels were unfeasible. The Damned had issued their most ambitious album to date on a label which had supported them throughout 1980, but less than a month after its release they were at a dead stop. In 1981, as it had been when they reformed in 1978, they once again had to start from scratch. This time, though, they would be doing it after compromising their relationship with Chiswick Records, the label which paid for their first demo in 1976.

The Black Album

It's an enduring tribute to Chiswick Records – and Roger Armstrong in particular – that the label, an independent despite its ties with EMI, had such faith in The Damned that they bore with the band while *The Black Album* took shape. The label's paperwork shows that the recording of demos began on January 11, 1980[130] and the album sessions finished on August 19.[131] It cost money: the bill for recording at Rockfield, one aspect of bringing the album home, totalled £15,874.15.[132] The album could have been a single set but 'Curtain Call' was included, stretching it out to a three-sider. Then, it become a double proper with the addition of its fourth side: a specially recorded live concert. Topping it all off, David Vanian designed the sleeve. It'd be churlish in the extreme to suggest Chiswick was not behind The Damned.

The resultant album was unwieldy. But it was a landmark, the peak of The Damned's ambition: encapsulating all aspects of the band. While the live side doesn't bear repeated listening and mostly serves as flash-frozen proof that Captain more than had chops as a guitarist on stage and had no problems with the Brian James-era songs, sides one to three were stuffed with pop songs infused with psychedelia, prog-rock leanings and plain old all-out attack.

As it had been with *Machine Gun Etiquette*, there was recycling and the drafting-in of guest lyricists. 'Sick Of This And That' was another old Whitecats song; new bassist Paul Gray had previously recorded a demo of 'Hit Or Miss' with Eddie & The Hot Rods[133]; 'Drinking About My Baby' pre-dated the *Black Album* sessions and was first heard on a John Peel session recorded November 16, 1979. Reversing this, 'Silly Kids Games' later echoed through Captain's 1985 solo single 'Come On Down'. Giovanni Dadomo again contributed lyrics, this time to 'Dr. Jekyll And Mr. Hyde'. 'Therapy' had lyrics by Fay Hart, who first met the band in Los Angeles in April 1977.[134]

Then, there were songs where outside inputs had more of an impact than lyrics. Despite its band-only writing credits, Rat says then-recent hitmaker and all-round music business powerhouse BA Robertson co-wrote 'History Of The World (Part 1)'. "He was a really nice guy," recalls Rat. "He wrote the melody, because all Captain had was the backing sequence." Of 'Wait For The Blackout', Rat says "I wrote the music. Billy Karloff[135] wrote the melodies, Captain – well, Nick Lowe actually – wrote the middle break. It's off a Nick Lowe song, it's stolen. I won't say which one."

When it was issued, *The Black Album* had, like *Machine Gun Etiquette*, all its songs credited to the band overall: Scabies/Sensible/Gray/Vanian. Dadomo, Hart and Karloff's names were added to the songs they contributed to. Robertson's was not.

Another credit firmly identifying this as The Damned's own album was "all songs produced the Kings of Reverb – P. Gray, C Millar, R. Burns, D. Vanian." The only exception was 'History Of The World (Part 1)', where "production and synthesizers [were] by Hans Zimmer Esq".

'History Of The World (Part 1)' was not the only track to incorporate a synthesiser. After opening with the irresistibly poppy 'Wait For The Blackout', *The Black Album* bedded in with 'Lively Arts', which featured synth as instrumental colour and rhythmic punctuation. As songs segued into each other, it was evident The Damned had moved on. 'Silly Kids Games' was reflective, underpinned by acoustic guitar, sported Beach Boys-style wordless harmony vocals and was sung by Captain. Rock as such was still unquestionably core to the band – in 'Hit Or Miss', 'Sick Of This And That', and the break and choruses of 'Drinking About My Baby' – but much more was going on. *The Black Album* was about disregarding boundaries.

While 'Twisted Nerve' developed the style of *Machine Gun Etiquette*'s 'These Hands', the new song had a creepier atmosphere and more sparse instrumentation – aided by Gray's sinuous bass. Although more traditionally constructed, the elegant 'Dr. Jekyll And Mr. Hyde' was as ambient and even more measured. '13th Floor Vendetta' (which had lyrics directly quoting from the quirky horror film *The Abominable Dr. Phibes*) was of a piece with both 'Twisted Nerve' and 'Dr. Jekyll And Mr. Hyde': each song demonstrating that within the framework of The Damned, David was coming into his own.

Side two of *The Black Album* finished with the Who-like and Hendrix-influenced 'Therapy'. For American buyers, this is where the album ended. The Damned's first album to hit their home audience was a single set: the IRS label did not release sides three and four[136], a lapse noted in *Creem* magazine where Gene Sculatti said, "The bad news is that this, their first American record, has been severed at the cervix from its beautiful British sister. Over there it's a double album." He preceded that statement with, "The good news is that England's surviving punk pioneers have released their most accessible album to date. Songs like 'Dr. Jekyll' and 'Wait For The Blackout' represent the monstrous Vanian, Scabies and cohorts at their darkest, densest best. The band has never written, played or recorded as strongly."

As well side four's live tracks, America was missing side three – the entirety of which was taken up by 'Curtain Call'. Over its 17 minutes, this portmanteau aural drama was unlike anything else The Damned had recorded

"Vanian had it all in his head," recalls Captain of 'Curtain Call'. "Almost all of it was hummed in my ear and transposed to guitar. I like that we tried to push things a bit. We were up all night, chopping tapes up, opening a piano, banging it with drum stick. I'd be in the plate reverb room and Vanian would be in there with headphones. I added the melancholy tune that precedes the instrumental section and then everybody was chipping in until the piece was complete. Somebody suggested adding some manic fiddle playing and we spun in a chunk from Rimsky-Korsakov's *Scheherazade*, which might have been easier if there had been samplers in those days. There weren't, so it was all hands on deck manipulating a 20-feet long piece of ¼ inch tape around pencils and the like while we attempted to record it in the correct place on the multi-track. By the time we were working on this track it was pretty much me, Dave and the engineer doing all-nighters. I remember dear Ratty getting a little impatient at the time we were spending on it, so in a final big push we completed it during a one big session ending at noon the next day. We celebrated by having too much to drink in the local pub."

With *The Black Album*, The Damned felt they could do anything. Ambitious? Yes. But also confirmation they were at a peak – one which would be hard to scale again.

CHAPTER TEN

Death Reports Unconfirmed

On Friday November 13, 1981 The Damned released the *Friday 13th EP*, their first record in a year. Despite the return to the shops, focus was lacking. The EP hit the racks a week after *This Is Your Captain Speaking*, Captain's own EP and his first solo record. Also vying for attention and issued on the same day as the *Friday 13th EP* was a new album titled *Another Great Record From The Damned: The Best Of The Damned*, The Damned's first compilation.

Another Great Record From The Damned: The Best Of The Damned, was on Chiswick's Ace imprint and included tracks from the Stiff-era band and the Algy Ward line-up, but had a cover photo of the current Damned with Paul Gray. The Lu Edmonds configuration was pictured on the back but not heard. On the inner sleeve, there was a photo of the Henry Badowski version of The Doomed, which had not even recorded. While positive that The Damned's history was being celebrated – as they always did by playing 'New Rose' and 'Neat Neat Neat' live – this was a befuddled release which also meant The Damned were competing for retail space with their own past and suggested they were now a heritage act.

And Captain Sensible was now a solo artist: a second distraction from the *Friday 13th EP*. Even so, their new record charted at 50, one place higher than the previous year's 'History Of The World (Part 1)'. The return to vinyl a year after their non-chart last release – November 1980's 'There Ain't No Sanity Clause' – and the other records were evidence for neither a flawless marketing strategy or unified outlook.

★ ★ ★

How The Damned now fitted in with British pop was unclear. Pop was now more fragmented than ever and tribalism was rife. In broad-brush terms, a second wave of punk had split into what were later termed street punk and anarcho-punk. The former, initially branded Oi!, was grassroots-driven, and had mostly evolved in suburban and non-London areas. Despite the support of weekly music paper *Sounds* it was never embraced by metropolitan taste-makers. The same went for anarcho-punk, whose figurehead band Crass defined a direction that never intersected with the mainstream. In 1980, The Exploited – who fitted neither category comfortably despite being punkier-than-punk – had supported The Damned, ensuring their headliners' awareness of the ebb and flow of what punk had become.

In the summer, the record defining the mood of the season was The Specials' prescient 'Ghost Town', the eerie and inadvertent soundtrack to British social unrest that culminated in riots. The Damned's former manager Rick Rogers was steering their career. Contrastingly, shinier fare was surfacing. Although they had played Canning Town's edgy Bridge House pub – which regularly booked Oi! stalwarts The Cockney Rejects – Depeche Mode's synth-pop was beginning to chart. The Damned themselves played the Bridge House in April 1981.

Although much of The Damned's most-recent music was unclassifiable as punk and they appeared to stand apart from anything voguish, the inspirations for the more questing material on *The Black Album* paralleled those driving the Sixties-influenced Liverpool bands The Teardrop Explodes and Echo & The Bunnymen. The latter had also recorded at Rockfield with Hugh Jones and were as fascinated with The Doors as The Damned. The Teardrop Explodes' Julian Cope would write *Tales From The Drug Attic*, a piece in *NME* in December 1983 on psychedelic music that enthusiastically extolled what had also fired The Damned up.

Plugging The Damned into anything of-the-moment beyond knee-jerk responses to them as "punk" was impossible. Their past was inescapable and always coloured their present. With their relationship with Chiswick Records now on the rocks, they also lacked the infrastructure to even try repositioning how they were perceived. While John Millar's examination of the label's books had confirmed that The Damned were indeed in debt, as the label had claimed, the band's insistence on this financial scrutiny compromised any relationship between them and Chiswick. With affirmation that any income from record sales was offset against the debt, the relationship was now barely viable. As usual, the only source of ready cash was playing live.

In the public-facing world, stories in the music press of their demise were denied. Other titbits were fed to the weeklies. A new album had apparently been recorded and was to be issued in the autumn. The band had now left Chiswick and were about to sign a new deal. The Damned were to celebrate their fifth anniversary in July with a concert trailed as "The History Of The Damned - 5 Years". Henry Badowksi, Brian James and Algy Ward were to join them on stage. American dates were set for May. They were also said to be considering an offer for a six-week tour of America.

The drip-feed reporting confirmed The Damned existed and that they were active. But they combined truth, bluff and counter-bluff. They were still signed to Chiswick and moving to a new label was not contractually possible. There would be a fifth anniversary show, but the imminent American tour was an invention. A new album had not been recorded. In fact, following a few British out-of-London dates in late April with the resolutely punk-motivated Anti-Nowhere League as support[137], The Damned were booked to play Finland and West Germany. In Berlin, where they played a residency, David was slipped LSD at one show. He drifted on and off the stage as the band played the songs with Captain on vocals.

It was a metaphor for The Damned's status during the first half of 1981. They existed, but how sustainable they were was anyone's guess. In December 1980 they played the 3,500-capacity Hammersmith Odeon. In March 1981, it was the smaller Hammersmith Palais to an audience of 2,200, across the roundabout from the Odeon. The next month it was Canning Town's Bridge House pub, with its capacity of 560. It was hardly new for them, but The Damned's fortunes were declining.

★ ★ ★

While his band's future was uncertain, David and his wife Laurie were featured in the short-lived London music magazine *Trax*, in a March 1981 article focussing on their style. A strong supporter of the scene around the club Blitz, the weekly covered fashionable bands like Depeche Mode, Spandau Ballet and Ultravox. David and Laurie showed off their dimly lit Islington flat, its mannequins, the clothes designed and made by Laurie. David said, "I suppose old-fashioned gear is becoming new fashion right now through people like Spandau Ballet and the Blitz Kids, although I was wearing those dress shirts with the full sleeves and frilled edges, frock coats and white face make-up years ago." The Damned were mentioned in passing twice. There was nothing about what David's band was doing.

Captain was also looking beyond the boundaries of The Damned. Early that month, he had seen the moody synth-pop band New Musik play Croydon's Fairfield Halls. His girlfriend Christiane was a fan and played their records at home, and although initially unconvinced he had grown to like them. He enjoyed seeing them live and met the band's leader Tony Mansfield after the show. The March 8 encounter was significant.

Captain also used the period of The Damned's relative immobility to add production to his resumé[138], as Rat had done in 1980 with Anti-Establishment, The Bouncing Flowers, The Satellites and Victim. "I always wanted to be a producer and wield all that power," he said. "Giving musicians a lot of stick is good fun." Already a fan of the all-female Cambridge band Dolly Mixture, he became their producer. After first seeing them at Camden's Music Machine, he was a regular in their audience.

"Captain was brought to see us by our agent, he used to hang out with The Damned," says Dolly Mixture's bassist and co-singer Deborah

Wykes. "Captain loved it and kept turning up at other gigs saying 'I've got to produce you.' He thought we wrote good songs." Although they had released one major-label single, Dolly Mixture were unhappy with how they had been marketed and not listened to. Ready for a fresh start, they signed with Paul Weller's Respond label and became its first band to issue a record, the 'Been Teen' single.[139]

In April, they played with The Damned for the first time at Fulham's Greyhound pub. "Playing with them was uncomfortable as everyone wanted to see them," recalls Deborah. "The audience spat at us, they spat at them, they spat at us big time. It was the ethic at the time. Captain encouraged it."

With Paul Gray by his side as co-producer, Captain and Dolly Mixture were booked into The Kinks' north London Konk Studio to capture the band's yearning Sixties-influenced post-punk songs. "Captain's input was constant," says Deborah. "He loved getting the right sound, spent hours getting the right guitar sound, drum sound, vocal sound. He talked all the time. Constant. Paul Gray wasn't as noisy. Paul was always concentrating, there as somebody to lean on, to consult. It was all about making us better. Captain was such an interesting person, all the things he used to observe about everyday life and people. He observed everything and used to make sense. He was really into politics, told us lots of things we didn't know. Tried to train us how to be good at interviews. He relished the chance to do some sort of performance at interviews."

Captain also became curious about the anarcho-punk band Crass – initially as he had seen their name on the leather jackets of much of The Damned's audience. After making contact, he spent six days recording with them on what became *This Is Your Captain Speaking*: Crass's Penny Rimbaud played drums and Dolly Mixture contributed vocals. The three tracks were recorded evidence for a political engagement which became more and more plain. '(What D'Ya Give) The Man Who's Gotten Everything' had shades of 'I Just Can't Be Happy Today' and lyrically questioned acquisitiveness. 'The Russians Are Coming' was an anti-war, pro-peace song attacking accepted dogma. The EP's final track was the hymnal 'Our Souls To You' which rejected the idea of divine retribution. While working with Crass, Captain found the food they ate tasty, realised there was no need to eat meat and became a vegetarian. The EP's sleeve featured a photo of Captain's face superimposed on the head of a rabbit.

While Captain pursued his own paths, despite still being under contract to Chiswick The Damned signed to NEMS, with whom Rat's father John Millar had been negotiating.

"They ran off and did the deal with NEMS and we pointed out they did it while they were still under the auspices of our contract," recalls Chiswick's Roger Armstrong. "They were still contracted to us. There was a good year to run. There was an intention to do a third album with us. They made the *Friday 13th EP* while they were still signed to us."

Their new label had few connections with contemporary music. The gritty, past-their-sell-by-date rock band Nazareth was with them in 1980, but NEMS' bread and butter was exploiting Black Sabbath's back catalogue. It was far-removed from its days under Beatles manager Brian Epstein. Following his death in 1967, a record label was launched under the NEMS name but beyond some Bee-Gees-related singles it never had a high or even medium profile. Nonetheless, The UK Subs also landed there in 1981. They and The Damned were the last active bands on their books. NEMS folded in 1983.

John Millar, who was now managing the band, obtained an advance from NEMS and Rockfield Studios was booked. Cementing the relationship between him and Captain, New Musik's Tony Mansfield was secured as the band's producer. He arrived in Wales with engineer Pete Hammond to find cornflakes tipped on the floor, coffee poured over them. The band had smeared the studio kitchen with eggs. Hammond left that night, as potential *Black Album* producer Alvin Clark had hours after his arrival at Rockfield in 1980.

As the sessions continued, Captain wanted to incorporate the distinctive Sixties sound of the Vox Continental organ. Paul Gray knew a man with one, someone he first met at a performance by racy dance troupe Hot Gossip. This was Roman Jugg, then in The Missing Men, a reconfigured version of Welsh punk band Victimize.[140]

"Paul rang me up," recalls Roman. "They were doing the *Friday 13th EP* and said they wanted a Vox Continental and could they borrow mine.

I didn't play on it though. They made me feel welcome at Rockfield, asking my opinion about things. I loved it. I was fascinated, watching Captain in the studio. I was dodging grapes that they were throwing."

★ ★ ★

The sense of boundaries being extended in the studio contrasted with the fifth anniversary show, booked for London's Lyceum on July 5.[141] No former band members joined in and the set list included the first album's 'I Fall', 'I Feel Alright', 'Neat Neat Neat' and 'New Rose', as well as material from *Machine Gun Etiquette* and *The Black Album*. *Music For Pleasure* was snubbed. The support bands were The Anti-Nowhere League, Ruts DC and Vice Squad. 'Love Song' was played twice. 'Ballroom Blitz' and 'In A Rut' were aired. Former Hawkwind member Nik Turner joined them on stage for the encore and their line-up was bolstered by ex-Dexys Midnight Runners keyboard player Pete Saunders, who had also played in Auntie Pus's band.

Amongst the few one-off shows which followed were two benefits, following on from one played in November 1980 at the Hope & Anchor under the banner "Blanket Coverage", to raise money to provide warm bedding and pay heating bills for old people in the Borough of Islington. The new benefits were in Manchester for the Campaign for Nuclear Disarmament and in Sheffield, where free tickets were available to the unemployed. The goodwill contrasted with 1979, when Captain's stage guitar strap bore the words Sod The Whale, his riposte to the Save The Whale Campaign.

A national tour was announced two weeks before the release of the *Friday 13th EP*. News items in the music weeklies also reported the signing with NEMS. Their support band, The Anti-Nowhere League, were issuing their debut single 'Streets Of London'/'So What' to coincide with the dates. As if to further stress that punk – or what it had become – was in for the count, on November 14 London's Rainbow was hosting a ten-band bill under the banner "Woodstock Revisited" with, amongst others, Angelic Upstarts, Anti-Pasti, Auntie Pus, Charge, Chron Gen, Eraserhead, and Splodgenessabounds. The "Christmas On Earth" festival had already been announced – "punk rears its extraordinary head again" said *Melody Maker* – for Leeds in December. The Damned were to headline over many of the same bands.

Despite who they played with, the *Friday 13th EP* once again defined The Damned as a band with no musical affiliations with the then-contemporary take on punk. Its lead track, 'Disco Man', was catchy, hard-edged pop. 'The Limit Club' was a searching examination of broken thresholds directly addressing the death of Ruts singer Malcolm Owen. Paul Gray's 'Billy Bad Breaks' was inspired by the book *Snowblind: A Brief Career in the Cocaine Trade*, a non-fiction account of drug smuggler Zachary Swan. 'Citadel' was a cover of a track from The Rolling Stones' psychedelic album *Their Satanic Majesties Request*, which in late 1980 Captain had talked about covering in full. Tony Mansfield's' pin-sharp production further ensured the EP was far removed from any notion of what punk ought to be.

Attaining a position any higher in the charts than the 50 it reached was impossible as NEMS lacked the resources to promote the EP. "Things started to get terrible shaky with NEMS," says Rat. "The money wasn't there." The label's shaky foundations became more and more evident as the tour continued. Cheques they had made out to cover coach hire and the PA system bounced.

The tour was also noteworthy as it was Roman's first time playing live with the band. "I got a call from Rat," he remembers. "He asked, 'Do you reckon you can handle it?' I wasn't a keyboard player but really a guitarist and thought, 'Fuck me, I'm going on tour with The Damned.' I was more overwhelmed by playing music in front of a lot of people rather than being in the band. I remember asking for the set list, and saying I play it like this. Nobody told me what to play. 'Wait For The Blackout' had no keyboards on the record, so I played along with it. No one ever said stop, so I kept playing and played on all the songs. No one questioned what I did. I remember at the end of the tour I said, 'It's been great,' but they never said I was in the band."

"Multi-talented," says Rat of Roman. "A great guitar player, a really good keyboard player. He had a really good ear for music. One of the problems The Damned always had was finding a keyboard player. Roman was really easy to have around, no ego clash, a great sense of humour. He was a welcome injection as he was talented, knew what the band was about, where it could go. I knew right from the beginning that this was a creative person who was interesting. He looked great, looked like one of the band the day he arrived. He naturally fitted in." Roman's debut tour with The Damned ended at London's Lyceum, where the American hardcore band Black Flag were added to the bill. It was the first time they had played the UK.

At the Lyceum, Captain told Black Flag that he liked them but that the audience would, as singer Henry Rollins recalled, "probably hate" them. Captain's advice was to play and it would be fine. They were on first, were barely acknowledged, were spat upon and drew no applause. With this, early in the evening of Sunday December 6, 1981, The Damned introduced American hardcore to Britain.

Two weeks later, it was time for "Christmas On Earth", the 11-hour punk festival at Leeds' Queen's Hall. The Damned were headlining to an audience estimated at 7,000. The bill also included Anti-Nowhere League, Chelsea, Chron Gen, Exploited, GBH, Outcasts, UK Subs, The Vice Squad and the lesser known The Insane, Lama and Tröckener Kecks. Black Flag were there too, and had a food fight with Captain. Late that night, after Captain had finished The Damned's set in a sleeveless dress, Black Flag found their rental company had repossessed their hire van from venue's car park. The only bands to help were The UK Subs – who loaded their gear into their truck – and The Damned, who offered them a ride in their coach back to London.[142]

The year ended with a low-key Christmas eve show at Fulham's Greyhound pub and Captain and Rat joining Ruts DC's New Year's Eve show there to air 'What D'Ya Give The Man Who's Got Everything' from Captain's solo EP. Talk of recording a new album early in 1982 remained that as NEMS was in no position to fund anything. The band appeared to be drifting apart. Rat had the roles of Germany's air defence minister and Winston Churchill in a stage production of Hawkwind member Robert Calvert's *Hype*.[143] Rumours he had left The Damned were reported in *Sounds*.

Low finances meant they were playing one-off dates to make money. After meeting at noon in a Hammersmith pub before getting in the van to Manchester, Captain, who arrived drunk with Paul Gray after a studio session with Dolly Mixture the night before, taunted Rat about the size of his nose and pulled his chair from under him. Moments after getting in the van, tempers flared and, leaping over Captain, Rat ran off into the street. Corralling UK Subs drummer Steve Roberts, they made it out of London by 6 p.m. Captain explained Rat's absence to fans in Manchester by saying he had broken his leg. A week later, Rat said, "The divorce lasted a day, it was one of those pathetic, childish squabbles."

A North American tour was set for February and early March. "The first time I went to America was the first time I got on a plane," recalls Roman. "Me and Rat checked our bags in: 'Where's the others?' Our luggage was on the plane. So me and Rat get on the plane, fly to New York, go to the booking agency and tell them some lie about Dave. We fly back the next day, I go back to Wales, to my parents. Not a word from Dave. He might have had a very good reason. Then, later, we go back to America. We were paying for it every time."

Ultimately, the five weeks of American dates was little more than a low-budget exercise in marking time, but the featured support bands read like a roll call of America's emerging hardcore underground: The Necros and the pre-Laughing Hyenas outfit Negative Approach in Chicago; Bad Religion, No Crisis and TSOL in California.

In Madison, Wisconsin the opening band was rising Minneapolis outfit The Replacements. Their Yes-fan guitarist Bob Stinson had been converted to the idea of punk after being played *Machine Gun Etiquette* by bandleader Paul Westerberg and was impressed with Captain's guitar playing. Stinson later said, "Captain Sensible! I ripped him off good." In Madison, Captain told Stinson to stop wearing flares and to "look and act the part" on stage otherwise no one would notice him. Seeing Captain in his pants or naked in front of an audience showed the guitarist that the British visitor was fearless. Captain was a prime influence on Stinson, who went on to take the stage in a dress, his underwear or anything else which came to hand. Once again, while there, The Damned had an impact on America's grassroots music scene.

Rekindling the impact they had on their home country was another matter. Their short-lived association with NEMS was at an end and after a show at London's Lyceum in March 1982, they took until September to return to the stage. They didn't play to an audience for six months. In 1978, it had taken the group less time to reform.

CHAPTER ELEVEN

Captain Masquerades As Granny's Favourite

After returning from America in March 1982, The Damned did as they had at the beginning of 1981: they apparently became no more. NEMS' financial problems again meant they had no label and Captain and Rat were following their own agendas. Each contributed solo tracks to the anti-nuclear *Wargasm* album, issued in April. The following month saw Rat beginning to play live in Foxes & Rats, with Ruts guitarist Paul Fox and bassist Martin Connelly.[144] The trio's goal was to recreate the Sixties with a repertoire including Hendrix cover versions. Dolly Mixture's second Captain and Paul Gray-produced single, 'Everything And More', was issued. After working with him as the producer of the *Friday 13th EP*, Captain recorded four solo tracks with New Musik's Tony Mansfield. Individually, Captain and Rat's actions implied their ties with the band were at breaking point. David had retreated to the shadows.

Rat's father, John Millar, was still the band's manager and was actively trying to find a label. "John Millar had struck me as being mysterious," recalls Roman. "A very striking man. This great shock of grey hair, this rambling mansion, his eyes would follow you around. I don't know how much influence he had. Of course, I wasn't in a position to ask. He was more mysterious than Dave."

One label in the frame was Bronze, but the money on offer was too low. Paul Gray's girlfriend, however, worked in the music business, knew the label's management and used her influence to get the offer upped. Once the deal was done in March, John Millar stepped down. The ink was on the paper: his work was done. "Paul Gray's girlfriend wanted to manage the band," says Rat. "She and Paul thought there could be more happening for The Damned than there was. So there was this political shift going on. I wasn't going to give anything away unless I was convinced it was going to work." After his father left the role, Rat took over as manager.

Bronze Records had an eclectic but unchallenging roster that included Manfred Mann's Earth Band, venerable rockers Uriah Heep and Sally Oldfield, the sister of Mike. The label had been founded in 1971 by Gerry Bron, who formerly worked for Vertigo Records. When punk arrived, the label's mainstays remained Manfred Mann's Earth Band and Uriah Heep (who Bron had brought to Bronze from Vertigo). Beyond a deal with the American label Red Star which led to issuing records by The Real Kids and Suicide, Bronze had not had a brush with anything remotely punk apart from, arguably, Motörhead. When The Damned were signed, the label's acts most in tune with them were all-female metal band Girlschool and, indeed, Motörhead.[145]

The Damned's new label paid for time at RMS Studios to record demos[146] and then issued the 'Lovely Money'/'I Think I'm Wonderful' single in June 1982. Co-produced by the band and Tony Mansfield, its top side criticised the jingoism surfacing in the run-up to the Falklands War. It featured the voice of former Bonzo Dog Doo Dah Band member Viv Stanshall, entered the charts on July 10, spent four weeks there and peaked at 42. On June 26, Captain's first solo single 'Happy Talk' began its chart run. It was also produced by Tony Mansfield.

★ ★ ★

The solo demos Captain recorded with Mansfield generated interest. Initially, Captain negotiated a deal with the independent label Cherry Red for an advance of £3,000 but he went on to rack up a studio bill of £10,000 while recording finished tracks. After securing concert promoter Andrew Miller as his manager, the tapes were shopped to A&M Records, whose biggest band was The Police. A&M wanted an album and agreed to an advance of £40,000, instantly swallowed up paying the studio bill, Cherry Red, Mansfield, Dolly Mixture (who sang on the sessions) and Miller's percentage. With what was left, Captain bought a second-hand car and a used synthesiser. By the second week of July, the money – which he had insisted the label pay in used £1 notes – was gone.

Together with Mansfield, Captain recorded songs that weren't a stylistic fit for The Damned at former Procol Harum member Matthew Fisher's Old Barn Studio in Kenley, near Croydon. Robyn Hitchcock, formerly of Damned support band The Soft Boys, contributed guitar to 'Brenda' and Dolly Mixture were also heard. 'Wot' unashamedly nodded to Grandmaster Flash's 'The Message'[147] and was rap with a rhythm inspired by a building-site jackhammer outside a hotel which had kept Captain awake while on tour in America.[148] 'Gimme A Uniform' was further evidence of a fascination with rap. While anti-materialistic and anti-war political outlooks distinguished 'Yanks With Gun', '(What D'Ya Give) The Man Who's Gotten Everything' and 'Gimme A Uniform', sweet melodies and lyrics imbued with longing and nostalgia defined what was, at its core, a psychedelic pop album. Most surreal was the country-slanted 'Who Is Melody Lee, Sid?' which revisited Captain's placards-aloft presence at the 1978 Vicious White Kids Electric Ballroom show. 'Croydon', a sensitive musical autobiography, was the album's highlight.

As an afterthought to the sessions, Mansfield decided a cover version should close the album. Captain suggested either The Kinks' 'Waterloo Sunset' or Pink Floyd's 'See Emily Play' but the producer told him to go home and look through his parents' records for something weird. He returned with a copy of the soundtrack to *South Pacific* and 'Happy Talk' was chosen. Mansfield and synth player Rob Bowkett concocted a backing track during an evening session while Captain was at the pub. He came back drunk, and sang the vocals in five minutes. A&M instantly knew it had to be a single.

"We just thought 'Happy Talk' was a bit peculiar, quite funny," recalls Dolly Mixture's Deborah Wykes. "Tony Mansfield seemed quite excited about it. Captain then rang up and said his manager had said 'love it, darling, love it'."

Reviewing 'Happy Talk' in *Melody Maker*, Vic Godard – who, with his band Subway Sect, had played the 100 Club Punk Festival in 1976 – declared, "It's got to be number one hasn't it? It's so brilliant. I think, like me, he really likes the song and thinks it should be brought out again. You might not like it, but you'll find yourself humming it everywhere you go." He was right. 'Happy Talk' got into the charts at 33 and Captain was invited onto *Top Of The Pops*. In white shorts, with a stuffed parrot perched on his shoulder, a seagull flapping its wings above his head and with Dolly Mixture in wigs joining him, the appearance propelled the single to number one where it stayed for two weeks, replacing Charlene's country-pop schlock 'I've Never Been To Me' and preventing The Steve Miller Band's 'Abracadabra' from reaching the top spot. Irene Cara's 'Fame' supplanted 'Happy Talk' as Britain's best-selling single in the week of July 17.

Captain was national news: the day before Britain saw him at number one on *Top Of The Pops*, he was interviewed by Sue Lawley on the BBC's news compendium programme *Nationwide*. The *Daily Mirror* said, "Ray [Burns] is a self-confessed weirdo who is called Captain Sensible because it's the opposite of what he really is."

Looking back at the Damned-free, separate persona which had emerged Captain says, "'Happy Talk' is such a monster most people don't bother checking out the self-penned songs, some of which are as pure pop as any I've heard and that I'm still very proud of."[149] A solo Captain running alongside the newly signed Damned both distracted attention from them and acted as PR for them. Which of the two would win out was, as yet, an impossible call.

Speaking to *NME* as 'Happy Talk' sat at number one, Captain said, "I love The Damned. They're the most important thing in my life and I'd much rather this was a Damned success than mine." He told *Sounds*, "The Damned were the first real punk band and they'll be the last, whatever happens. We'll always be together. I'm doing this solo album and single as it allows The Damned to be as hard and aggressive as they want to be, and my solo career can give me new freedom outside the first and finest punk band."

"I didn't think 'Happy Talk' was a particularly great idea," says Roman, by then embedded in the band and ready to record the next Damned album. "Captain was astute though. He always spoke very fondly of The Damned. He always put himself in a position where he could always come back to the band."

"None of us knew that Captain had a solo thing," says Rat. "It was a surprise. We didn't know anything about it until 'Happy Talk' came out. You can't go from Captain Sensible in The Damned and 'fuck the world' to being Mr Smiley, Granny's favourite. But in a way it was kind of natural, as we'd always had this pop sensibility."

★ ★ ★

NME caught the rift between the "Mr Smiley, Granny's favourite" Captain and who he actually was. He told them, "I've come to realise that if I've got a voice and there's people willing to listen then I've got to say how disgusting some of the things I see are" and went on to bemoan newspapers' incessant coverage of the Royal Family, the lack of democratic representation in a Britain run by elites, that missiles, American military bases and the Tory government should be kicked out, and that the country was "run by advertising men". But he conceded, "In every interview I've done [with newspapers] I've made my point but they won't listen. I've got to continue making reasonable statements in the hope that someone will listen because that's the only way to change anything." The weekly's Amrik Rai sneered that "reasonable statements will never change a thing. But a good wheeze is what the Empire needs. Long may the new Captain's 'Happy Talk' rule the waves."

Competing for his time, The Damned were booked into Rockfield again to record their new album, their first for Bronze. Although the solo Captain continued working with him, Tony Mansfield was not their producer. They were reunited with Hugh Jones, who ended up credited as co-producer on seven tracks.[150] Rat says Jones had recently "done Adam & The Ants [Jones engineered the *Kings Of The Wild*

Frontier album] and had a bee in his bonnet about being a hot shot. He found us really hard to work with. We were all really different [from each other]. Captain would work until five in the morning, then I'd come in and do the drums."

"Paul Gray's girlfriend was there," says Roman of the sessions. "I was enjoying the process, learning, watching Hugh Jones and I could see there was something wrong with Rat. I can only tell what I saw. We were recording a Paul Gray song, 'The Pleasure And The Pain', and I was sitting in the TV room with a cup of tea. Hugh Jones came in and said, 'Someone's got to sort this out, Rat's just hit the bass player.' I thought this was a bit weird. There was a big row going on. I went to see how Paul was and he wouldn't answer the door to his room. He had barricaded himself in. I asked Hugh and he said there was friction in the studio, there was a lyric about being inside and Rat said, 'How can you write a lyric about being inside?' Rat's girlfriend arrived, Paul's girlfriend arrived and there was a big slanging match. It was all blown out of proportion. Rat agreed to leave and go back to London. He went, then it was just me and Captain and Dave and Paul. It was one of the most peaceful times I remember. Rat and Paul made up, but you could tell it wasn't right – a line had been crossed by both of them."

"I didn't really think 'The Pleasure And The Pain' was relevant to us," explains Rat. "The lyrics: 'these feelings deep inside me'. It was Paul's song. It was too personal for me and I didn't relate to it. There was a big dispute in the studio, because I didn't want to do it. But in the end we were happy to have enough songs for the album and have a feeling of variation." The album was completed.

At the time, Rat said, "I threw him [Paul Gray] out because I couldn't be bothered playing with him, but he's back. Let's just say the rules have been straightened out and the game's easier to play now."

While the fault line between Rat and Gray had resulted in physical confrontation, the gap between the band and Captain's solo ventures needed plugging. 'Wot!', his second A&M single, had been issued in August. It charted at 26 in the UK and there were two *Top Of The Pops* appearances[151] but this was small beer compared with its success in France where it became a massive seller over January to March 1983.[152]

The band had not played live since the end of March 1982 and were planning dates to coincide with the release of the new album in September. Yet the draws on Captain's time meant he was hard to pin down so the joint decision was reached that his manager, Andrew Miller, take care of him and the band in an attempt to bring the increasingly conflicting schedules together.

Given what was happening, sharing the same manager was reasonable but what actually transpired was that The Damned's records were played off against Captain's. His album, *Women And Captains First*, was released by A&M on September 3; The Damned's *Strawberries* was in the shops a month later as 'Croydon', Captain's third A&M single, was also issued. It didn't chart, but neither did 'Dozen Girls', The Damned single issued immediately before *Strawberries*.

Rat was also pondering a new direction which was soon abandoned. He had recorded a song aimed at children. Credited to The Lollipops, 'The Naughty Gnomes' featured the lyric, "There's yellow teethy from Hampstead Heathy".

In *NME*, Charles Shaar Murray reviewed *Women And Captains First* with consideration. "Sensible is quite content to make records that sound dumb, but which obviously aren't," he said. "*Women And Captains First* draws on three sources: the warm, rumbustious clowning of his two hit singles, an enormously likeable variety of psychedelic whimsy (a la '66 Kinks or '67 Pink Floyd) and a righteously indignant series of attacks on things that are genuinely brutal, ugly or stupid. In 'Yanks With Guns', Sensible touches on areas previously investigated by The Clash in 'I'm So Bored With The USA' and Costello in 'Watching The Detectives', but the song derives its power from far more contemporary observations on the growing invasion of Europe as well as the more obvious issue of cultural imperialism. Elsewhere – on 'Gimme A Uniform' – he tackles an issue previously dealt with by Gang Of Four and Pete Townshend, but he scoops the lot of 'em here: no one has stated the basic issue more baldly than this. 'Just gimme a uniform,' he sings, 'and I won't be responsible, I'll do what the hell they want me to.' On the other side of the fence, we find Sensible getting up The Morning After and bemoaning the state of his kitchen in 'A Nice Cup Of Tea', delivering his autobiography in 'Croydon', evoking an absent girlfriend in 'Brenda' and – in what will probably be his next hit – fronting a hot Dixieland band on 'Nobody's Sweetheart'. *Women And Captains First* is a charming and admirable bit of plastic, and its creator is obviously sensible like a fox." Despite the admiration Shaar Murray had not mentioned The Damned, whose new album was ready for release.

With *Strawberries* out, The Damned began touring in early October 1982. For the first time, attention was paid to the staging. A pulpit was constructed around Roman's keyboards, David wore a priest's dog collar and the band were accompanied on stage by three female fans they had met at 1981's Christmas On Earth show. Angel, Jezebel and Rockabox were dressed as nuns. David described the shows as "The Damned's religious Sunday service" and said, "With all the things we've been through, I always feel frightened of being optimistic: it's [now] the best music, the best show, everything."

"It was the first time Captain was not the focal point all the time," explains Roman. "Captain was the most flamboyant, the most attention-seeking. When the nuns came on, it drew attention to Dave. I think Captain was happy with this as he was doing his [solo] thing and it took pressure off." 'Happy Talk' was not performed at every show and, if it was, it was tacked on as an encore.

"I don't think there were many people there who were 'Happy Talk' fans," says Rat. "It was always a toss-up between the Vanian dollies and the herberts down the front who liked gobby old Captain who was drunk – a very divided audience. But Captain got stick. You'd expect some stick from an 18-year-old down the front who's committed his lifestyle to your group. We did 'Happy Talk' to show Captain we weren't pissed off at him about it."

Reflecting on the balance between the two draws on his time, Captain says, "I absolutely went for it and had some fun times as Britain's most unlikely pop star. I did everything I could do, but both the [The Damned's and the solo] schedules were so intense. I virtually never slept."

'Happy Talk' had not been recorded with any intention of it becoming a success. At their end of year shows, The Damned ran through it in their encores alongside cover versions of 'Ballroom Blitz', 'Be Bop A Lula',

'Hippy Hippy Shake', and 'Pretty Vacant'. Like those, it was an adjunct to the band's repertoire. Captain's solo venture was something other, a diversion from the main order of business. Yet his media presence was increasing.

In November, Captain had appeared on the Midlands commercial channel Central's Saturday morning kids TV show *The Saturday Show* with juvenile reggae band Musical Youth. The previous month saw him offering his views on BBC2's topical youth show *Speak Out*, where his fellow talking head was the anthropologist Dr Desmond Morris. Listings guide *The Radio Times* billed him as "zany pop star Captain Sensible". In late November, he was amongst the celebrities answering the phones for BBC1's *Children In Need* appeal. 'Happy Talk' was reprised on Christmas Day's *Top Of The Pops* seasonal special. Three days later, he was a panellist on BBC1's *Pop Quiz*. The other pop stars on the special edition also exhibiting their knowledge of pop history were David Essex, Hank Marvin, Leo Sayer, Mari Wilson and Duran Duran's John Taylor.

A solo Captain tour planned for early December was cancelled. In October, Rat had said Captain "is killing himself, he's doing too much work. He wants to take it easy." Captain describes his solo agenda as "Hardly sleeping, breakfast TV slot, promo in Europe, fly back to do a Damned gig the same evening. That was typical stuff."[153]

★ ★ ★

As Captain struggled with his own diary, The Damned had problems with Bronze. "They ran out money," says Rat. "Also, they had no idea how to promote the band. The head of marketing would turn up and say, 'Hey guys, baseball caps!'" 'Generals', drawn from *Strawberries*, was issued as a single after the Nuns tour and didn't chart. The Damned and Bronze Records parted company in February 1983.[154]

Another setback arrived in March as they were about to begin a British tour when Paul Gray left. He had been approached by the metal band UFO, who were doing a farewell British tour and asked if he would play with them.[155] He had their management tell The Damned he was leaving.

"He left because I had slapped him [at Rockfield]," says Rat. "He waited until the night before the tour to tell us, but luckily we had seen it coming. He didn't have the decency to tell us three months before." At no notice, Roman's friend Bryn Merrick, who had also been in Victimize, was asked to replace Gray.[156]

"When Paul left, I said I knew a guy," recalls Roman. "Doing so meant it was another headache for the band not to worry about. The bass player wasn't that important to The Damned."

It wasn't an intentional merger, but The Damned now comprised three of their own original members and half of the Welsh band Victimize. Merrick played his first show with The Damned on March 19, 1983 in St Albans. Although planned as the fourth date of the tour, it became the opening night as Gray's sudden departure forced three cancellations.

"I had met Bryn and heard him," says Rat. "It was 'make the call'. He was there because he could do his job and was better at it that anyone else. It wasn't that Lemmy, kind-of clunky sound everyone was doing. First and foremost, Bryn was a great bass player. One of the beautiful things about being in The Damned is making people's dreams happen. Here's the ticket, get on the train."

Strawberries

The release of The Damned's fifth album – Paul Gray's second with them and their first in two years – was in danger of being overshadowed by Captain's burgeoning solo career. His album *Women And Captains First* came out a month before *Strawberries* and, thanks to 'Happy Talk', he was a household name. Issuing The Damned's album tie-in single 'Dozen Girls' at the same time as Captain's 'Croydon' 45 muddied waters even further. Whatever Captain said to the music press about The Damned being "the most important thing in my life", it was hard to determine where one began and the other ended. Had The Damned become an extension of the solo Captain? Or was he an aspect of who they were?

The questions were partly answered by the chart statistics. *Women And Captains First* rose no higher than 64 on the album chart. *Strawberries* hit 15, The Damned's highest ranking to date. Of course, they were helped by being a band which was seen live and Captain, despite his increasing ubiquity on television, was not touring. The crossover between The Damned's following and those buying a version of a song from the soundtrack to *South Pacific*, an album which held the number one spot in *Melody Maker*'s album chart for a record 115 weeks from November 1958, was limited. 'Happy Talk', written by Richard Rodgers and

Oscar Hammerstein II, had been in the nation's consciousness a lot longer than The Damned. For now, The Damned and Captain Sensible co-existed as discrete entities without detriment to the band.

Captain was behind *Strawberries'* title. "He would get fed up with the abuse, gobbing, cans being thrown," recalls Rat. "So there was a saying that went round the tour van: 'It's like giving strawberries to pigs.' When it came to the album, it was, let's call it *Strawberries To Pigs*." The phrase wasn't used in full but the cover image of a piglet with a strawberry upon its head reflected Captain's view.

Although *Strawberries* arrived on Bronze, a new label for The Damned, there was continuity as most of the album was recorded in Wales at Rockfield, where its predecessor *The Black Album* had been completed for Chiswick. The studio's staff engineer Hugh Jones worked on both albums.

Change did come, though, with the songwriting credits: unlike *Machine Gun Etiquette* and *The Black Album*, songs were no longer given as penned by the band overall. 'Generals' and 'Pleasure And The Pain' were solely Paul Gray's. The other ten were shown as Vanian/Sensible/Scabies compositions. Gray's assertion of an individual identity – which secured him a separate income stream from publishing to the rest of the band – was telling. He was a man apart. Furthermore, this time there were no outside contributors to the writing and no songs plucked from figurative drawers or memory. There was also a focus on the snappy with no wig-out codas, as there was on *The Black Album*'s 'Therapy', and no equivalents of the epic 'Curtain Call'. *Strawberries* was lean.

David sang Gray's pair of songs but his own identity was most perceptible in 'The Dog', inspired by the character Claudia from the 1976 Anne Rice novel *Interview With The Vampire*.[157] Rat says, "'The Dog' is all Dave, killer. The backing tracks were brilliant, outstanding. Dave and Captain went outside the studio to get the dog noises as there was a dog next door, but there was this big black dog standing outside the studio. Spooky." With lyrics by Captain, 'Gun Fury'[158], despite not immediately suggesting it, drew its main riff from Pentangle, the jazzy British folk-rock band. 'Don't Bother Me' and 'Life Goes On' were Captain's, and he duly sang them.

The album's back cover noted "This is a synth-free album", an announcement marking *Strawberries* as distinct from its predecessor.[159] *The Black Album* had employed synthesisers on 'History Of The World (Part 1)' (played by the track's producer Hans Zimmer, who added it after the band had completed their work), 'Curtain Call' and 'Lively Arts'. However, musical exploration was not on hold. Parts of the rhythm track of *Strawberries*' closer 'Don't Bother Me' cropped up over the album as one song ended and another began. "There's a noise between the tracks," explains David. "What nobody knows is that it's a toilet being flushed. We had a bet we couldn't put a toilet on there, and we did. I used a conga with an egg whisk and slowed it down with loads of reverb on 'The Dog'. We used jeans being torn, things being whipped. We always wanted to find something we could add that would make a difference."

Other aspects set *Strawberries* apart. Simon Lloyd from The Members contributed trumpet and alto saxophone to 'Generals' (his playing bled into 'Stranger On The Town'). On 'Pleasure And The Pain', Dolly Mixture's Rachael Bor guested on cello. And, now he was in The Damned's orbit, Roman Jugg was credited with "keyboard solos".

Strawberries opened with 'Ignite', a blast which hinted at 'Love Song'. 'Under The Floor Again', with its Sixties influence and sitar-sounds (sourced from a synthesiser, whatever the sleeve said) was not a surprise. Nor was the galloping, rollicking 'Dozen Girls'.

However, three tracks showed The Damned had moved on again. 'Stranger On The Town' was their first and unexpected glance towards soul, and prefigured the mod-R&B-soul sound of The Truth who charted in 1983.[160] This was The Damned's pop album and, as such, steered its way through the contemporary currents. The moody, sensitive 'Life Goes On' was of a piece with the then on-the-rise Tears For Fears and also suggested the latter-day Teardrop Explodes (and even The Cure). The song also appeared to have an afterlife when its main instrumental refrain perhaps resonated through Killing Joke's 'Eighties' (issued in April 1984) and then Nirvana's 'Come As You Are' (first released as an album track on *Nevermind* in September 1991: Nirvana allegedly knew of the similarity of their song to 'Eighties').

With the release of *Strawberries*, The Damned had much to ponder. Neither single drawn from the album – 'Dozen Girls' and 'Generals' – had breached the Top 50. *Strawberries* itself did. They were still a live draw. Yet Captain's new solo career inevitably generated uncertainty.[161] There was friction between Rat and Paul Gray as the album was recorded. Instability was surfacing. A new band member seemed on board. Roman Jugg played on *Strawberries* and then toured with the band.

And then there was Bronze Records. Although the label had an interest in selling The Damned – early copies of *Strawberries* were enhanced with a desirable scratch and sniff lyric sheet which faintly smelt of something sweet, maybe a strawberry – it was struggling. No one knew it, but the relationship between band and label did not have long to run. If a step had been taken back, it may have become apparent that the relationship between Paul Gray and the band did not have long to run either. And no one knew how Captain's relationship with the band would change. The Damned were in flux – again. Nonetheless, *Smash Hits*, the fortnightly catalogue raisonné of British pop, reviewed *Strawberries* glowingly. It was "the kind of pop album Paul McCartney would be pleased to have has moniker on. 9 out of 10."

But *Strawberries* was out, and was yet another tremendous album – and not *The Black Album* part two or *Machine Gun Etiquette* part two. Where The Damned headed next musically was anyone's guess, but who would be in the band when they got there was easier to figure out. The signs were there. Some were conspicuous: Captain's path, Roman's arrival, the newly apportioned writing credits. Other signs were behind the scenes: the conflict with Paul Gray, the viability of Bronze.

The *Strawberries* version of The Damned was unlikely to last much longer.

CHAPTER TWELVE

There Were Cobwebs

The Damned were now founder members Rat Scabies, Captain Sensible and David Vanian, and Roman Jugg and Bryn Merrick. With Merrick's predecessor Paul Gray, they had been with Bronze for 11 months and released three singles and an album for the label. Over the same period, for A&M, Captain had issued the same and was better known than the band he was in.

In the early months of 1983, the French success of Captain's 'Wot!' ensured A&M wanted more from him. He had a four-album deal, actually signed with his management: Captain was not signed directly to the label. Both parties had interests in keeping the golden goose laying. With Captain's attention directed elsewhere, The Damned had a vacuum to fill.

It was plugged at the end of April when a band called The Nightmares played Fulham's Greyhound. This four-piece was a pseudonymous Damned shorn of Captain which featured Roman on guitar rather than keyboards and Merrick billed as "Grimm". "We had down time as Captain was so busy," says Roman of how the first Nightmares show came about. Captain had, a week earlier, also played The Greyhound at a benefit in aid of World Weekend for Laboratory Animals with Dolly Mixture as support.

If anyone had assessed what was happening, there was one conclusion: Captain Sensible had nothing to do with The Damned and they were over. "I had a manager who plainly didn't want me to do The Damned," recalls Captain. "He'd fill my diary so full that to do both careers I'd have to drive myself completely into the ground. Which is what happened."

The next month, during a repeat visit to the pub's stage, The Nightmares' cover-version-heavy set featured The Monkees' 'I'm A Believer' and 'Last Train To Clarksville' along with American Sixties garage rock and psychedelic nuggets like The Electric Prunes' 'I Had Too Much To Dream (Last Night)', The Human Beinz's version of 'Nobody But Me', The Others' 'I Can't Stand This Love Goodbye' and The Rockin' Ramrods' 'She Lied'. Britain's musical past was represented by The Beatles' 'Sgt. Pepper's Lonely Hearts Club Band', The Rolling Stones' 'Citadel' and The Yardbirds' 'Evil Hearted You'. For the encore, The Damned's own 'Born To Kill', 'Love Song' and 'Smash It Up' were played, each of which gave Roman a first chance to play guitar on songs where he'd previously contributed keyboards. Although the musical spirit echoed Rat's Foxes & Rats outings a year earlier, The Nightmares were different – this was most of The Damned.

David had also been seen without The Damned for the first time at an all-nighter hosted by the Scala Cinema billed as *No Rest For The Wicked*. His short solo appearance came between films, a juggler and belly dancer, the Wet Paint Theatre Co and the bands Blood & Roses, Brigandage and Carcrash International (who featured members of Crisis and Sex Gang Children). Although the term had yet to become common currency, it was an early manifestation of goth. A scene was emerging which shared David's outlook.

NME was paying attention. In February, it had featured Blood & Roses, Brigandage and Sex Gang Children in a cover-feature article awkwardly identifying a new form of punk: "positive punk". Other bands mentioned included Danse Society, Rubella Ballet, Southern Death Cult, The Specimen (the house band at The Batcave, the London club they opened in July 1982), UK Decay and The Virgin Prunes. The writer, Richard Cook, pointed to a unifying interest in "mystical/metaphysical imagery", "the sub-world of Crowleyan abyss" and personal style taking in backcombing, blue hair, long black skirts, red trousers and bootlace ties: dressing up. The Doors were, said Cook, an influence, as were Siouxsie & The Banshees and Adam & The Ants.

As a label, positive punk never caught on but Cook had identified what would become known as goth. David was not the only person from the punk generation of 1976 to whom the description goth would be applied retrospectively. Siouxsie had grown into and embraced the style, as had the pre-hit Adam Ant. But David was the only candidate from British punk's year zero with a claim to be the original goth. He had never adopted a look – he was who he was, and had been such from the beginning.

Both strands of The Damned – the love of Sixties garage and psychedelic music, and the as-yet uncodified goth – were brought together in May, when *The Whip* album was issued. Conceived as the soundtrack to an imaginary film, the compilation sought to evoke a "life drenched with unrestrained savagery and menace... a strange world [of] angels and gravediggers". Blood & Roses were heard. So were Brigandage and Sex Gang Children. David contributed 'Tenterhooks', reviewed in *NME* as a "concerto noir crossing the threshold of Doors psychedelia". He and Roman wrote the song, which featured Dolly Mixture's Rachel Bor on cello. The backing band was credited as Naz Nomad & The Nightmares, who were also heard on an unlisted track titled 'Just Call Me Sky', named in tribute to Sky Saxon, the leader of Sixties garage-psych band The Seeds. Without being credited as such, *The Whip* showcased The Damned's Sixties and not-yet-known-as goth sides.[162]

Acknowledging their twin-track identity, they played the Hammersmith Palais in July with Blood & Roses and Le Mat – the latter from the new psychedelic scene – as their support bands. Also on the bill were Brian James' new band Lords Of The New Church.[163] 'Happy Talk' was not performed.

★ ★ ★

The Hammersmith show came on the back of an American tour organised by Andrew Miller. Beyond being notable for giving Merrick the opportunity to party hard for the first time, the late May to late June

199

visit was marked by a shoestring approach and inappropriate bookings which led to Miller's dismissal as The Damned's manager. The nearest they got to Manhattan was Brooklyn.

Though Captain was sustained by his solo work, finances in America were short. "As soon as the tour manager got the tour float he spent it on cocaine and sold it back to Captain and the band," recalls Rat of the tour. "We're all sitting in the tour van sharing Wendy burgers and a bag of fries between us and Captain overtakes us in a Cadillac limo. We get to the hotel, only a motel, a Howard Johnson's, but Captain would hire the bridal suite. 'Come up to my room.' He's got the champagne on ice, and that still didn't finish the relationship with him off. We got back, saw Andrew Miller. 'Where's the money?' 'There's no money.'"

At home, the solo ventures continued. Captain issued a new solo single, 'Stop The World', as did Rat, a mail-order only version of Sandy Nelson's 'Let There Be Drums' recast as 'Let There Be Rats'.[164]

All three founding members of The Damned now had solo releases out. After a headline booking at a one-day punk festival proposed for Knebworth in August was cancelled, there was nothing on the band's books. Again, Rat took on the management.

A handful of dates in September culminated in another Hammersmith Palais headliner. Though an accountant was appointed to look after the band's finances, there was little sign The Damned were a going concern. Year-end dates – including top-billing at a punk festival in Leeds – did not move things on.

Nor did the November release of Captain's second solo album, *The Power Of Love* and a steady flow of reissues and repackagings. In 1981, Stiff had issued a package of the four sell-through singles and followed it in February 1983 with a double-album set collecting *Damned Damned Damned* and *Music For Pleasure*. Chiswick had reissued *Machine Gun Etiquette* and *The Black Album* (as a single album of sides one and two only) in 1982, and also issued the Shepperton live recordings as a stand-alone album along with a string of back-catalogue singles. In November 1983, the band itself released *Live In Newcastle*, an album drawn from an October 1982 show at the city's Mayfair venue. The Damned's past and present were competing as never before.

External observers at that moment could have assumed The Damned were exclusively about looking back. Playing punk festivals did nothing to suggest otherwise. So did – to whatever degree they had control over it – the increasing amount of archive vinyl. And with only 'Wot!' having charted in the UK after 'Happy Talk' and *The Power Of Love* missing the charts, Captain's solo career also gave the impression of having stalled. As Captain began the new year appearing on kid's tea-time TV pop show *Razzmatazz,* Rat was told that a possible deal for The Damned with MCA Records had fallen through. Where 1983 had begun with at least the reassurance that being signed to Bronze would help them flourish, 1984 began with nothing.

Still, Naz Nomad & The Nightmares had recorded a Captain-free album over five days at Wapping's no-frills Elephant Studios in the first week of December and there was news The Damned were in the running as a guest on the BBC comedy show *The Young Ones.*

★ ★ ★

In April 1984, Captain regained lost commercial ground when 'Glad It's All Over', the opening track from *The Power Of Love*, became a single. As it was released, he told *NME*'s David Quantick, "I do have a hankering to be a pop star." His biggest homeland solo hit since 'Happy Talk', 'Glad It's All Over' was a pointed comment on the Falklands War: an anti-war contemplation ruing the jingoism fomented by the campaign. The B-side was less serious. 'Damned On 45' was a medley – in the style of the Stars On 45 singles – of 13 Damned songs and two solo outings which Captain had knocked up in three hours.

'Glad It's All Over''s passage into the charts was helped by Captain's ubiquity on British TV via his ad for breakfast cereal, co-starring his real-life aunt Sadie. As the chirpy 'Puffin Billy' played (the theme to the BBC's *Children's Favourites* radio programme in the UK and the *Captain Kangaroo* theme in the US), an even chirpier beret-wearing Captain leapt energetically from his bed after a night's sleep to vigorously declare, "Jolly sensible my auntie… the Weetabix Breakfast Box, a sensible choice."

The surreal apotheosis of Captain's ubiquity as an object of fascination had come at 8.12 a.m. on November 22, 1983 when *TV-am*, Britain's new breakfast television show, lit on looking at him and his home for their *Through The Keyhole* slot. Uber-patronising roving presenter Loyd Grossman had no idea where he was visiting, who lived there and, to entertain viewers, drew conclusions from what he saw. Like the rest of the nation, Captain saw the report for the first time as he sat across from studio presenter Anne Diamond on a sofa while it was being broadcast.

Grossman began in the garden of Captain's parents' house with "the fattest, the meanest and ugliest black rabbit in all of England". After passing judgement on the streetscape he took his etiolated voice indoors and said the "general effect is rather like being in the ante-room of a chop suey house in Crouch End". Captain's bedroom was like "an ill-organised jumble sale" and, with its wallpaper of Smurfs and animals-dressed-as people, and stuffed toys, suggested someone very young or "possibly someone very old who doesn't realise it yet". He wondered if the contrast between soft things and "nasty and aggressive things" (a bullet belt and an army helmet) meant the occupant had a split personality and concluded this was the room of a person who "presents a fairly aggressive face to the outside world but at home is sort-of very childish and likes to be cuddled as it were" and was "possibly someone who is a professional musician".

After the excruciating item, Diamond remarked, "It's not quite the place I thought many people watching would expect Captain Sensible to live in, maybe a palatial mansion in Surrey is more fitting." Magnanimously accepting Grossman's verdict Captain said, "I'm exceptionally childish, I'm in a business, the music business, where you can be a perpetual schoolboy, you don't actually have to grow up. Which is mainly why I'm doing it." Although 'Happy Talk' was the default when music came up in the chat, he did remind Britain that "for seven years I've been in a group called The Damned" and pointed out that they "have had some hits as well".

The Damned themselves had assembled in toto at Wapping's Elephant Studios on January 19 to record a new song for *The Young Ones* which Captain had been meant to write with Roman. Each member of the cast was a fan and had wanted 'Help' to be performed. As the horror-themed episode was inspired by the hot topic of video nasties – supposedly shockingly offensive, violent films released for home viewing on VHS video tape – it was decided to record a fresh song.

"Captain said, 'Tell you what, we'll write a song,'" recalls Roman. "He said come down. I went down to his parents' house and he's lying in bed with his cricket-bat guitar watching cricket on TV. 'Right Captain, what you got?' 'Nothing.' We were supposed to have this thing demoed. I had something which was to nick this song 'I Must Be Mad' by The Craig.[165] When I got home the first thing I saw was a Pink Floyd LP and 'Careful With That Axe Eugene', so that became the first line. Me and Dave finished the lyric." 'Nasty' was the first track The Damned had recorded for release since 1982, when they had been at Rockfield making *Strawberries*.

"I was astute enough to realise that we would earn money from publishing," says Rat about choosing to do a new song. "So we asked to be sent the script. Roman wrote it. As it was *The Young Ones*, 'Nasty' and the horror thing, we had pale faces for the filming. There were cobwebs. We are the damned. I looked at us and thought: 'That looks fucking great, this is our image', Dave and three people who are on the same page as him, what Dave had been all along. And Captain." When the show was broadcast on May 29, 1984, a new Damned was revealed, four of whom shared a unified, gothic style.

Looking back on the band's new look, Roman says, "That show was the perfect time for the transition in the image. That is where the rift came as Captain was on his own. Captain was just there as the token guy."

"Rat said at the time, Vanian's doing well, we'd better dress like him for a bit," recalls David. "They started wearing Victorian clothes. I thought it was very funny. To look a certain way takes a bit more work and I'd be smirking while they all stood in front of the mirror crimping their hair. I never asked them to do that."[166]

Without Captain, a bid for a life apart from the band called The Damned was made in the last week of February when Naz Nomad & The Nightmares' *Give Daddy The Knife Cindy* album appeared on Chiswick's Big Beat imprint.[167] "Captain's solo career had meant that we'd had do some things without him," says Rat. "One was the Naz Nomad record. It was hard for Captain to be in the band as he just wasn't available. And we got used to the idea of being without him."

In a sleeve looking like the soundtrack album for a Sixties exploitation movie with photos of regulars from Soho's Alice In Wonderland club, ...*Cindy* was crammed with vibrant versions of freakbeat, garage rock and psychedelic songs and while not quite sounding as though it was from 25 years earlier, it was a fine tribute to the music inspiring The Damned.

"Me and Dave chose the songs," says Roman. "Our love of psychedelic music ran through the veins of the band, probably least so in Rat. We were in a situation where Captain was getting more and more distracted with the solo thing and if you do an album, you can do gigs. For me, Naz Nomad was more fun than The Damned where there was no feeling of stability in the line-up, Bryn was a new bass player, you didn't know if Captain was going off or not."

The ruse of *Give Daddy The Knife Cindy* being by an obscure band – one from the Sixties – was propagated by Big Beat, whose press release said the album was originally issued by the Love Vibrations label as the soundtrack to a film directed by one Quarry Richards. The band members were Nick Detroit (Rat), Buddy Lee Junior (Bryn), Naz Nomad (David) and Sphinx Svenson (Roman). David and Roman undertook a front-cover interview for *Sounds* as their alter-egos, pedalled some yarns about what they had been doing since the fake band's demise and even got themselves up for photos in the roles they had assumed, down to the grey in their hair.

With Naz Nomad & The Nightmares hitting the shops and Captain bedding himself in as a long-term solo proposition on the back of 'Glad It's All Over' hitting the Top 10 in April, Rat was considering the implications of being invited to jam with Jimmy Page at west London's Nomis Studios. He got on well with Page and hadn't initially realised he was being auditioned for the band that became The Firm.[168] In mid-February, he learned it wasn't going any further. Three months after that, he turned down a concrete offer from The Truth, the mod-inclined band which had evolved from R&B outfit Nine Below Zero.

David was also scratching a solo itch. On March 12, a show at Victoria's The Venue was billed as the "first solo project by Dave Vanian of The Damned". Although it was cancelled, ads for the show reinforced impressions The Damned had been shelved.

As the new extracurricular opportunities came and went, Rat met aspiring manager Andy McQueen, who was pushing for 'Wiped Out' from his solo 'Let There Be Rats' single to become an easily available A-side. McQueen felt that if a video was made, it stood a chance of becoming a hit. Rat quickly learned the enthusiastic entrepreneur had bigger ideas: The Damned could capitalise on their global status.

"Captain found Andy McQueen," says Rat. "He said, 'I've met this bloke I think should be the manager of The Damned.' McQueen was quite brilliant, the ideas, the way he thought, really direct. He was going to go to CBS, get a million, he said, 'You're worth it.' Full of confidence, brash. I was convinced he was the right guy."

McQueen became their manager in April and organised a session at Roundhouse Studios on May 12 to record a track to accompany 'Nasty' as a single. Again, Captain was meant to come up with a new track but hadn't. David and Roman had to look for something to tape and chose 'Thanks For The Night', a track from the previous year's solo Captain album *The Power Of Love*. It had a history and had been demoed as 'Thanks For The Favour' in 1982 when it was potentially in line for *Strawberries*. Rat wasn't happy with the recycling as it implied The Damned were a Captain Sensible covers band, but went ahead and played on the single anyway. Logic may have indicated that 'Nasty' – promoted on national television via *The Young Ones* – was the top side, but it was not.

Released on the band's own label, 'Thanks For The Night' was a fair seller and charted, but without a budget for radio plugging and no live dates hung around its release, the single's lifespan was short. [169]

Reuniting in the studio as The Damned and appearing on TV brought enough of a boost to help negotiations with CBS about signing. "We did some demos and they were well received," recalls Rat. "CBS were interested, which I thought was perfect for us. They really liked everything. They said they wanted to come and see a show."

Captain didn't turn up for rehearsals to prepare for a showcase date booked for Madrid on June 15. He also didn't travel to Spain so Roman took over on guitar. Rat had been told the contract was ready for signing the following week. CBS were in Madrid and the show had gone well but the label wanted to see the band with Captain. Another date was arranged, at Exeter University on June 29 while 'Thanks For The Night' was still in the charts.[170] "It was a nightmare night," says Rat. "The support band spilt beer all over the monitor desk. We played and the whole deal just died."

"I had been told the deal with CBS was done," recalls Roman. "After two weeks I asked Rat was going on: 'They're avoiding our calls.' I then heard they weren't convinced about us signing as Captain was in the band – the conflicting interest between him solo and the band. I was told that at Exeter Captain had said to [CBS head of A&R] Muff Winwood, 'I don't care about money'. That's what swayed Winwood, he wouldn't want to sign somebody who would throw it away." On July 5, The Damned were formally told that CBS were passing. A week earlier, Rat had told *Sounds*, "We all decided we wanted to become that force again. We've all adopted a more serious attitude towards our art: and I use the term in a comical sense. The problem was that we weren't too serious ourselves."

"Finally, an A&R guy told me that they didn't like Captain being a distraction from Dave," adds Rat about CBS turning the band down. "They felt that the 'Happy Talk' persona of Captain had become overpowering." After CBS passed, Andy McQueen began talking to Warner Brothers.

Renewed interest from MCA also offered hope. The label had a new A&R man, Steve Kutner, who had joined them from RCA.[171] A long-time Damned fan, Kutner had tried in 1980 to sign them to Magnet, the label he was with before RCA but had been rebuffed. "When I went to Magnet in 1980 I thought 'History Of The World' was a masterpiece," says Steve. "I played it to the head of marketing, as I had heard they were available. 'What do you think of this, it's great.' 'Who is it?' 'It's The Damned.' 'Fuck off.'"

Four years on, Kutner still held the torch and set up a meeting to feel out whether a signing was possible. Unfortunately, the label's head of

A&R, Lucien Grange, missed the meeting as he had forgotten about it. Rat felt it was the fault of the band's manager, Andy McQueen, and pushed for him to be fired. For now, any dealings with MCA were on hold.

The Damned – with Captain – played what was only their fifth show of the year, headlining an outdoor all-day event on Saturday August 4 in south London's Brockwell Park before 40,000 people in support of the Greater London Council, an institution the Conservative government was in the process of abolishing. Earlier that day, Captain had appeared live on BBC1's Saturday morning kid's TV show *The Saturday Picture Show*, which went on air at 9 a.m. In the evening at Brockwell Park, a bottle chucked from the crowd hit Captain in the testicle area as they left the stage.

After Brockwell Park, Rat concluded that McQueen was in breach of contract as wages asked for had not been paid. Without telling him, the rest of the band decided they couldn't progress with Captain: a guitarist who wasn't committed and was a solo act. They would continue without him.

A couple of days later, Rat met MCA's Steve Kutner for lunch. At the same time, Captain remained supportive of McQueen as he saw him as committed to the band. If the manager went, so would he. "I got a phone message from Captain," remembers Roman. "He had said, 'I'm leaving The Damned. Take my advice, I would leave too if I was you.' I had no idea why he would say that." He had made the call on August 20. David and Roman were phoned with the news. Rat was not. Brockwell Park had been Captain's final show.

Captain Sensible had left The Damned.

★ ★ ★

Looking back on leaving The Damned and the pressure of balancing solo commitments with being in the band, Captain says, "I'll hold my hand up and admit the solo career can't have helped. I understand my colleagues if they were pissed off, but as an ex-bog cleaner I wasn't going to tell the bloke from A&M to stick his contract up his arse. I ended up having a breakdown of sorts, in a clinic for exhaustion, took ages to recover and when I eventually did get myself back together both careers had gone."[172]

Once again, The Damned were a four-piece band. Roman Jugg and Bryn Merrick had not been there from the beginning. Rat Scabies and David Vanian had. It wasn't quite like 1976 or the reformation in 1978, but this was a new beginning.

A 30-date tour planned to begin in September with Hanoi Rocks and The Sid Presley Experience as support bands was dropped. "I can't remember if an actual decision was made to carry on," says Rat. "But we hadn't been working and we needed money. We never got any royalties and lived on fresh air, so we needed what we got from gigging. We didn't want Captain out of the group. We could work the two careers together, and that's what we did for two years but it got increasingly difficult. [Captain's manager] Andrew Miller didn't care about The Damned as there wasn't enough money in it. And after *The Young Ones*, it was obvious that Dave's persona could lead the band comfortably."

CHAPTER THIRTEEN

Not A Fucking Pop Band

Progress was implausibly fast after August 20, when Captain told the band he was leaving. Faster than it had been the last three years; faster even than in the months after the band formed in 1976. Eight weeks after he left, The Damned signed to MCA Records. The deal was done on October 10, 1984.

Like Captain's label A&M, MCA was an American-owned multinational with a global reach. Earlier in the year, the band's now ex-manager Andy McQueen had wanted them to capitalise on their internationally known name and the opportunity to do exactly this had come.

In the UK, MCA's principle business was bringing American-signed acts to a British audience and 1984 saw them exporting former Eagle Glen Frey and Bee Gees stalwart Barry Gibb (who may as well have been American). The hefty amount of country on their books (including Reba McEntire, The Oak Ridge Boys, Kenny Rogers and Don Williams) was balanced against upbeat soul acts (New Edition and Shalamar were bankers amongst their roster) and rockers like Night Ranger, Stone Fury and Triumph. Their edgiest signings were Tom Petty & The Heartbreakers and Rat's old acquaintance Joan Jett and her Blackhearts. They also had The Fixx, a British band whose recent American success, coming on the back of MTV's exposure of their videos, overshadowed their British profile. Albeit a minor aspect of their portfolio, The Fixx did prove MCA brought US success for current British bands.

Other local signings by MCA's British arm included Bronski Beat, Nik Kershaw, Musical Youth and Kim Wilde. Any way it was looked at, the label was corporate, mainstream and safe.

Steve Kutner, the MCA A&R man who engineered The Damned's new deal, was a long-term fan – it was this, more than anything, which mattered. He had tried to bring the band to Magnet, where he had worked in 1980, and attempted to do the same with MCA earlier in the year when Captain was still in the band. Now, as one of a new team at the label, he achieved a long-held ambition.

"I told [MCA's head of A&R] Lucien Grange I wanted to sign The Damned and he said, 'You're fucking mad,'" recalls Steve. "He said, 'You cannot sign The Damned as your first signing with me as the new director of A&R and a new American MD. How are you going to explain you want to sign a band who were hot in '77?' I didn't care who the audience was, I just wanted to sign them. The head of marketing said he would not work with this band. No one wanted to work with them." Nonetheless, Steve got his way and – for the first time – The Damned shook hands with the corporate, mainstream and safe.

"When you take a piece out of the jigsaw and try to piece what's left together, it made what was left stronger," reflects Roman on the effect of Captain's departure. "You wouldn't have a guy with a beret taking his clothes off and telling jokes on the other side of the stage to Dave. I've never heard Dave Vanian tell a joke on stage. In effect, once you took that out you didn't have two frontmen. All the attention now went on Dave. You've got a platform where you're projecting the singer, the image of the band and the songs. You've got something to sell."

"We were conscious that The Damned were renowned for changing horses midstream, progressing as musicians," adds Rat, stressing that losing Captain was an opportunity. "You do it to be creative. You don't do it to learn ten songs and play them for the rest of your life. I could have joined an orchestra if I'd wanted to do that." The immediate change was to switch Roman from keyboards to guitar, his first instrument, as a show was booked at Nostell Priory, a Yorkshire stately home surrounded by parkland which was hosting a four-day music festival over the summer bank holiday weekend. The Damned were headlining the first night, Friday August 24. Captain had left the Tuesday beforehand.

Roman had played guitar in The Damned without Captain in the line-up for the Naz Nomad & The Nightmares album and live, when the Sixties cover versions were supplemented with 'Born To Kill', 'Love Song', 'Smash It Up' and 'Neat Neat Neat'. Now, he had three days to learn the whole set. "When Captain left, Rat and Dave came round my flat – seeing Dave in broad daylight! – and said that it occurred to them that I could play guitar as there were shows booked," says Roman. "Nobody had rung from the band confirming Captain had left. They just said, 'We're coming to see you.' I didn't see anything different in their attitude. Nothing was said whatsoever about Captain leaving."

At Rat's father's house, they set up in the garden and ran through the set. Roman says, "The first try was awful but by the third it was OK." At Nostell Priory, they were preceded on stage by Doctor & The Medics – with whom Roman had often played keyboards. Their guitarist Steve McGuire became The Damned's temporary keyboard player. The show went off without a hitch.[173] No announcement was made to the crowd or anywhere else that Captain was no longer in the band but the absence was – in a fashion – addressed in the music press.

Rat told *Melody Maker* that the band was not splitting, this was a flexible arrangement with Captain and, if he had songs, they will be used: "He won't leave entirely, Captain's personal schedule is unlikely to fit with ours all the time." In the same report, Captain was quoted as saying, "I'll always continue to work with The Damned." His first public appearance after leaving was to sing 'Glad It's All Over', 'Happy Talk' and 'Wot!' in the living room of the winners of a competition run by London newspaper *The Evening Standard*.

After the Yorkshire show, the band's joint bank account was close to tapped out. Roman thinks the balance was either £300 or £400.

The choice was stark: divide the money up between themselves or use it for the band. With no manager, no gigs on their books and without Captain, this was a point to pack it in. Instead, a new booking agent was engaged and, as Roman had a new song, the money was used to book Pathway to record a demo. "We were aware that there wasn't a lot of lifespan left in The Damned and it was time to take it seriously," says Rat.

The new song taped was 'Grimly Fiendish', which Roman had initially demoed by playing piano to a click track. "I couldn't claim credit," says Rat. "Roman wrote it. We'd never done one of those Madness-type songs, a London-type song. It was born from sitting around saying 'let's do one of those'." Steve Kutner heard the demo, thought the song was a hit and paid for more tracks to be recorded.[174]

'Grimly Fiendish' became Steve's leverage to sign The Damned to MCA. "The first piece of paper I signed for The Damned was when I signed on the line for MCA," recalls Roman. "Rat had seen Captain Sensible being Captain Sensible with the backing of his record company: selling himself as Captain Sensible. Rat was trying to make a career, but both Dave and Rat were very very hesitant about putting their signatures on the MCA contract. It meant you had to knuckle down, to toe the line."

"MCA's managing director said, 'This is a fucking great first signing, you'd better be sure,'" recalls Steve of the reaction to bringing The Damned to the label. "Their reputation was terrible, no one at the company wanted me to sign them, they had split up a million times. One person transformed the whole situation. One person, and one person only. Rat Scabies. When Rat came to the building everyone was absolutely petrified, but he was a legend. The first time he came in, everyone loved him. He was brilliant, all the people in the record company fell in love with Rat. They expected him to be difficult to deal with but when he hadn't had a drink he was genuinely a lovable rogue."

Steve also got the measure of the rest of the band. "Once I met Dave, I understood he was the brains behind *The Black Album*, without a doubt.

'Curtain Call', all that was him. Dave was the musical driving force behind the band, by a million miles. Dave was a nightmare though, he'd never turn up. The most unreliable man ever. Roman was quite quiet, good musically. I liked Bryn, he was just a dope who liked to drink a lot and always fell out with Rat. Bryn was lovable and Rat would torment him all the time."

After the signing, the next piece of business was securing a manager. Rat wanted and had contacted Andy Cheeseman, who had begun working for Jake Riviera's label F-Beat in 1982 but was latterly employed as a pub barman after he'd put the music business behind him. Rat's persistence paid off, convincing Cheeseman that the band were serious and that he was prepared to give two years to become a rich and famous pop star. "The Damned became very businesslike in 1984," says Rat. "In 1976, 1977, 1978, we were juvenile delinquents. We didn't have any self-worth or value. It wasn't the same band any more."

'Grimly Fiendish' was released on March 18, 1985. With its title reference to cartoonist Leo Baxendale's villain Grimly Feendish[175], vocal quotes from The Who's 'A Quick One, While He's Away' and dark yet gently humorous tone helping ease its route to an audience, MCA ensured the single attracted as many sales as possible and co-opted some Stiff-style marketing for the press ads: "After 9 years, 11 managers[176], 5 labels and numerous lunches – they're back with a great Damned single." The first 4,000 picture sleeves were signed by the band. There were two 12-inch single editions, a gatefold seven-inch and a seven-inch picture disc.

Of the multiple formats, Rat says, "That was what was happening at the time. That was how you broke bands in those days. To a degree we had control over what came out, we were part of the decision. But the record company chose all the singles. I always thought they knew best. We did discuss it, but if they had a suggestion I thought they knew their stuff."

Press reactions to 'Grimly Fiendish' were favourable. *NME*'s Danny Kelly declared it "a hit" and noted the influence of Pink Floyd's 'Arnold Layne' and the similarity with Madness. *Sounds* said it was "ominously pretty".

British television viewers got their first look at the new four-piece Damned on March 12 when BBC2's *Whistle Test* broadcast the 'Grimly Fiendish' video. More extravagant than anything they had ever done, MCA's coffers paid for a promo featuring the band in their ruffle-shirted glory with crimped hair, dandy-esque clothes and extras playing out a Dickensian story of ordinary folks taking revenge on a bad man. While their happy faces confirmed The Damned were having a ball at the filming, Steve says making "the video was nightmare. We filmed in Docklands, really early in the morning, it was freezing. We had brandy and the band got really drunk. In one part of the video Dave walks with a flaming torch and he set fire to his hair and the set. He got really pissed."

Three days after the *Whistle Test* airing, the video was also shown on *Breakfast Time*, the BBC's cosy morning news-and-chat show. The following week's *Whistle Test* saw The Damned play 'Grimly Fiendish' and 'Shadow Of Love' live in the studio. There were no upsets, and no smashing as there had been on the show in 1979. The raised profile meant *Top Of The Pops* featured the 'Grimly Fiendish' video on March 28 when other hit picks included Phil Collins & Phillip Bailey's soul-lite 'Easy Lover', Go West's electro-soul 'We Close Our Eyes', Alison Moyet's tasteful cover of 'That Ole Devil Called Love' and Frankie Goes To Hollywood's 'Welcome To The Pleasuredome'.[177] High gloss recordings all, and The Damned needed a large dash of this to compete.

MCA had done their job: The Damned headed to 21. "When 'Grimly' charted, I remember ringing my brother up and saying we're on *Top Of The Pops*," recalls Roman. "It still had that meaning. It was massive."

It was as if punk had never happened and, appropriately, *Smash Hits'* writer Dave Rimmer's book *Like Punk Never Happened* was published in October 1985. The magazine Rimmer wrote for was now the dominant force in the propagation of British pop and his book, although focussing on Culture Club, charted how punk had been central to and – Wham! excepted – was a major influence on Duran Duran, Frankie Goes To Hollywood and Spandau Ballet, the bands defining the "new breed of British pop stars": bands which had "come of age during punk, absorbed its methods, learnt its lessons – but ditched its ideals." Culture Club's drummer and business brain Jon Moss had auditioned for The Clash and had been in The Damned. Of his spell as Rat's replacement, he told Rimmer, "It wasn't really me."

Now, though, the door swung the other way and The Damned were throwing their lot in with what Rimmer called the "New Pop".

★ ★ ★

MCA had no intention that 'Grimly Fiendish' would be a one off. They wanted follow-up hits and an album had to be recorded.

The band wished to work with 'Grimly Fiendish' producer Bob Sergeant again, but Steve says he instead "wanted to get someone who could get the best sounds, a really good current sound. We were a major record label and we wanted the album to be huge." He felt Jon Kelly, who he knew from the Chris Rea records he had worked on at Magnet, was right. Up to this point, Kelly had worked only with solo acts, including Kate Bush and Paul McCartney. "They weren't overly keen," recalls Steve of The Damned's first encounter with the suggested producer. "We had a meeting, Jon walked out and I asked, 'What do you think?' Rat said, 'Wanker, he ain't making our record.' I sat down with Dave and said Jon understands vocals, understands keyboards, everything you want. The quid pro quo with Rat was recording at The Who's studio, Eel Pie." In mid-April, recording what became *Phantasmagoria* commenced.

Despite the initial friction Rat says, "We all liked Jon. He was good and easy-going, knew his stuff. He was technical minded and very much went for a pop, non-aggressive feel. If Brian James had played guitar, the songs would have had a different sort of impact. The production is aimed at the mainstream. For me, it was a lot of work, as suddenly people were getting used to hearing things in time. We started afresh with *Phantasmagoria*." A national tour was booked from late May into mid-July. The Damned knew they'd be working hard.

Catching up with the band in Aberdeen on June 2, *NME*'s David Quantick noted that The Damned's wilderness years were epic and that he had no idea Roman had been with them for four years and Bryn for two. David said, "Success would be all the more appreciated from the nine-and-a-half years of struggle, we'll enjoy it," and Rat told Quantick, "I've always believed that The Damned can become one of the major boring bands of the world, that then becomes the dinosaur that becomes obsolete. Hopefully, I'll love it." Seeing them in Birmingham on June 20, *Sounds* witnessed what they concluded was "a clinical operation: sanitised, antiseptic and coldly calculating".

The Cure-like 'Shadow Of Love' single was issued June 10 in multiple formats and *Phantasmagoria* followed on July 15: on limited-edition white vinyl and then, a month later, as a picture disc. In the single's video, a cowled, mysterious lady and a black cat prowled around a dolls house, inside which the band ran through the song.

Reviews of *Phantasmagoria* were at odds. *NME* said they were "panto-freaks" who "make you wish they'd stayed in the pub" but *Melody Maker* was seduced. "A fine rock band have come of age," said the paper's Mat Smith. "The Damned have at last produced their meisterwork. *Phantasmagoria* is, quite simply, The Damned's finest moment [and their] two-fingered salute to all those doubters, detractors and record companies who have kept them away from us for far too long." *Sounds* was more measured, saying it was "smooth!" and that "all this moody mysterioso stuff works better in the small doses provided by the 45 format. Damned fans will love it."

At David's insistence, the sleeve featured a specially commissioned photograph by Bob Carlos Clarke, then most well-known for his erotically slanted images of women which often featured fetish wear. He had photographed nudes for the high-street porn monthly *Men Only* and his first book, *Obsession*, had been published in 1981. His second, the polished *The Dark Summer*, followed in 1985. For The Damned, Clarke photographed model Susie Bick at London's Kensal Green Cemetery in an image he titled *Dreamkeeper*. She later married Nick Cave. *Phantasmagoria*'s packaging was as high-gloss as its sound. The white vinyl edition helped the album to 11 in the charts, while 'Shadow of Love' reached 25.

"It was how Dave saw the album," says Steve of what was released. "How Dave heard the album, the artwork was all Dave. It was all Dave.

Rat was a lot more about business. Within the record company, the ones who counted were Dave and Rat. Roman was good in the studio, because he kept things together when Dave wouldn't turn up."

Speaking with *Melody Maker*, Rat quipped, "We're certainly this week's flavour. Nobody wanted to know us two years ago when we had nothing." He also noted that the band's fans had stayed loyal, while David declared he favoured Peter Cushing over Christopher Lee and that he liked *Wuthering Heights* as it represented an English way of life that has disappeared.

Phantasmagoria sold well, more than enough to be awarded a silver disc for 60,000 sales. MCA wanted photographs of the band being presented with the award. "Rat was quite emotional about it, the first time they had got any recognition," recalls Steve. "At least, he was until he got pissed and set my office on fire. We went out for lunch after the photos, then we're all sitting in my office and Rat had got over being happy and was saying, 'Who gives a fuck, fucking silver disc, we're a punk band.' I was behind my desk and there was a huge rubber plant. Rat said this is what we used to do when we were a proper punk band. He sprayed lighter fuel over my desk and set fire to it. The tree caught fire. It was hard work."

Contemplating dancing with the mainstream and the marketing, Rat says, "Because it's the first time you're doing it, you don't realise how much fun you should be having. It becomes a small, insular world quickly. You're always doing something more important than setting the drums up. If you nip off to the pub you get found quickly as people would be out of a job. Once being in the band becomes every waking moment – when you suddenly have a value – you take on delusions of importance and you get used to certain things. If there isn't a cold beer that's a problem. I remember my wife later on saying we need some milk, I said, 'Send someone.' That's what you did."

★ ★ ★

Cracks were appearing. 'Shadow Of Love' had been drawn from *Phantasmagoria* as a single and had been a hit. MCA wanted to extract another album track. The label's American office favoured 'Is It A

Dream'. But Rat did not want the album to spawn a third single. "I went to Rat and Dave," says Steve. "Rat said, 'No more singles off the album. We're not a fucking pop band. I don't want to rip anyone off.'"

America was to be prepared for the new, business-friendly Damned and, whatever Rat thought, a new single was key to the strategy. After continental European dates in September and October, they were scheduled to play New York in November and a couple of Californian shows in December.

As he had with securing Jon Kelly to produce the album, Steve looked to Dave to get what the label wanted. "Dave had talked to me behind everyone's back about maybe doing a solo record," explains Steve. "We had a plan some time in the future to do 'Eloise'. I said if you let me put out 'Is It A Dream' we can do 'Eloise', I'll give you a budget. Rat liked the idea of having a single that was not on the album." Duly released as single, 'Is It A Dream' charted at 34 in September to keep the pot boiling.

'Eloise' was recorded with Jon Kelly in December.[178] "It was a nightmare track to record," recalls Steve. "It was originally twice as long as what came out. Dave was a bit of a nightmare not turning up for his vocals. They went off to America, so Jon Kelly had to mix it on his own."

The song, originally a massive cross-European hit in Autumn 1968, was written by Paul Ryan for his brother Barry, twin sons of dance-band singer Marion Ryan. Breathless, huge-sounding and fully orchestrated, it defined pop as drama. Looking back to *The Black Album* and *Machine Gun Etiquette*'s proposed bonus EP's Walker Brothers cover version, choosing to cover it was not such a surprise.[179] In April 1985, David had told BBC Radio 1's Janice Long, "Barry Ryan and Paul Ryan have been sadly forgotten. Everyone waxes lyrical about Scott Walker which is marvellous but this is absolutely superb. There's a tension in there, it starts off pretty but it grabs you after a while" when introducing Ryan's 'Eloise' on her show. Back in 1980, he had told the fanzine *Allied Propaganda*, "maybe we'll do a cover of 'Eloise'". Despite getting what he wanted, Roman recalls being told by MCA that David had called the label to ask for the single not to be issued.

ith friends. Rat with Motörhead's Lemmy and The Adverts'
aye Advert at The Roundhouse. April 24, 1977.
UL SLATTERY/CAMERA PRESS

With family. Rat with his father and future Damned manager
John Millar, who sports Adverts, Damned and Grateful Dead
badges. Backstage at The Sundown. August 17, 1977.
ERICA ECHENBERG/GETTY IMAGES

Edmonds' (left) first UK show as a member of The Damned, at The Sundown. August 17, 1977. ERICA ECHENBERG/GETTY IMAGES

Rat's sudden departure meant The Damned had an ad-hoc, two-week long line-up with Johnny Moped drummer Dave Berk (second from right) behind the kit. October 1977. PICTORIAL PRESS LTD/ALAMY STOCK PHOTO

Dave Berk's place on The Damned's drum stool was taken by future Culture Club drummer Jon Moss (second from right). Backstage at The Roundhouse. November 1977. ROBERTA BAYLEY/REDFERNS

e Damned reform as The Doomed. Their only promotional photograph parodied *Damned Damned Damned*. Captain had
itched from bass to guitar, and new short-stay bassist Henry Badowski is top right. October 1978. CHALKIE DAVIES/GETTY IMAGES

David Vanian paying tribute to actor Max Schreck's Count Orlok from the 1922 film *Nosferatu, eine Symphonie des Grauens*. April 1979. DENIS O'REGAN/GETTY IMAGES

New York, beginning a tour during which stages were wrecked and audiences castigated as knowing "fuck all about punk".
gy Ward, Henry Badowski's replacement, is seen on the right. June 1979. ACE RECORDS

viously unseen promotional shot for the 'Smash It Up' single, taken at a British Rail warehouse behind Kensington's Olympia.
tober 3, 1979. ACE RECORDS

THE DAMNED

Chiswick

Singles — Love Song/Noise, Noise, Noise/Suicide · CHIS 112
Smash It Up/Burglar · CHIS 116
I Just Can't Be Happy Today · CHIS 120

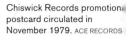

eviously unseen shot from
w bassist Paul Gray's (on the
t) first photo session with The
amned. Planned for the sleeve of
e shelved British 'White Rabbit'
ngle, the session was later used
r the cover of the 'History of the
orld' single. April 1980.
E RECORDS

id caught on camera by Rat during the *Black Album* sessions at Rockfield Studios. June 1980. RAT SCABIES

Unused shot from the *Black Album*
cover session. October 1980.
ACE RECORDS

Promotional session for Chiswick
Records. The label – to which
The Damned was contracted – w
unaware the *Friday 13th EP* was
about to be issued by
another imprint. November 5, 198
MICHAEL PUTLAND/GETTY IMAGES

Rat was not convinced by 'Eloise'. "Dave had always thought about doing it with The Damned," he acknowledges. "But as a cover, 'Eloise' wasn't such a proud moment. It never sounded finished to me."

Wooing America began in earnest. They spent the last couple of days of February and the whole of March touring the States. In the US, the sets played were generally the same night-to-night with little of the typically Damned randomness. Encore versions of 'Pretty Vacant', The Doors' 'Riders On The Storm', Johnny Kidd's 'Shakin' All Over', 'We Love You' and 'Wild Thing' were played, as well as regular outings of Iggy Pop's 'Lust For Life'. In Boston, there were old-style manglings of The Cult's 'She Sells Sanctuary', The Doors' 'You're Lost Little Girl', Public Image Ltd's 'Rise', Kenny Rogers' 'Ruby Don't Take Your Love To Town', U2's 'Sunday Bloody Sunday' and ZZ Top's 'Sharp Dressed Man'.

Following their Denver show, the band's touring keyboard player Paul Shepley bailed out for a few days after he and Rat had argued. Both were stressed: Rat with setting up his drums and Shepley dealing with his temperamental digital keyboards and synthesisers. The Damned were still not operating to a template.

Rat told the American music trade paper *Billboard* that being with MCA was "the first proper record deal we've had. None of the other organisations – Stiff, Chiswick, Bronze – really had any sort of clout internationally." When it was pointed out that "the biggest hurdle they face in promoting the moody ethereal album [*Phantasmagoria*] is their own notoriety", Rat acknowledged, "people still think we're a three-chord band. We've learned to control ourselves. You can't help growing up," he concluded.

The *Los Angeles Times* ran an article headed "The Damned's back and it's better than ever" which said "*Phantasmagoria* is a big surprise. Instead of vicious, goony songs riding on metallic overdrive, the new Damned songs are melodic, orchestrated pop gems, closer to the Beatles-influenced school of imaginative eclecticism than to the slash-and-burn theatrics of the bad old punk days." To the paper's writer, former member of early LA punk band The Bags Craig Lee[180], Rat confessed of the band's early days "all of a sudden you're getting free alcohol, free drugs – how can you resist it? I couldn't. So I tended to make the most of it. It was the drink, always the drink… but eventually your realise it's not that much fun being a pain to everyone around you."

★ ★ ★

'Eloise' had been issued on seven- and 12-inch on January 27, 1986 and became The Damned's biggest hit, reaching number three in the British charts. A second, sales-stoking edition of two 12-inch formats came in February.

Coincidentally, The Damned's version was publicised when Robin McCauley, who had sung on the previous year's Far Corporation version of 'Stairway To Heaven', also issued a version. He said The Damned's 'Eloise' has "got absolutely no chance of making it in the charts". Asked about the competing versions, Barry Ryan said, "I like The Damned best, it's even better than mine."

It was at number three during the week ending February 22. The first American date was five days later. While the band had not vanished from the UK before the single was promoted, the scheduling underlines that the profile-raising spike in sales was unanticipated: they were out of the country when 'Eloise' was at its chart peak. Despite being issued on 12-inch in America, it did not chart there. The US version of *Phantasmagoria* also had not. In the UK, MCA released a new blue-vinyl *Phantasmagoria* packaged with a 12-inch single of 'Eloise' to capitalise on the hit.

The Damned were now aiming for a global audience. From America, they headed off to New Zealand, Australia – where 'Eloise' peaked at eight; it hit 18 in New Zealand – and then Japan. "With 'Eloise' and *Phantasmagoria* promoted again on the back of it, you see your workload," says Roman. "Physically we weren't in great shape by then, drinking far too much."

In Sydney, a drinking session at the Sebel Townhouse Hotel culminated in each member of the band being thrown out, one-by-one. Merrick was first, then David, followed by Rat. Sting's band were also there, as he was in town playing, and Roman was the last to be ejected after he fell, face down, onto their table. He went back to his band's hotel. Merrick, however, ended up in a pool hall where, perhaps in his imagination, he became separated from his hat. Blotto, the bass player, went back to look for it, kicking in the pool hall's glass door. He was set upon, arrested and flung into a cell. Charged with assault, he was freed after a fine was paid and was able to play the band's late April Japanese dates. The Dammed were already there without him.

"Bryn was beginning to jeopardise what we were doing," recalls Rat. "When he couldn't play properly because he was hammered or locked up in a police cell he was costing an extra few thousand bucks to get him out to shows because he wasn't travelling there with the rest of us."

Then, The Damned learned MCA wanted a new album. "We came back home and had a meeting," says Roman. "We were told, 'You've nine days off. Then you go to Denmark to record a new album.' We hadn't written anything."

Phantasmagoria

For the first time since 1979's *Machine Gun Etiquette*, a Damned album was released after two hit singles had paved the way for it. Back then, it was 'Love Song' and 'Smash It Up'. Now, in 1985, it was 'Grimly Fiendish' and 'The Shadow Of Love'. *Phantasmagoria* was a reaffirmation.

Captain Sensible had gone. Paul Gray, bassist since 1980, had left in early 1983. Roman Jugg, initially their keyboard player, had switched to guitar. His friend Bryn Merrick had replaced Gray. David and Rat were the constants. Half The Damned were there from the beginning. The other half had been in Welsh band Victimize.

How the new Damned sounded had already been telegraphed. Keen Damned watchers already knew four of the album's nine tracks before its July 1985 release. 'Grimly Fiendish' was dark, particularly English pop with Sixties leanings. 'The Shadow Of Love' was smoother than older songs and more grand. Both had been singles. The album's 'Is It A Dream' had been recorded for a John Peel session in July 1984, while Captain was still with the band. It was broadcast on August 6, two weeks before their first live show without him. They didn't play live after that for just over eight months[181], but the new 'Street Of Dreams' and 'There'll Come A Day' entered their

223

live sets from May 1985. 'Grimly Fiendish' and 'Shadow Of Love' were performed on BBC2's *Whistle Test*.

Phantasmagoria was by a Damned which was all on the same page, operating as a single entity with a cogent identity and the focal point of an evident frontman. This time, there was marketing collateral too. Copies of *Phantasmagoria* came with an A4 sheet advertising mail-order merchandise: five different badges, two T-shirts, a sleeveless T-shirt, a "ladies size only chemise", a scarf, a poster and the programme for the recent UK tour. All for sale, and all Damned branded. The band's fan club, the Flashman Society, had been reactivated: for a £5 membership fee fans received a badge, band biography, membership card, a photo and a quarterly newsletter.[182]

Undoubtedly, The Damned meant business. This much was already evident from the multiple formats in which the singles of 'Grimly Fiendish' and 'The Shadow Of Love' had been issued. But could they back this up? Could they recoup the investment which MCA had made in them?

Looked at coldly, the answer was probably yes. They were selling more records and touring more widely than ever. Shows were sell-outs. Their audience numbers had increased. They were more popular than former mainstay Captain Sensible. There was also now a codified fashion style which David represented, even though he had been its lone, unrecognised pioneer or originator: goth or, as it was originally dubbed, positive punk. One look at *Phantasmagoria*'s sumptuous, mysterious sleeve imagery confirmed this band had a firm grip on how it was seen.

But all of this needed the music. Without it, MCA had little to sell and The Damned were stuck with 'Grimly Fiendish' as a false (re) start. Happily, beyond being an exquisite object, the original album of *Phantasmagoria* came up with the required goods.

After kicking off with Gary Barnacle's late-night saxophone for 'Street Of Dreams', the album and the song found their feet within moments. This was pop – dark and moody, but pop. It was also modern. Digital instruments were apparent. Jon Kelly's production was clean, and highlighted elements bringing out the melodies and driving the songs forward.

Musically and atmospherically, *Phantasmagoria* built from The Damned of *The Black Album*'s '13th Floor Vendetta', 'Dr. Jekyll And Mr. Hyde' and 'Twisted Nerve'. Though *Phantasmagoria* had less of an edge than *The Black Album*, it was its belated and logical successor. As the packaging – the first thing anyone finding the album encountered – confirmed David's strong hand, so did the music. Everything fell into place to endorse his conceptualisation.

Even so, all nine tracks were credited to Jugg/Merrick/Scabies/ Vanian in varying orders. 'Street Of Dreams' was as by Scabies/ Vanian/Jugg/Merrick: an individual song's prime composer was noted first. So, 'Shadow Of Love', given as written by Vanian/ Scabies/Jugg/Merrick, was more a David song than by another band member. 'Is It A Dream', written before Captain left the band, was credited to Scabies/Jugg/Vanian/Merrick/Sensible. "Doctor" was appended to the band's names for 'Grimly Fiendish': this was Clive Thomas – Doctor of Doctor & The Medics (Roman had a working relationship with him and his band – all five received an equal payment of the songwriting money for 'Grimly Fiendish'). Roman sang 'Edward The Bear', which was credited to Jugg/ Scabies/Merrick/Vanian even though David was not heard on it. Album closer 'Trojans' was credited to Merrick/Jugg/Scabies/ Vanian despite being an instrumental which David was also not on. As far as the songwriting was concerned, it was equal shares for all even if some band members were less active than others.

Phantasmagoria's singles were successful. The album itself was a success too: artistically, as it unambiguously stated the identity of this reconfigured Damned, and also commercially. Everyone had what they wanted: the band, their champion Steve Kutner and MCA, the label he worked for. The future looked rosy. Except, it turned out not to be.

CHAPTER FOURTEEN

The False Dawn Of 'Eloise'

The raised profile and success brought by *Phantasmagoria* meant The Damned's label MCA wanted more. It also meant they were now a crossover band, appealing to goths and punks as much as pop fans.

"The audience had become divided between the 'New Rose', 'Smash It Up' fans and the 'Eloise' fans," explains Rat. "We'd play 'Smash It Up' and all the punks would be down the front, then we'd play 'Shadow Of Love' and all the little goth kids would come down and push them out the way. The 'Eloise' audience hadn't seen a burning drum kit before. We realised we had this fragmented audience. All of this is The Damned. Dave had come into his own. He was so good at it. We had to become something different to what we were to pull it off every time. It was going great. But we all knew that we couldn't keep doing it."

That was of no concern to MCA, who wanted to keep the wheel turning by greasing it with more product. Steve Kutner retained tried-and-tested producer Jon Kelly and booked PUK, a residential studio in Denmark.

Located in Gjerlev, in central Jutland, north Denmark, PUK was in the country and more isolated even than Rockfield. A fully digital studio, it was a 32-track set-up with a Fairlight keyboard, a snooker table and tennis court. But it wasn't the state-of-the-art facilities or leisure opportunities which led Steve to choose it. "It was nothing to do with digital," he says. "The problem was Dave would never turn up. Jon Kelly said the only way to do it is somewhere residential. We booked it for a month, Jon went out to set it up, we bought the tickets, Dave didn't turn up."

"For the first month I was the only one there," recalls Roman. "Bryn came out with me, then he had to go off with his wife to sort something out. There was nothing for Rat to do, so he didn't come out. 'Where's Dave?' That's when I did the backing track for 'Alone Again Or' as I was so bored. We had half-arsed demos we'd done in our little breaks. We had half ideas." Gradually, they assembled. Rat came and began contributing to backing tracks and then left. David arrived. Bryn returned.

In the down time, the band members who were there raced around the local fields on the studio's pair of Suzuki 125 motor-trikes. "That was as exciting as it got," says Rat of the trikes. "But we did get very good at snooker."

★ ★ ★

The faltering sessions in Denmark were interrupted by a 10th-anniversary show in north London for their fan club, on July 1 at the Town & Country in Kentish Town. 'Anything', which became the new album's title track, was played live for the first time. At the end of the month, after a pair of festival dates in France and Italy, work on the album was again disrupted by two more anniversary shows, in a tent set up at north London's Finsbury Park. On the second night, Captain joined them for the encore run-though of 'Smash It Up'. It was two years and a week since he had last played with The Damned. "We were trying to build bridges with the Captain," says Rat. "There may have been seething resentments in the background but we never fell out with him even though he'd left the band."

This wasn't a lasting reunion but a one-off glance back at the past. The main business was finishing the new album. After backing tracks were completed in June, David came to Denmark but wasn't prepared. "Jon Kelly called me and said, 'He's here, he's got no lyrics,'" recalls Steve. "*Anything* ran over and over while Dave wrote lyrics. Expensive."

"We went to over £300,000 on this record," explains Rat. "Why the fuck didn't anyone get us out of there after a few weeks as we didn't have any songs? As an overall strategy, you owe the record label money. Then MCA were going, 'Fuck, you've spent too much.' But I knew it wouldn't be a bad thing as they would have to promote the record." As the clock ticked on an album which was barely taking shape and eating up money, Steve left MCA. The band's only supporter at their label was gone.

"The new people at the label didn't really like the band very much," says Rat. "We were someone else's signing. Then the new people would disappear after a few months. I remember one of them said Dave and I should dress in Nazi regalia and cause trouble – I couldn't believe that anyone would suggest that." More satisfactory promotion came when BBC2's *Whistle Test* filmed the band at PUK and caught them on the Suzuki trikes and motoring through a commanding version of The Doors' 'LA Woman'.

Roman thinks the band was on a downslide while in Denmark. "All the way through the recording of that album, in everyone's mind was 'this is not good'," he says. "We were in denial about it. Yet we went ahead with it. 'Psychomania' would have been a great song, if it was done in the right way – but it sounded like Bruce Springsteen. By then, we didn't have the man on the inside at MCA."

"*Anything* has some moments I'm quite proud of," adds Rat. "I really like 'Anything' and 'Alone Again Or'. 'In Dulce Decorum' is one of the best things we did, but none of the tunes on the album had any commercial appeal. The drag was that we'd been out touring for too long and we weren't sure what we wanted to do next. All MCA were saying was, 'The studio's costing too much, hurry up and get out.' In some ways, I saw *Anything* as our difficult second album."

"*Phantasmogoria* was fantastic but after that we'd been on tour constantly and were then asked to record a new album," says David. "We needed a break, to clear our heads. Instead the manager had his advance and was building his swimming pool, and wanted some more [money]. We didn't have the songs and it did us more harm than good. The *Anything* album could have been so much better but we were knackered and it caused us a lot of problems. The English and US sides of the business began arguing, the people who signed us had left and the last album hadn't done very well. We had to dust ourselves down and start again."[183]

'Anything' was chosen as the first single from the new album, and released on November 6. Previewed prematurely on August 29 on the BBC's *Rock Around The Dock* television show – where they also performed 'Eloise' with the full Royal Philharmonic Orchestra – it scraped into the Top 30 but had none of the impact of its predecessor, 'Eloise'. A new mix of 1984's 'Thanks For The Night' included on one of the 12-inch versions hardly suggested a coherent release strategy for this album. Neither did issuing the single a month into the lengthy October/November British and Irish tour. *Melody Maker* reacted to their November 12 Hammersmith Odeon date by saying The Damned "haven't got a clue about punk anymore". Of the same gig, *Music Week* concluded "Britain's own DC Comic-book group" had a "well-crafted, now musically mature sound [which] should surely make the group a worthwhile proposition in America".

Indeed, this was how MCA saw The Damned. The label paid for an astonishing eight-page, pull-out advertorial – though tagged as such, it looked as if it was part of the paper's usual editorial pages – in the issue of *Music Week* from two weeks before the album's release. Under the headline "Blessed Are The Damned", the PR puff declared "the strength of their following and the potential to crossover in the US were the principle factors that convinced MCA to sign them. Now with the force and astute guidance of a major company behind them, The Damned are confident of their ability to achieve their true potential."

Amongst the achievements listed in *Music Week* was that their recent US tour had sold out and done better business in America than The Cult, further confirming The Damned were regarded by MCA as fit for the American market. An instrumental version of 'In Dulce Decorum' had been heard on *Walk-Alone*, an episode of *Miami Vice* broadcast across America on October 17. The first words of the paid-for article were "after 10 years in the business The Damned are still the rough boys waving the flag – and proud of it".

Anything the album was issued on December 1. The critics were ambivalent. *Melody Maker* said it featured "some excellent pop songs" and *Sounds* identified an overt tilt towards the American market: "America's heartland devours its AOR fodder, which this LP rejoices in being. America will eat up this cute melange."

As 1986 ended, Naz Nomad & The Nightmares – not The Damned – played two pre-Christmas shows at the Klub Foot nights at Hammersmith's Clarendon. Nothing from *Anything* was performed. No Damned songs were. The audience saw The Damned hurtle through the MC5's 'Looking At You' and 17 Sixties garage-rock, sixties punk and psychedelia cover versions.

If anything, it suggested The Damned were trying to close the door on their time with MCA and forget all about *Anything* weeks after it was released.

★ ★ ★

The Damned's 10th year as a band had come and gone. They first played live on July 6, 1976. That anniversary had been celebrated with London shows at the Town & County and Finsbury Park. Stiff Records also acknowledged the band's history by issuing *The Captain's Birthday Party* album in June 1986. A ham-fisted archive release, it was titled as if it was a recording of their April 1977 Roundhouse show but was actually compiled from tracks taped there with the no-Rat, Jon Moss and Lu Edmonds line-up the following November. It was one of Stiff's last gasps. The label – or rather its parent company Elcotgrange – had met with its creditors on August 18, 1986 to declare debts of over £3.5 million.[184]

Not a man to give up. Dave Robinson then formed Stiff Records Ltd, a new company, and urged the creditors – of which he said he was one – to stick with him. The major debtors were Island Records, who had partnered with Stiff again from January 1984 to August 1985 with a 50% investment when they took Robinson on as one of their own directors, and the Mechanical Copyright Protection Society – the latter's claim meant acts on the label had not been paid for sales of their records.

Despite Robinson's entreaty, Geoffrey Christopher Antony Morphitis was appointed as Elcotgrange Limited's liquidator on September 26.[185]

Stiff had gone bust. Its assets were up for sale. Ten years and six days earlier, The Damned had recorded 'New Rose' for Stiff.

Most of Stiff's catalogue was bought by Jill Sinclair, the chairman of the Sarm group and ZTT Records, and wife of producer Trevor Horn, through Cashmere Ltd, a specially set up company. She paid £305,000 and kept the label in the market but did not secure The Damned's Stiff catalogue.

"When Stiff went bankrupt, we said, 'Let's buy our catalogue,'" recalls Rat. "It was the *Phantasmagoria* line-up then and the conversation came with Roman and Bryn. 'This isn't you, why should you own these recordings?' 'Well we're promoting it, we're out there playing 'New Rose''. So, magnanimously, they said it should be a sixth each. I asked Brian and Captain if they wanted to do it and even offered to lend them the money to do it, but they both said no. We spent £8,000 and we had to recoup that. Then, later, Roman and Bryn agreed to sell it to me and Dave. At the time, Captain said it felt wrong to pay for his own work, why should he give money for it."

Asked about being offered a stake in the rights to The Damned's Stiff catalogue, Brian James says, "I was offered but had no money. I would never take out a loan, be in debt, I don't like the worry. Just one of those things."

The Damned, in the form of Fanpack Limited, the company they had already formed on July 23, 1986 to oversee their merchandising, now owned their Stiff catalogue. The directors were Mr Christopher Millar, Mr Roman Jug (sic), Mr Bryn Merrick and Mr David Vanian.[186] Mr Christopher Millar was also the company secretary. The catalogue was swiftly licensed to Demon Records and the first release, by the end of 1986, was a reconfigured *The Captain's Birthday* with the new title *Not The Captain's Birthday Party*?

As a way to mark ten years of The Damned, the business dealings were unlikely but no more so than MCA's promotion of the video for the this-close-to U2/Simple Minds 'Anything' single as "the first nude promo". David was seen in a shower singing as the rest of the band careened around a room sitting at a flying table while trying to eat a medieval banquet. For his role, David endured six hours in the shower.

★ ★ ★

Next, in January 1987, MCA issued the album track 'Gigolo' as a multi-format single and, again, they wanted another album. *Anything* was barely out and the label wanted more. "The end was never there," says Roman. "We were getting really really tired. Then you start physically suffering. Give us a break." In the promo video for 'Gigolo', as fluffy toys rained down upon them, Rat, Roman and Merrick looked barely engaged. Only David had some life in him.

"We sold more records, we had bigger audiences," adds Rat. "In those few years we outpaced everything The Damned had done before but, as we did it, we knew it was a fickle, hollow victory."

Once they realised a new studio album was a non-starter, MCA explored the possibility of releasing a live set. The November 12 Hammersmith Odeon show had been recorded on a 24-track mobile studio, but the tapes were archived and the idea abandoned. With no new songs and the knowledge that completing *Anything* in Denmark had increased their debt to the label massively, the band suggested they recorded demos at Elephant, the small Wapping studio where the Naz Nomad & The Nightmares album was completed. The label agreed and so, in January 1987, The Damned took musical stock on a restricted budget. Tracks were roughed out at Elephant, but nothing amounted to a finished recording and most of what was taped were vocal-free backing tracks as, for much of the time, David was not there.[187] Even so, there was the skeleton of a new album.

Instead of building on the foundations of what MCA wanted – a new album – The Damned set out on a continental European tour immediately after the time at Elephant. For six weeks, they slogged through Sweden, Denmark, West Germany, Italy, Spain, France, Belgium and the Netherlands. Two weeks off were followed by a month in New Zealand, Australia (where the bulk of the dates were played) and Japan.

"I got really dulled with two years of doing mostly the same set," says Rat. "Certain parts of the set, we could go walkabout. That's why we did 'Looking At You'. The *Phantasmagoria* and *Anything* songs didn't really stretch out. With 'In Dulce Decorum' we had to use the Emulator and if the wrong disc was put in, we'd be playing 'In Dulce Decorum' and the brass parts of 'Psychomania' would come in halfway through. The discs took so long to load in, an eternity."

MCA looked back to *Anything*, decided more promotion of the album was necessary to recoup the costs of recording in Denmark and chose 'Alone Again Or' as the next single. Issuing another cover version made business sense as it may have tapped into buyers of 'Eloise', but Roman says, "I always shied against doing another cover. For MCA: dollar signs."

The label organised a video shoot in Australia, at Broken Hill where the *Mad Max* films and ads for Castlemaine XXXX beer had been made. The pilot of the plane hired to take The Damned to this remote spot fell asleep at the controls and was woken by Roman. The preposterous promo – the nadir of the MCA videos and probably the most expensive to make[188] – featured Roman perched on a ladder with his guitar, David in a Zorro mask, Rat and Merrick in spaghetti western gear, a twirling flamenco dancer, a tanker truck, a man riding a motorbike and a small aeroplane swooping over the desert landscape.

Rat hadn't known the Love song until Roman had played it at PUK a year earlier. "I'd never heard 'Alone Again Or' before. I thought Roman had written it while I was back in London from Denmark for a few days. When I got back and they played me it, I thought Roman had knocked it up in a moment of inspiration." As a single on seven-inch, 12-inch and CD, it sold reasonably well and hit 27 in the UK charts.

There were only three British dates over June, July and August 1987, and a festival appearance in Sweden as well as another London show as Naz Nomad. No American tour was booked for 1987: MCA's declared strategy of aiming The Damned at America had come to nothing and 'Alone Again Or' had not set the table for anything. The Damned may as well have ceased to exist.

Late October and early November saw them working their way around the UK on the back of 'In Dulce Decorum''s release as a single – though this was a new mix, the song had been on the B-side of 'Alone Again Or' – a full year after it had been featured on *Miami Vice*.[189] And, still, MCA wanted that third album.

In October, MCA was appeased when a strategy to recoup some of their investment surfaced. "I came up with the best-of idea pretty much to sell the back catalogue," says Rat. "But MCA only wanted tracks from singles and albums which had been successful."

It was agreed The Damned would issue a career-spanning double compilation album for the Christmas market. The new *Light At The End Of The Tunnel* best-of was accompanied by a nine-track VHS tape of the band's promo videos (from 'New Rose' to 'Alone Again Or': there were no videos for 'Eloise' and 'In Dulce Decorum') and an approved biography of the same name by *Melody Maker*'s Carol Clerk, a long-term supporter. In the band's fan club magazine, *Light At The End Of The Tunnel* was trailed as "our ultimate compilation album", suggesting some sort of conclusion.

Phil Smee designed similar covers for the album, biography and videotape, and the book's publishers Omnibus Press met with MCA to co-ordinate a promotional campaign. "It didn't work out," says editor Chris Charlesworth. "The book came out fine. Carol did a great job under duress. We went for a meeting with a few people from MCA, talked about joint advertising and agreed to meet again in a couple of months. Nobody from the first meeting was at the second meeting. They'd all left the company, every single one. We just decided to put the book out regardless."

After *Light At The End Of The Tunnel* spent a week on the album charts in December, the year was rounded off with a show at Brixton's Academy and little sign The Damned were a going concern.

★ ★ ★

The beginning of 1988 became another of The Damned's low points. MCA had lost interest, but the contract between the band and label stood. A few live dates were played – a cover of John Leyton's early Sixties Joe Meek-produced musical psycho-drama 'Johnny Remember Me' was featured.

Then, in June, MCA let The Damned go. The label had cut their losses. The official band statement said, "We were dissatisfied with the way MCA marketed us as a pop product rather than a band. The

Damned has always been more interested in making good records rather than hit records and in quality rather than quantity; and as we wanted to start afresh the band decided to part company with our long-suffering manager – Andy Cheeseman."

"They dropped us," says Rat. "It wasn't a big drop. Kutner had left, we weren't worried about not being with that organisation. A new managing director, who hadn't signed us, didn't care." None of the music papers, even the biz-focused *Music Week*, reported the news.

Instead of starting afresh, the Town & Country Club was booked for two shows on June 12 and 13 which featured the original Brian, Captain, David and Rat configuration of The Damned playing one set of *Damned Damned Damned*, 1976-vintage songs. This was followed by a second set without Brian, during which Captain switched to guitar with Bryn Merrick on bass and Roman on keyboards for *Machine Gun Etiquette* and *Black Album* material. Brian joined in on the encore of 'Looking At You' and The Rolling Stones' 'The Last Time'.

Rather than this being the last time, a couple of shows with the current line-up were followed by a truncated, one-set version of the Town & Country revisitation of the past reprised at the second day of a massive Amnesty International benefit at Milton Keynes Bowl on June 19.[190] Over the two days, Aztec Camera, Go West (who had been recording in Denmark at PUK at the same time as The Damned in 1986), Howard Jones and The Icicle Works also appeared. Post-Live Aid, there was a glut of large-scale charity shows[191] but this was the only one featuring a handful of 1976-era punk veterans.[192] Mick Jones' Big Audio Dynamite and a solo Joe Strummer were also at Milton Keynes, as were Motörhead and The Stranglers.

Looking back at re-joining The Damned for the Town & Country and Milton Keynes shows, Brian says, "Out of blue, Rat said, 'Do you fancy doing some reunion gigs?' There was a lull in Lords Of The New Church and I thought, 'Yeah, that'll be fun.' I never played the songs with the Lords. It sounded good at the rehearsals. It was selfish, fun, playing all those old songs again."

Tagged as *Final Damnation*, the tapes – both audio and video – of the second Town & Country show were first issued in 1989 and became a mainstay of the ever-increasing, always confusing Damned archive reissue catalogue. Beyond this, despite reverting to the Bryn, David, Rat and Roman band after the reunion shows, this was the point where the live Damned explicitly began reordering the building blocks of their own past as they saw fit. Although Rat was at this point trying out a renewed liaison with Brian as jazz-inclined duo The Stink Insects, he was also working out how The Damned would make some headway. After Milton Keynes, an appearance at a festival in Lausanne, Switzerland which also featured the hard-edged, high-energy punk/R&B band The Godfathers gave him pause for thought.

"We were drained," he says. "We were all worn out. Then we did the show with The Godfathers in Switzerland. I really wanted [their guitarist] Kris Dollimore to play with us as I thought we'd dried up, to put some life in this band. It needed an injection of new life. Bryn was a pain in the ass and Roman just wasn't interested. The idea wasn't to get rid of Roman. I knew Roman would never stop playing guitar in The Damned." The thought was put on hold as the most perplexing conceptualisation of The Damned yet was about to play.

A week after the Swiss festival, on September 6, The Damned played London's Limelight Club. A Damned no one had seen before. One entirely conforming to David's vision. "It was Dave's thing about moving into the Fifties," notes Rat. "That was what he thought we should be doing." The Final Damnation shows had reanimated The Damned's own past. Now, it time to reanimate other musical pasts.

At the Limelight, Bryn and Roman had their hair combed back in quiffs. David was in biker leather. No Damned songs were played. Cover versions included Eddie Cochran's 'C'Mon Everybody', Peggy Lee's 'Fever', Roy Orbison's 'Pretty Woman', Elvis Presley's 'One Night With You', Gene Vincent's 'Be Bop A Lula' and the Link Wray instrumental 'Rumble'. There was no alter-ego, as there had been with Naz Nomad & The Nightmares. The Damned were a covers band.

Some American west coast dates in October mixed the rock'n'roll covers with familiar Damned songs but this shift and the reunion shows crossed a line. In February 1989, like the Naz Nomad-style pseudonymous Damned, a show was played as The Phantom Chords at south London pub The Cricketers, where more rock'n'roll–slanted material was performed. The Damned had become an animated jukebox, rummaging through their own past and David's particular tastes. Rat then set off to America to find The Damned a record deal. Rather than that, he managed to set up a tour for July in the spirit of the *Final Damnation* shows.

★ ★ ★

On Rat's return from America, there was a band meeting. "We met in a café in Kensington Church Street, me, Bryn, Dave and Rat," remembers Roman. "Vanian said, 'I'm leaving The Damned.' Rat said, 'What are you two doing?' I said, 'I'll probably work with Dave.' I turned to Bryn who said, 'I'll probably work with Dave.' So Rat said, 'Unofficially then, I've been sacked from The Damned.' Dave said, 'We're not going to be called that.' Rat said, looking at me but speaking to Dave, 'Will you do these shows in America?' Dave said yes. Rat said, 'You can pay for my meal' and walked out. So that was it."

Rat remembers it differently, that Bryn, David and Roman came to his house. "They had a biker mate of Bryn's as security, as they thought it was going to kick off," he recalls. "All three of them informed me that they'd left The Damned. Then and there. It was already done, they'd made the decision. I couldn't say anything. They were going with Dave in The Phantom Chords, there was no doubt about that. Roman was the one with the respect to tell me what was going on. Dave saw Roman as the writing talent, which he was. And he took Bryn."[193]

David and Rat had been together in The Damned from the beginning. They were the only constants. Now, their partnership was broken. The Damned was over.

Anything

In early summer 1986, The Damned were in a situation similar to that of 1977. It was a different line-up then, but history repeated itself. Their record label demanded an album when they weren't ready. This time, MCA wanted a follow-up to *Phantasmagoria* so sent them off to make an album when they were ground-down from touring. Also, there were no new songs. Before recording *Music For Pleasure* in 1977, they had some. Now, they had none.

On the positive side, an expectation The Damned were able to magic-up an album from thin air demonstrated an impressive faith in the band as a creative unit. As did – despite being chosen to ensure David was there for the sessions – booking a state-of-the-art studio in Denmark. MCA were behind the band. They were an investment to nurture. What became *Anything* was intended to consolidate the success of 'Eloise'. It was also, of course, meant to be more successful than *Phantasmagoria*.

One pair of shoulders bore most of the burden. Roman's. He was the first to arrive in Denmark, was there longest and, with *Phantasmagoria* producer Jon Kelly shaping the finished recordings, he found himself in the driving seat of The Damned's new album. For every song on *Anything*, his name came first in the egalitarian credits: Jugg/Scabies/Merrick/Vanian. As it was with *Phantasmagoria*, the album included an instrumental – 'The Portrait'– on which there was no evidence of David. He was still credited as one of the writers though.

Anything opened with its title track. For those familiar with the band, 'Anything' the song was bewildering. A riff and a series of crescendos in search of a melody, it could have passed for a Simple Minds song: one where hugeness of sound was paramount. David even seemed to buy into this with a vocal style drawing from both the Minds' Jim Kerr and U2's Bono. The album closed with another of these exercises in 1986-style stadium rock, the even-more melodically weak 'Psychomania'.

In between 'Anything' and 'Psychomania', *Anything*'s seven other tracks were as varied stylistically as they were – often – not fully formed. The album's credits suggested it may not be coherent and it was not. In addition to Jon Kelly, mixing was credited to Nigel Walker and Ken Thomas. Session keyboard player Blue Weaver (an expert with early digital keyboards) also appeared. With the instrumental 'The Portrait', the undeveloped nature of the melody wasn't such a problem as it was about setting a mood rather than making a mark as a traditional song. But, despite the delicate piano refrain and the polished production, it felt unfinished: a sketch. The same went for 'Restless'. The vocal melody was thin – and adding female vocals to echo David singing the title did not fill the song out. Most problematically, 'Restless' did not go anywhere. It wandered through its too-long five minutes.

However, 'In Dulce Decorum', which followed – despite more distracting Simple Minds touches, David's strained lead and some digitally generated backing vocals – was a proper song and as good as *Phantasmagoria*'s best tracks. The Damned had not fully given up the ghost. And notwithstanding its meandering and pointless album-only introductory section, the directly Syd Barrett referencing 'Gigolo' showed they still had the goods when it came to writing and recording a fine – if too glossily produced – pop song. The spy-theme sounding 'The Girl Goes Down' nodded back to *The Black Album*'s 'Twisted Nerve'. 'Tightrope Walk' was another unformed mood piece, this time with vocals. Which left 'Alone Again Or', a bright cover of the Love song: the album's most energised moment and manifestly – from MCA's 'Eloise'-bolstered perspective – a single.

Anything was problematic, but not entirely awful. This was a Damned album and, at times, recognisably so but it had been hijacked by the period's big production style and undermined by its weak songs. In the *Music Week* advertorial trailing the album, MCA's head of marketing said, "The Damned are now poised for maximum impact" and mentioned Duran Duran and Tears For Fears. The label's ideas about where *Anything* was taking them were far-fetched. Building on who they were would have made more sense than suggesting part of Duran Duran's audience may be theirs.

Still, the album was well designed. The pop-up figures which emerged on opening the sleeve were nice, as was the painted wooden carving made for the front cover. *Anything*'s packaging and artwork placed the band in a fairground setting. The photo inside the gatefold sleeve was distorted, as if seen in a hall of mirrors. But beyond linking the merry-go-round feel of the intro to the album version of 'Gigolo', it was hard to trace a connection between the design and the musical contents.

Anything was more likely to undermine The Damned than sell them.

CHAPTER FIFTEEN

A Not So Final Curtain

The end had come. It was announced in May 1989. Naturally, uncertainty accompanied the declaration. In *Sounds*, the news was reported under the heading "The Damned break all records". Ostensibly, "The Damned, the first punk band to reform, have become the first punk band to disband twice. They've decided to call it a day after 13 turbulent years and almost as many line-ups."

Then came the kicker. "But the original line-up of Dave Vanian and Rat Scabies plus guitarist Brian James[194] and the inimitable Captain Sensible have got back together for a series of farewell gigs. And long-time bassist Paul Gray will find himself guesting with his own band." British gigs were announced for June and July, along with the intention to play summer dates in America. Instead of vanishing, The Damned were stepping into rock's equivalent of *The Time Tunnel* to double-dial-up 1976 and 1977, and 1980 to 1982.

No reasons for the split were given in *Sounds*[195] but *Melody Maker* faithfully related the behind-the-scenes events: "The split happened after Vanian walked out of the group, taking bassist Bryn Merrick and guitarist Roman Jugg. All three are expected to continue working together. Scabies' plans are as yet unknown." Expect Scabies' plans were known: as it had been with the 1988 *Final Damnation* shows, he was behind the reunions. Whatever David had done, Rat was going to keep The Damned – or a version of it – going.

In the event, not only were the British dates played and American shows undertaken in July – to the same revue-style format as *Final Damnation*: a set by the original band followed by another from the Paul Gray line-up[196] – there were also UK shows in October and five more British shows in December. The latter were unconvincingly tagged "We Really Must Be Going Now". There were even a smattering of Naz Nomad & The Nightmares shows in October. It was hard to grasp how The Damned had called it a day and even tougher to see when David would find the time to work with Bryn Merrick and Roman on whatever he was planning.

One thing was certain. The Damned were no longer about advancing creatively. They were now dedicated to addressing their own past – and appealing to that section of their audience – rather than making new music. The way the split was announced accepted this. And as to how Roman Jugg and Bryn Merrick fitted in? They soldiered on in the resurrected Naz Nomad & The Nightmares.[197] Both had been in the most commercially successful Damned line-up but neither was invited on board for the farewell shows.

The fluidity makes pinpointing when The Damned ceased to be a functioning unit as opposed to a heritage band (i.e. one solely addressing its past) difficult. The first explicit winding back of the clock came in June 1988 with the *Final Damnation* reunion shows. These coincided with being dumped by MCA. Yet, Roman contends he felt the end had come while in Denmark at PUK Studios in summer 1986. Even so, when demos of new songs were recorded at Elephant Studio in Wapping in January 1987, looking towards the future was on the agenda then. There were markers, but conceding the end had arrived only came after David told Rat, Roman and Merrick that he was leaving the band.

Nevertheless, this being The Damned, David was back on stage with them at the end of June 1989 opening a tour advertised as "The Final Curtain". Twenty-five years later, he was still on stage with The Damned with no final curtain in sight.

★ ★ ★

Following a year mostly taken up by the hybrid farewell-reunion shows, David's new band, the Fifties/early Sixties-styled Phantom Chords, made their live debut proper in May 1990. Roman Jugg was the keyboard player, Bryn Merrick the bassist, Brendan Moon the guitarist and Clyde Dempsey the drummer.[198] A version of the John Leyton/ Joe Meek song 'Johnny Remember Me' was issued as a single[199] to coincide with this and other dates: they supported The Stray Cats at north London's Town & Country.

Despite playing regularly throughout 1990 and 1991, The Phantom Chords never took off. Merrick was dismissed in September 1991 due to his drinking and there were further line-up changes, though Roman stayed with the band up to the end of 1995. A second single, a version of 'Town Without Pity'[200], was issued on the small Camden Town label in 1992 and an album – credited to David Vanian & The Phantom Chords – released by Chiswick's Big Beat imprint in 1995.[201] The Phantom Chords travelled a bumpy road.

Captain's progress was also uneven. He had been dropped by A&M after 1987's 'Revolution Now' single[202] but remained active. The year before, he was cast as the Billiard Maker to sing 'The Snooker Song' in Mike Batt's stage adaptation of the Lewis Carroll poem *The Hunting of the Snark*. Although a May 1988 single, 'The Snooker Song' went on to attract national attention in 1991 as the theme to the BBC TV quiz show *Big Break*. It did not become a 'Happy Talk'-type distraction, impeding whatever else Captain wanted to do.

The 1989 Damned reunion shows had coincided with the release of Captain's first post-A&M solo album, also titled *Revolution Now*. Rat appeared on it. So did Paul Gray, Dolly Mixture's Rachael Bor[203] and Henry Badowski (who co-wrote 'The Coward Of Treason Cove').[204] It appeared on Captain's own label Deltic[205], which he launched in 1988. The money made from his time with A&M was poured into the venture, which hit the buffers in 1991. Records by Brotherhood Of Lizards (a psychedelically inclined duo featuring former Cleaners From Venus main-man Martin Newell), Johnny Moped, Sixties-ish pop group Smalltown Parade, ex-Advert TV Smith and The Damned's 'Fun Factory'[206] single were amongst those Captain issued on Deltic.

As for what traded as The Damned, once the 1989 shows were played, the next year saw nothing. There were no appearances in 1990. Perhaps The Damned really had bowed out.

★ ★ ★

While Captain's Deltic label headed towards its final releases and David endeavoured to create traction for The Phantom Chords, examination of the history of British punk was beginning with a detail usually applied to sociological studies. The 15 years elapsing since 1976 had to be an anniversary of note. The Damned just about got their due.

Some foundations had been laid. Cash-in books were published over 1977 and 1978 (the best of which were Caroline Coon's *1988: the New Wave Punk Rock Explosion* and Fred and Judy Vermorel's *Sex Pistols: The Inside Story*) but the first heavyweight book-length consideration of punk as a phenomenon was published in 1985. Dave Laing's *One Chord Wonders: Power and Meaning in Punk Rock* (an Open University Press publication) was academically dense yet stimulating. The tone is caught in his discussion of 'New Rose'. Laing said, "[the song] foregrounds the singer's elation rather than the 'her' with whom that feeling is associated". Of The Damned's name he asserted that "to say 'Damned' rather than 'Condemned' [curious: was this ever put forward as the name for the band?] was to evoke an extra layer of the supernatural in a media context to invoke the 1969 film by Visconti which caused a ripple of excitement or censure for its lurid presentation of Nazi decadence." And so on. As per its title, the book was about meaning and looking for it – even if it was not necessarily there.

A less brow-furrowing analysis came in 1987 with The Damned's own authorised biography – another first for them: they were the first British punk band to have an official book.[207] Carol Clerk's *Book Of The Damned: Light At The End Of The Tunnel – The Official Biography* was a headlong rush through the headlines to date and also the place to learn about a member of Anti-Nowhere League mucking about with a carrot. The band were paid an advance against royalties and owned the copyright, but subsequent entreaties by Clerk to publish

245

updated editions ran aground when The Damned's request for a further advance was not met by publisher Omnibus Press.[208]

The next one worth adding to the shelf was Sex Pistol Glen Matlock's almost anniversary-marking 1990 autobiography *I Was a Teenage Sex Pistol*.[209] The Damned featured. He illuminated the nature of the relationship between Malcolm McLaren and Jake Riviera: "McLaren got them [The Damned] on the [*Anarchy*] tour, despite the fact that he couldn't stand their manager. Jake came from a pub rock background and had no time for Malcolm who he saw as little more than a jumped-up schmutter merchant, with no understanding of the music or the business. Malcolm thought Jake was a real pleb. They hated each other." Without mentioning The Clash, Matlock also caught the punk rock pecking order: "Like it or not, these two enemies had ended up managing the number one and number two punk bands in the country."

All these broke the ground for what came in 1991, 15 years on from 1976. Jon Savage's *England's Dreaming: Sex Pistols and Punk Rock* was and remains the definitive statement on the evolution of British punk and brought context (including the international context) which, to date, had been lacking. He also teased out regionalism and ripple effects. Savage had written for *Sounds* and *Melody Maker*, was on board early and had his own punk fanzine in 1976. Of course, *England's Dreaming* was not about The Damned but concerned with Malcolm McLaren and the Sex Pistols. Everything else was core, but ultimately the book was about the beginning, middle and end of the Sex Pistols. Savage clarified the nature of The London SS properly for the first time and, even-handedly, placed The Damned as central to British punk. Memorably, he said "The Damned was the Bash Street Kids of punk; their lack of calculation and insistence on high-octane, hell-raising fun meant that their rapid rise was bedevilled by the impossibility of any planning. The Damned went out there and pulled faces at the world as if there was no tomorrow."

Four years later, in 1995, The Clash were subjected to exhaustive scrutiny for the first time in Marcus Grey's essential *Last Gang in Town: The Story and Myth of The Clash*. Grey laid it all out: the background of each member of The Clash, which bands they were in beforehand and the dynamic between Malcolm McLaren and Bernard Rhodes. The London SS were fundamental to the story, and The Damned were again shown to be central to what became British punk rock.

But neither *England's Dreaming* or *Last Gang in Town* were about The Damned. They were a building block in the story. And once the Sex Pistols and Clash were up and running in the narratives, The Damned were dropped off in a narrative lay-by.

John Lydon was also unconcerned with The Damned as an entity in their own right. In his 1993 autobiography *Rotten: No Irish, No Blacks, No Dogs*[210], he had no truck with them. "We never saw ourselves as being in a punk movement," he stressed. "What the rest of them were up to was neither here nor there. They weren't there at the beginning. They just came in and sat on our coattails. Rat Scabies and The Damned, he used to say, 'My band is better that yours!' Yes, Rat. He used to roadie for us." By the time the loquacious Lydon put out a second autobiography, 2015's *Anger Is an Energy: My Life Uncensored*[211], the ever-capricious Sex Pistol shifted ground to perhaps accept punk as a movement. But he still wasn't mad-keen on The Damned. "We [the Sex Pistols] weren't the first punk band to sign a deal. The Damned did that some time before us, which was bizarre – using our punk moniker and beating us to the alleged punch."

The historiography of British punk carved out in the years 1990 to 1993 recognised The Damned's centrality and that they were there from (close to) the beginning. Even so, there was scant interest in what happened to them after 1977. After then, The Damned were of little concern to the story of British punk.

★ ★ ★

The Damned returned to the stage in September 1991. *England's Dreaming* had been published 15 years on from 1976 and, after their last shows in December 1989, they were also marking the anniversary. Following a couple of British Damned shows, David put The Phantom Chords on hold to join Brian[212], Captain, Rat and Paul Gray in America for a month-long US tour. The format was familiar: a set by the original four-piece followed by one with Captain switching guitar and Paul Gray playing bass. There was no keyboard player. It did not go to plan. Brian bailed out after the third date, at Washington DC's 9.30 Club.

On stage, at the end of the first set on that third date, Captain introduced 'New Rose' as "This one's written by Guns N' Roses." The band knew the then-massive Guns N' Roses were considering recording a cover version and Brian, as the writer, had no desire to jeopardise it happening. Reacting to Captain's remark, Brian threw down his guitar and left the stage. He told Captain that any money coming his way would be good for his family. The tour continued without him.[213] Washington was the last time Brian played anywhere with a band billed as The Damned.

In the event, Guns N' Roses' 'New Rose' was released on November 1993's all-covers *The Spaghetti Incident?* album together with versions of songs the metallers liked or considered integral to their DNA: songs from punk precursors The Stooges and The New York Dolls toughed it out with tracks originally recorded by Fear, The Misfits, The UK Subs, post-Pistols outfit The Professionals and The Dead Boys.[214] *The Spaghetti Incident?* was a worldwide best-seller. The songwriters whose material Guns N' Roses' chose to record enjoyed a financial windfall. The album was also an acknowledgement of America's debt – and that of Guns N' Roses' home city Los Angeles in particular – to British punk rock; The Damned's early influence on west coast punk (and how it bled into metal) had not been forgotten.

Without Brian, The Damned continued playing into summer 1992: sometimes, Naz Nomad & The Nightmares – David, Rat, Roman Jugg and Phantom Chords bassist Donagh O'Leary – were the support band. The Phantom Chords also undertook strings of dates. The Damned's default status as a heritage band was duly confirmed.

★ ★ ★

Once the reunion shows were over[215], and with Brian unlikely to take the stage again with Captain, Rat began casting around for a new outlet. A new Damned was in the offing.

Rat was playing with Brian in an impromptu, unnamed outfit alongside Killing Joke bassist Raven and guitarist Alan Lee Shaw.[216] Rat and Shaw had a new song called 'Testify'. The quartet never went anywhere, but Rat kept working with Shaw. They hooked up with former New Model Army bassist Moose (Jason Harris) and thought about finding a singer. As a trio, they recorded some instrumental demos which they played to David. He didn't like them. Then Rat found out The Godfathers had split and cast his mind back to when they played with The Damned in Switzerland in 1988. Godfathers guitarist Kris Dollimore was duly ushered in to what was turning into a band. The songs were worked on more, played to David and, this time, he came on board. Exit Shaw.

The new David Vanian, Rat Scabies, Dollimore and Moose Damned made their public debut on BBC Radio 1's Mark Radcliffe show on November 23, 1993. A version of 'Neat Neat Neat' was accompanied by three new songs: 'Testify', 'Never Could Believe' and 'I Need A Life'. A week later, they played a low-key London show in north London at Tufnell Park's Dome as The Damagement. Always the bridesmaids, The Phantom Chords were – once again – put on hold.

This, then, was The Damned now seen in Britain, America, continental Europe and Japan. Although a couple of Phantom Chords shows were played in 1994, it was a full-time band until March 1995, after which David brought The Phantom Chords back to life. The last time the Vanian, Scabies, Dollimore and Moose Damned were on stage was July 1995.

As reconfigurations of The Damned went, this was the most curious to date. The guitarist and bassist had no historic ties with The Damned. Old songs were played live, including 'Disco Man', 'Gun Fury', 'Love Song', 'New Rose', 'Nasty', 'Noise, Noise, Noise' and 'Smash It Up'. New ones included 'My Desire', 'Not Of This Earth', 'Running Man' and 'Tailspin'. Most of the lyrics and much of the new music was by the departed Alan Lee Shaw. None of it was Dollimore's, though he was the guitarist. The sound was hard, with a 12-bar blues edge. In Damned-world, it had no immediate stylistic precursor and, in general, did not relate to anything The Damned had done before. But at least it wasn't wholly about the past.

Recording sessions were undertaken while the band was touring Germany.[217] The all-new tracks were issued in November 1995 in Japan as the instantly contentious *Not Of This Earth* album. David has said he understood it as a Japan-only release issued to generate income to make another album. Effectively, he has said, these were demos to be further worked on and that Captain was going to play on them too. Rat and Alan Lee Shaw have said David wanted to be given songwriting credits even though, they maintain, he had no input. When it was issued, all the album's songs were credited to Rat and Shaw.[218] David has also said it "wasn't a Damned album", that he wanted his vocals erased and its release meant he felt he was "being shafted".

Inevitably, the *Not Of This Earth* Damned ground to a halt and David directed his attention back towards The Phantom Chords. Then, in 1996, Rat issued the album in the UK on his own label under the title *I'm Alright Jack And The Beanstalk*.[219] It also came out in America. Of Rat and his own involvement with the *Not Of This Earth/I'm Alright Jack And The Beanstalk* album, David said it was "a bitter, horrible, twisted end to our friendship".

David and Rat would not work together again.

★ ★ ★

Commercially, the past now held even more appeal. But marketing The Damned's history as a unified entity was tricky. If the *Not Of This Earth/ I'm Alright Jack And The Beanstalk* album is excluded, The Damned's official discography was still a muddle. By the time it was released, The Damned had made seven albums: *Damned Damned Damned*, *Music For Pleasure*, *Machine Gun Etiquette*, *The Black Album*, *Strawberries*, *Phantasmagoria* and *Anything*.

They had come out on four labels: Stiff, Chiswick, Bronze and MCA. Stiff no longer existed, and the rights to The Damned's recordings had been sold as part of the bankruptcy process. Chiswick – under the name Ace – was still trading. Bronze was not and its catalogue was sold on. MCA was no longer a stand-alone concern and, in due course, became part of the Universal group. Even if singles and EPs on other labels and future changes of hands were ignored, this was all very untidy.

With 'Happy Talk' an unexpected [hi]t, Captain plays up for the [n]ational press in his bedroom at [hi]s parents' house. July 1982.
[NI]LS JORGENSEN/REX/SHUTTERSTOCK

[A]t MIDEM, the French music [b]usiness conference, Captain [lar]ks about with Dolly Mixture [l]eft to right: Rachel Bor, [D]ebsey Wykes, Hester Smith). [Ja]nuary 1983.
[M]ILLS PRESS/MICHAEL/REX/SHUTTERSTOCK

The Damned record without Captain as Naz Nomad & The Nightmares at Wapping's Elephant Studios. Bassist Bryn Merrick (Paul Gray's replacement) photographed by Rat as the *Give Daddy The Knife Cindy* album is taped. December 1983. RAT SCAB

Rat captures Damned keyboard player Roman Jugg tackling guitar at the *Give Daddy The Knife Cindy* sessions. December 19
RAT SCABIES

...eviously unseen shot for *Sounds* to promote the 'Thanks For The Night'/ 'Nasty' single. Though Captain was still in the band, ...y David and Rat attended the photo session. June 1984. PAUL SLATTERY

What became The Damned's final promotional shot with Captain in the band. David at the front and behind, left to right, Roman Captain, Bryn, Rat. August 1984. RAT SCABIES

No one knew it then, but Rat was photographing Captain's last rehearsal with The Damned. His jumper quotes lyrics from the recent 'Nasty' single. August 1984. RAT SCABIES

Reflective self-portrait by Rat. August 1984. RAT SCABIES

Captain's first engagement after leaving The Damned: singing to backing tracks of his songs in a newspaper competition winner's living room. September 1984.

On the set of the 'Grimly Fiendish' promo video. David set his hair alight. February 1985. RAT SCABIES

The Damned

orld-wide success. On tour, in Chicago. March 17, 1986. PAUL NATKIN/WIREIMAGE

two 'Eloise' vocalists. Rat catches Barry Ryan and David during The Damned's appearance on TV programme *The Tube*.
cember 19, 1986. RAT SCABIES

David poses for Rat's camera at Elephant Studios, Wapping. January 1987. RAT SCABIES

Back to the beginning. The original Damned reunited in June 1989. KEITH MORRIS/REDFERNS/GETTY IMAGES

The Clash were the subjects of 1991's retrospective box set *Clash On Broadway* as it was (relatively) easy to compile: while extant, they were with one label. Any such project with The Damned would be an organisational nightmare.

A parallel strand of reissues and archive releases further complicated matters. By 1996, the band's 20th anniversary, *Damned Damned Damned* had been reissued in the UK at least four times. Around ten live albums were available: some of which plucked bits from a few and added them together to make a supposedly new package. Whole albums of demos, never intended for release, were in the shops.[220]

Of course, there were good, diligent reissues amongst this onslaught but the net effects were: to obscure what The Damned were actually about; to render their history incomprehensible; to devalue the original recordings which were actually released; and imply – whether or not the band had anything to do with the releases – that they did not care about their recorded legacy. The Damned's catalogue was – and remains – in disarray and does them no favours.

The damage inflicted on their back catalogue was doubly unfortunate as it did little to rescue The Damned from knee-jerk perceptions. When 2001 came along – the 25th anniversary of 1976 – Britain got its first large-format, apparently all-encompassing glossy coffee-table punk rock book: Stephen Colegrave and Chris Sullivan's *Punk: A Life Apart*. The 100 Club Punk Festival was covered, but The Damned were not mentioned. Elsewhere, when they briefly were, the authors said, "The Damned were, in many people's eyes, an aberration, a punk cartoon." Whose eyes in particular was not divulged.

Yet The Damned were not going away. After *Not Of This Earth* was issued in Japan and before it re-emerged as *I'm Alright Jack And The Beanstalk*, The Phantom Chords were billed with Captain at north-west London's Mean Fiddler. It was December 9, 1995 and another new Damned wasn't far off. One which, bar a few line-up changes, outlived all previous Damneds.

Backstage, that December, Captain and David were chatting. David said it wasn't going so well for his band and wondered if Captain wanted to team up with him. Although he had issued the superb concept album

The Universe Of Geoffrey Brown in 1993, Captain was treading water. At this point, he was promoting the unwieldy and recently released double CD-album *Meathead*: an over-the-top science-fiction/fantasy tinged outpouring featuring 32 songs.

When David asked, Captain said yes. As the door on one long-time relationship closed – David's with Rat – another had been renewed. Live dates were set for February 1996.

★ ★ ★

Captain and David were back in the same band for the first time since Brockwell Park on August 4, 1984. The Essex town Harlow witnessed the reunion, the debut appearance of another new Damned. One in which Rat no longer played a part. The band he and Brian formed had shut him out.

In Harlow, on February 8, 1996 the newly reunited singer and guitarist were joined by Paul Gray, who had been playing in Captain's band. Drummer Gary Dreadful (Gary Priest) and keyboard player Monty Oxymoron[221] (Montgomery Gillan) were also transplants from Captain's band. 'Love Song' was played first, laying the table for a greatest hits set ranging through 'Dozen Girls', 'New Rose' and 'Plan 9 Channel 7'.

There were rebirthing pains. Two days on, in Birmingham, they had to be billed as "Dave Vanian, Captain Sensible, Paul Gray ex-members of The Damned" as Rat had claimed he had the rights to use the name "The Damned". Then, two weeks after Harlow, David did not turn up for the third comeback show at Cardiff's Hippo Club. On stage, a message was read out announcing, "That bastard Vanian has not turned up. We are appalled. If you leave now, you may have your money back. If you stay, the Captain and the rest of the band will play your favourites." Captain and the rest of the band did, but only after he referred to "that fucking bastard Vanian".

A couple of days later, for an all-punk bill at Kentish Town's Forum, David was back. Paul Gray though was soon off – for good. At the Forum, he was hit in the face by a glass chucked from the audience. He left and David's future wife, Patricia Morrison, stepped in as the bass player.[222] Now, the band were playing as "Dave Vanian & Captain

Sensible Ex-Damned". They became The Damned in September 1996. Garry Dreadful played his last show with them in December (also at the Forum). His replacement, Spike T. Smith[223], debuted with them in February 1999 and was gone by September when he was, in turn, replaced by Pinch (Andrew Pinching).[224] At different times, both drummers had been in British punk-metal band English Dogs.

The Damned were now Captain, David, bassist Patricia Morrison, keyboard player Monty Oxymoron and drummer Pinch. Just short of four years on from Captain and David agreeing to reinstate their working relationship at the Mean Fiddler, they had a line-up which was a keeper.

Once Captain and David had returned to stages together in February 1996, what they performed was about the past. There were airings of everything expected: 'Love Song', 'New Rose' and 'Smash It Up'. 'Eloise', released when Captain had not been in the band, was played. So was 'The Snooker Song'.

Whether it was Australia or Japan, the United States or a punk festival in Bath, a ticket bought entry to a mix-and-match show drawing on most aspects – *Music For Pleasure* never figured – of The Damned's past. Other itches were scratched – Captain released his *Mad Cows & Englishmen* solo album in 1996 – but this particular resurrected Damned was all about who they were, not who they could be.

★ ★ ★

Brian had retreated from public view after he bailed out from the 1991 American reunion tour. Living in France, he was content that Guns N' Roses had recorded 'New Rose'. The song was a classic, and acknowledged as such by a wider world than ever. Low-key solo recordings as The Dripping Lips confirmed that looking back was not on his agenda. Rat too was not part of The Damned. The Damned he created over 1993 to 1995 had been stopped in its tracks by the disorder surrounding the *Not Of This Earth/I'm Alright Jack And The Beanstalk* album. David's Phantom Chords cropped up again at the end of 1999 and in summer 2000, but his bread and butter was now The Damned with Captain and their live reiterations of who they were. But there were signs the past wasn't the only game in town. A new song, David's 'Absinthe', was played in 2000. 'She' and 'song.com', both written by Captain and David, entered live sets.

Confirmation that The Damned – Captain, David, Patricia Morrison, Monty Oxymoron and Pinch – was a creative entity came in August 2001 with the US-recorded *Grave Disorder* album. Dexter Holland, of American band The Offspring, had brought The Damned to his own label[225], Nitro Records. The 13 new songs were recorded at Venice, California's Mad Dog Studio with producer David Bianco. This was not small beer: Bianco was a hot contemporary producer and had worked with Teenage Fanclub and Buffalo Tom. Mad Dog was the facility favoured by singer-songwriter Aimee Mann. Once again, America's west coast embraced The Damned. *Grave Disorder* was a fine album, setting the dark off against Captain's poppy sensibility. It was also the most consistent album issued under the name The Damned since *Strawberries*.

Despite having to pull out of a March–April 2002 US tour as support to Rob Zombie – a musical mismatch the headliner's audience had little time for – The Damned had said they were not only about their past. Touring put dinners on their tables. This became more necessary after Patricia Morrison left the band in March 2004: she and David were to become parents. Her replacement as bassist was Stu West, another former member of English Dogs.[226] As it had been from 1984 when Roman Jugg and Bryn Merrick had both been in another band together – Victimize – before being in The Damned, it was again. Two former members of English Dogs were in The Damned.

The new line-up was another keeper. Captain, David, Monty Oxymoron, Pinch and West have remained together as The Damned which released the also-fine *So, Who's Paranoid?* album in 2008.

This is The Damned. The Damned which continues. A Damned without Brian and Rat. And a Damned which caused the Reverend Stephen Leeke of Cambridge's St Martin's Church to raise objections when they were invited to switch on the city's Christmas lights. "I do not think they are the best people to be switching on the Christmas lights," said the Reverend in November 2004. "I think perhaps it would be more appropriate for them to switch them off. It just seems to me to be a bit of a culture clash in launching the city's Christmas celebrations with a group who really haven't been renowned with looking at the positive side of life and Christian principles." The Damned switched them on.

Captain set out his principles in September 2006 when he launched the Blah! Party, a new political party dedicated to, as its press release put it, "chang[ing] the current political landscape and directly challeng[ing] the major political parties to forget spin and rhetoric and deliver on the promises that they make. The Blah! Party offers a real alternative for no-nonsense, straight-talking people who are disenchanted with the irrational and senseless aspects of everyday life and of modern-day politics."

"The Blah! Party simply demands accountability and honesty for the actions and decisions that are taken by individuals and politicians," said Captain. "We will fight for simple answers to straightforward questions. We believe in the right to an opinion, the right to question, the right to disapprove and the right to change things for the better – we want to see the current leading parties pull their socks up, stop spouting hot air, and actually deliver on their promises." The Blah! Party, which failed to attract serious support, became history. Captain, though, kept in the public eye by uploading a string of charming, self-made footage to the internet – much of it centring on his love of trains.

Anniversaries also came and went. Some were celebrated. Others were not. The 25th anniversary of *Machine Gun Etiquette* was marked in concert by the current Damned. In July 2006, the 30th anniversary of the first show was acknowledged when Brian, Rat[227], former Stone Roses bassist Mani and ex-Amen frontman Casey Chaos took the stage at London's 100 Club to play 1976-vintage songs. There were a few similar shows in 2009 and 2010 and more, in 2012 and 2013, under the banner "Scabies & James play *Damned Damned Damned*" – with singers and bassists as necessary. Brian and Rat were making the point that the story of The Damned was theirs as much as it was Captain and David's.

Messy. How much so became clear in 2015.

★ ★ ★

On March 18, 2015 a new film premiered at Austin Texas' South By Southwest festival. The director was Wes Orshoski, whose previous picture was the well-regarded documentary *Lemmy*, about Motörhead's then seemingly eternal leader. The new film was *The Damned: Don't You Wish That We Were Dead*, a band-authorised, feature-length examination of The Damned, the first in-depth biopic about them.

Captain was present at the premier. He had not seen the film beforehand. When Rat appeared on the screen, he shouted "rubbish". After leaving the auditorium as the film rolled, he returned, registering his disapproval by wandering the aisle offering sweets to the audience. David was also in Texas but did not attend the screening. His message to those gathered was "tell them I died this morning".

The history was there but Orshoski – a massive fan who spent three years on the project – was also presented with raw material laying out the conflicts between the members of the band. No one was shy, and the footage was used. It also caught the extremely sad way Paul Gray and Bryn Merrick – who died on September 12, 2015 – had been brought together when they were both treated for cancer at Cardiff's Llandough Hospital. Rat was seen saying his relationship with Captain was "beyond repair". Talking about how The Damned had messed up brought him to tears.

After the screening, Captain addressed the audience. "All bands have got these skeletons in the closet, and there's no exception. I love Brian, and Rat as well. That thing we did in 1977 will last forever but the only problem is there's only room for one guitarist in The Damned. At the moment it's me. It was Roman last week and it was Brian the week before. What can you do? I'm not going to give me job up because I enjoy it. It's a fucking good laugh. There's much more important things going on in the world than the history of The Damned. We're just a bunch of drunken cunts."

As a way of encapsulating a legacy, it was funny. Pithy too. But it did not sum it all up. Doing that would have kept him on stage for hours, much longer than the running time of *The Damned: Don't You Wish That We Were Dead*. There *are* more important things going on in the world than the history of The Damned but, as the audience and Wes Orshoski knew, the history of The Damned is important.

EPILOGUE

The Damned Brand

September 16, 2016. Brian James and David Vanian are seen on stage together for the first time since the bust-up in Washington on September 24, 1991. It's not an exact 25 years as the dates don't quite align, but they weren't reuniting to mark this but another two anniversaries: 40 years since the emergence of British punk and 40 years since September 1976's 100 Club Punk Festival.

Rather than playing, Brian and David instead sit side-by-side on chairs placed on the 100 Club's stage. They've been brought together by BBC television's early evening magazine programme *The One Show* for an item celebrating the anniversary of punk. Studio-based host Alex Jones introduces them as "[from] the band that started it all".

As the pre-recorded report moved into the field and onto the stairs of the 100 Club, Brian and David were introduced with a scrambled chronology ('New Rose' was apparently issued a few months after the festival). No matter, The Damned were getting their due. And the studio introduction was right. The Sex Pistols were already there, yet The Damned were the first: the first band to pick up the baton and, of course, the first to release a record.

"It was never us saying we want to do that before anyone else does. It was more a case of 'we were ready'," David told Britain's viewers about being the first on record.

257

"Even if it all stopped there," added Brian. "We did it."

The story of the band's formation was sketched out, with David stressing "it would be us against the world".

Each looked comfortable with the other. There was no uneasy body language. David was biker-bedenimed smart, in round-framed glasses with a professorial air. Brian was heavier than he had been but still had the air of a classic rock'n'roll guitarist. They were asked if they had been anarchists.

"No," Brian retorted. "Personally speaking, never. The only anarchy that I was interested in was on stage, the music. Where there's no bars. I love avant-garde jazz and I wanted to play rock'n'roll like that. I wanted freedom." As the item wound down, Brian was seen without David but with a pick-up band playing 'New Rose'. It was noted that Dave Vanian and Captain Sensible are still touring as The Damned. There was no talk of a reunion.

★ ★ ★

That the 40th anniversary of punk was worth marking was stressed by tying the *One Show* item in to the exhibition *Punk 1976–78*, running at The British Library, the national library of the United Kingdom. The story of punk was playing out in an institutional setting also exhibiting the *Magna Carta*, the nation's most significant constitutional document. On *The One Show*, The British Library's Andy Lineham said, "What punk did was question the status quo and look at the way things were done. To reflect the fact that punk was central to the culture in the late Seventies, it's very important that we collect the records, the print material, everything that goes with it so that people in the future can actually compare mainstream culture with the counter-culture."

Punk wasn't quite everywhere in 2016 but it was pervasive. In the capital, *Punk.London*, tagged as celebrating "40 years of subversive culture", was trailed as "a year of events, gigs, films, talks, exhibits and more celebrating 40 years of punk heritage and influence in London". Its sponsors included the Mayor of London. The *Punk.London* events included photographic exhibitions and the publication of a useful guide explaining "where to be punk in London". At The British Library, on June 8, David and Captain were interviewed on stage, in front of an audience. Rat's leather jacket was also seen in the library's *Punk 1976–78* exhibition.

The Damned – the Captain and David Damned – had a good 2016. They sold out the Royal Albert Hall on May 20. Brian and Rat were not in the audience. There were two strings of dates in America. They played Ireland, Norway, Portugal and Sweden. In early winter, billed as "The Damned featuring Dave Vanian and Captain Sensible", they toured the UK and played the whole of *Damned Damned Damned*. The tour was promoted as "celebrating the 40th anniversary of 'New Rose'".

The tour's promotional material declared "Punk legends The Damned have announced a huge UK tour taking in more than 20 towns and cities across the UK, and have revealed they are currently working on a brand new album for 2017. Celebrated as the most entertaining of the original punk bands, The Damned were the very first British band to release a punk single, the first to release an album and also the first to tour America. From the very first moment they started playing live in tiny punk clubs in 1976, The Damned quickly gained a reputation as a band who would always deliver an accomplished live set."

There hadn't been such a push since the MCA days. Percussion company Spaun manufactured a snare drum commemorating their 40th anniversary. The selling price of £506 included a pair of tickets to a show and the chance to meet the band. Signed wall clocks were on sale: 25 of them, at £20 apiece. £100 netted entrance to a "40th Anniversary Of 'New Rose' Celebration Q&A Event" at the Hope & Anchor where Captain would DJ and be interviewed by Jonh Ingham – who, for *Sounds*, wrote their first live review. The admission price also included a new pressing of 'New Rose' and a T-shirt. Another reissue of *Damned Damned Damned* was on the horizon.

This time though, The Damned had no record label behind them. Most of the promotion was in their own hands. Anniversaries sell and all power to them. But the media interest was mostly about the very earliest years. Except for fashion magazine *Vogue*, that is. In October, they marked David's 60th birthday with an article headed "Happy Birthday to The Damned's Dave Vanian, Goth Style Icon". "His flair for aesthetics has never waned," it said and pointed to "hair slicked back [in 1976], and single skeleton earring jangling; undead in appearance, yet so, so alive... the shock of white hair in a mane of black and frilled shirts circa 'Eloise' in the Eighties and later stylistic nods to steampunk and even silent film stars." He had, in 1976, "emerged with [his] macabre sartorial sensibilities fully formed".

★ ★ ★

Live, in 2016 on stages in America, France, Germany, Ireland, Norway, Portugal, Sweden and at home, 'Alone Again Or', 'Eloise', 'Shadow Of Love' and 'Street Of Dreams' were played: all released on MCA by a Damned which Captain was not in. 'Fan Club', 'Neat Neat Neat' and 'New Rose' were also played: all Brian James songs on which he originally played guitar rather than Captain.

Such is nostalgia. Boundaries are blurred. The difference between one thing and another is elided. The Damned playing live offered a direct line back to 1976, and a short-cut to any version of the band, from almost any era. In Austin, Texas, in March 2015, after the premier screening of *The Damned: Don't You Wish That We Were Dead*, Captain remarked that he had to accept that The Damned were a brand. And, as outlandish as it was, this is what 2016 confirmed. The name The Damned had become shorthand for anything or everything punk represented.

It was also shorthand for anything and everything The Damned represented, not all of which was necessarily punk in the classic, default or, even, any sense. Whether it was 'Happy Talk' – played live in 2016 – or the everlasting knowledge that they were the first British punk band to release a single. Or it could be *Machine Gun Etiquette*, a flawless, timeless rock album. The grandeur of 'Shadow Of Love'? Perhaps simply that they had a drummer called Rat Scabies?

Everyone has their own Damned. But no other band born in the Seventies has such a legacy, one which can be all things to all fans. More significantly, it's a legacy which ensures The Damned will always have their place in history.

Methodology And Acknowledgments

Everything in *Smashing It Up* is based on testimony and what happened. The text is written according to what the protagonists have said, was broadcast and reported, and what is in record label archives.

All unattributed quotes are from interviews conducted by the author and, in seven specific noted cases, Peter Watts, who kindly supplied transcriptions of interviews he conducted with Captain Sensible and David Vanian in 2016.

Quotes given in the present tense (i.e. says, explains, remembers, and so on) are from the author's and Peter Watts' interviews.

Quotes given in the past tense (i.e. explained, noted, said, and so on) are from interviews contemporaneous with the relevant part of the narrative. No after-the-fact print, broadcast or internet sources are quoted – in these cases, this is what was said at the time as events occurred, not quotes drawing on memory.

Contemporaneous raw information is plentiful. The Damned were blessed with a rolling news service in the music press reporting their activities from shortly after the band formed. In *Sounds*, Jonh Ingham reviewed their third live show. *Sniffin' Glue* interviewed them following the same show: their first interview. They developed in public and, being who they were, nothing was hidden. This went on until early 1978, when they first split. After that, interest was less abundant and interviews were usually pegged to record releases and tours. Nonetheless, The Damned were always good copy and worth covering. Press interest did not dry up.

The three prime press sources have been original hard copies of the music weeklies *Melody Maker*, *NME* and *Sounds*, all copies of which over the period March 1976 to February 1989 were combed through. As well as providing source material, they brought a chronology which, through comparison between the papers, is confirmed as accurate. The weekly *Record Mirror* was also valuable, as were the (usually dispassionate) *Music Week* and *Zigzag*, all – as was every other print source, bar two – scrutinised in their original hard copy form.

The Damned were well served by their regular supporters at the music weeklies: Carol Clerk and Allan Jones at *Melody Maker*, Giovanni Dadomo at (mainly) *Sounds*, Barry Cain (*Record Mirror*) and Jonh Ingham (*Sounds*). Nick Kent, Tony Parsons and Charles Shaar Murray (*NME*), Pete Silverton (*Sounds*) and Mat Smith (*Melody Maker*) were also adept chroniclers.

Of the British weeklies, after early 1978, *NME* had the least time for The Damned. Paul Morley's spectacularly patronising *NME* article *Damned & Deliver* (October 16, 1982) is – Morley's own perspective aside – the prime example of received attitudes towards The Damned informing how they were written about.

They did get a bum rap, and this has rung down through the years. For example, *Music For Pleasure* has been described as being panned when it was released. Not so. The contemporary reviews were critical, but did not treat the album badly and looked for positives. Similarly, in 1977, there was no consorting-with-old-farts hoo-hah in relation to Nick Mason being their producer. Just as learning this was instructive, so was finding the source of old chestnuts such as the one about *Damned Damned Damned* being speeded up after it was recorded. It was said in one malicious review, in *Zigzag*, and said nowhere else at the time.

Other useful publications were *Flexipop*, *Punk Lives*, *Smash Hits* and the fanzines *Allied Propaganda*, *Grim Humour*, *Ripped & Torn* and *Sniffin' Glue*. The American magazines/fanzines *Big Star*, *Search & Destroy* and *Slash* were trawled too, as were, in the only cases of exclusively online archive searches, the US trade mags *Billboard* and *Variety*.

In books, The Damned are either bit-part players or amongst the supporting cast in what are, often, accounts of lesser bands or about less important subjects. A shame. Beyond wanting to tell this important story, this was one of the motivations for writing *Smashing It Up*. The story of The Damned needs to stand on its own. Important and need are strong words, but they are the right ones. Books consulted are listed in the bibliography.

There is no one story of The Damned but, until any band members write their own, this is the one there is. In the introduction to his Clash biography *Last Gang in Town*, Marcus Gray noted, "It would be unwise to claim that *Last Gang in Town* tells the truth, the whole truth and nothing but the truth; but it should take you considerably closer to the truth than you are now." The same applies to *Smashing It Up*.

This is an extraordinary, memorable story. One of a band which never gave up. In their October 1980 press release for *The Black Album*, Chiswick Records said of The Damned that, "They've had enough bullets pumped into them to kill dozens of bands, yet they reappear stronger and more durable after each setback." As of writing in 2016, whatever anyone says about the (usually self-inflicted) "curse of The Damned", it remains the case.

Smashing It Up has come about thanks to all those who have told their stories, either to the author, to Peter Watts or to the writers who witnessed the narrative unfolding: the part of the narrative they were there to witness, that is.

Smashing It Up could not have happened without, at various and sometimes often times, interviewees Ray Burns (Captain Sensible), Lu Edmonds, Brian James, Roman Jugg, Chris Millar (Rat Scabies), David Vanian and Algy Ward of The Damned, as well as Roger Armstrong, Steve Kutner, Shel Talmy and Debsey Wykes.

It also would not have happened without (again) Roger Armstrong (who, after opening the filing cabinets, took even more time to dig out further detail), David Barraclough (Omnibus Press), Kate Booker (picture licensing), Sarah Burton (The Society of Authors), Chris Charlesworth (Omnibus Press), Peter Doggett, Russell Gould, Matthew Hamilton (Aitken Alexander), Anthony Keen, Peter Watts and my wife Joni Tyler.

Thanks are also due to Barry Cain, Antony Clayton, Andrew Czezowski, Larry DeBay, Lora Findlay, Thomas H Green, Steve Hammonds, John Ingham, Bill Inglot, Oleg Moiseeff, Amarinta Reeves, Wes Orshoski, Phil Smee, Bob Stanley, Richard Strange and Mark Stratford.

Without The British Library, its collections and its always helpful staff, *Smashing It Up* would not exist. The assistance of this outstanding institution cannot be understated. Long may it endure. And long may The Damned endure.

Bibliography

Balls, Richard, 2014, *Be Stiff: The Stiff Records Story*, Soundcheck Books

Burchill, Julie and Parsons, Tony, 1978, *The Boy Looked at Johnny: The Obituary of Rock and Roll*, Pluto Press

Carrington, Susan and Czezowski Andrew, 2016, *The Roxy: London, Covent Garden, 14 December 1976–23 April 1977*, Carrczez Publishing Ltd

Clerk, Carol, 1987, *The Book of the Damned: Light at the End of the Tunnel – The Official Biography*, Omnibus Press

Colegrave, Stephen and Sullivan, Chris, 2001, *Punk: A Life Apart*, Cassell & Co

DeSavia, Tom and Doe, John, 2016, *Under the Big Black Sun: A Personal History of L.A. Punk*, Da Capo Press

Frith, Simon, 1978, *The Sociology of Rock*, Constable and Company Ltd

Garner, Ken, 1993, *In Session Tonight: The Complete Radio 1 Recordings*, BBC Books

Glasper, Ian, 2004, *Burning Britain: The History of UK Punk 1980–1984*, Cherry Red Books

Gorman, Paul, 2008, *Reasons to be Cheerful: The Life and Work of Barney Bubbles*, Adelita Ltd

Gray, Marcus, 1995, *Last Gang in Town: The Story and Myth of The Clash*, Hal Leonard

Hermes, Will, 2014, *Love Goes to Building on Fire*, Viking

Heylin, Clinton, 1993, *From the Velvets to the Voidods: A Pre-Punk History for a Post-Punk World*, Penguin

Heylin, Clinton, 2007, *Babylon's Burning: From Punk to Grunge*, Viking

Heylin, Clinton, 2016, *Anarchy in the Year Zero: The Sex Pistols, The Clash and the Class of '76*, Route

Hinton, Brian, 1990, *Nights in Wight Satin: An Illustrated History of the Isle of Wight Pop Festivals*, Isle of Wight Cultural Services Department

Kent, David, 1993, *Australian Chart Book 1970–1992*, Australian Chart Book

Kent, Nick, 2010, *Apathy for the Devil*, Faber and Faber

Laing, Dave, 1985, *One Chord Wonders: Power and Meaning in Punk Rock*, Open University Press.

Larkin, Colin (ed), 2006 (fourth edition), *The Encyclopedia of Popular Music Vol 2*, Muze/Oxford University Press

Link, Roland, 2015, *Love in Vain: The Story of The Ruts and Ruts D.C.*, Cadiz Music

Lydon, John, with Zimmerman, Kent and Zimmerman, Keith, 1993, *Rotten: No Irish, No Blacks, No Dogs*, Hodder & Stoughton

Lydon, John with Perry, Andrew, 2015, *Anger is an Energy: My Life Uncensored*, Simon & Schuster

Marko, Paul, 2007, *The Roxy London WC2 A Punk History*, Punk77 Books

Martin, George (ed), 1983, *Making Music: The Guide to Writing, Performing & Recording*, Pan

Mehr, Bob, 2016, *Trouble Boys: The True Story of The Replacements*, Da Capo

Mercer, Mick, 1988, *Gothic Rock Black Book*, Omnibus

Mullen, Brendan with Bolles, Don and Parfrey Adam, 2002, *Lexicon Devil: The Fast Times and Short Life of Darby Crash and The Germs*, Feral House

Ogg, Alex, 2006, *No More Heroes: A Complete History of UK Punk from 1976 to 1980*, Cherry Red Books

Ogg, Alex, 2009, *Independence Days: The Story of UK Independent Record Labels*, Cherry Red Books

Panciera, Mario, 2007, *45 Revolutions (1976/1979) – Punk, Mod/ Powerpop, New Wave, NWOBHM, Indie Singles in the Years of Anarchy, Chaos and Destruction. Volume 1: UK/Ireland*, Hurdy Gurdy Books

Parker, Alan, 2007, *Sid Vicious: No One Is Innocent*, Orion

Paytress, Mark, 2004, *Vicious: The Arts of Dying Young*, Sanctuary

Rimmer, Dave, 1985, *Like Punk Never Happened: Culture Club and the New Pop*, Faber and Faber

Robb, John, 2006, *Punk Rock An Oral History*, Ebury Press

Rollins, Henry, 1994, *Get in the Van: On the Road with Black Flag*, 2.13.61

Sabin, Roger (ed), 1999, *Punk Rock: So What? The Cultural Legacy of Punk*, Routledge

Savage, Jon, 1991, *England's Dreaming: Sex Pistols and Punk Rock*, Faber and Faber

Savage, Jon, 2009, *The England's Dreaming Tapes*, Faber and Faber

Scapalo, Dean, 1997, *New Zealand Music Charts 1966 to 1996*, IPL Books

Spitz, Mark and Mullen, Brendan, 2001, *We Got the Neutron Bomb*, Three Rivers Press

Stark, James, 1992, *Punk '77*, Stark Grafix

Stubbs, David, 2007, *Ace Records*, Black Dog Publishing

Valentine, Gary, 2002, *New York Rocker: My Life in the Blank Generation*, Sidgwick & Jackson

Vermorel, Fred and Vermorel, Judy, 1978, *Sex Pistols: The Inside Story*, Universal

Endnotes

1   Though frequently identified as Dave Vanian, he refers to himself as David Vanian. Unless it is part of a quote, the latter is used here.

2   In the 1993 John Lydon book *Rotten: No Irish, No Blacks, No Dogs*.

3   Benn Brothers Ltd., *Newspaper Press Directory* (1975), 512.

4   The best and most detailed account of this aspect of The Clash's tangled prehistory is Marcus Gray's 1995 book *Last Gang in Town: The Story and Myth of The Clash* (see bibliography).

5   The British Government's New Towns Act of 1946 designated specific towns as under the control of development corporations rather than local authorities. These towns would then be expanded (often with the construction of alienating brutalist architecture and poorly planned housing estates) and settled by populations relocated from cities which were bombed during World War II. It was also a way of relocating populations from urban areas which were either overcrowded or seen as slums. As an exercise in social engineering it was, ultimately, seen as a failure. Existing communities were broken up and the New Towns were defined by anomie.

6   From June 1970's *Third* album.

7   Later, he was briefly in Kilburn & The High Roads.

8   Estimates of attendance levels at the festival vary, but the figure used here is from contemporary reporting quoted in Hinton (1990). See bibliography.

9   *Billboard*, October 13, 1973, 41.

10   Brian has never allowed this to be heard since.

11 Not a shop: Bizarre (nothing to do with the Frank Zappa-sponsored label of the same name) opened for business in February 1975 and allowed buyers to visit, but it was not a walk-in operation. Even so, records as seminal as The Flamin' Groovies, *Grease* EP (released in 1973), The Stooges' *Metallic KO* (released in 1976), The Velvet Underground's *White Heat* EP (released in 1977) and the 1977 reissue of the MC5's 'Borderline'/'Looking At You' single reached British shops through Bizarre. As did the first, independent, releases by Roky Erickson, Pere Ubu, Patti Smith and Television. It is no overstatement to say that the tremendously important Bizarre was integral to the shift in Britain's musical outlook (including the favouring of picture sleeve singles) which took place from 1975 to 1977. DeBay lived in London from 1972 and had previously worked for CBS. Before Bizarre, Crosby had been a researcher at the Harwell nuclear establishment.

12 The Certificate of Secondary Education was aimed at less-academic pupils as a verification they had been at Secondary School and was in widespread use at Comprehensive and Secondary Modern schools. More academically inclined pupils took O Levels at 16.

13 The dates given for Rat's pre-London SS tenure with Tor have varied but the earliest, and therefore most likely accurate, source is the family tree on the inner sleeve of the Johnny Moped album *Cycledelic*.

14 The only indication of what this sounded like came when The Damned began performing 'Fish', which was based around 'Portobello Reds'. Tony James has said he has tapes of The London SS in rehearsal, but he has never allowed them to be heard or said which line-up (or line-ups) was (or were) recorded.

15 Pub rock's first wave effectively had a line drawn under it in 1975 when three of the leading bands played their final shows: Brinsley Schwarz (with Nick Lowe in their line-up) called it a day on March 18, 1975; Kilburn & The High Roads, with Ian Dury, played their final show in June 1975 in Derby (Dury then formed Ian Dury & The Kilburns with a new line-up); Ducks Deluxe did so on July 1, 1975. Dr. Feelgood (who had been playing since 1971 but picked up momentum after they issued their first single: October 1974's 'Roxette'), Eddie & The Hot Rods (formed in 1973) and Graham Parker & The Rumour (formed in 1975) plugged the gap and, in differing ways and to different degrees, took pub rock out of the pubs. Members of and people associated with all of them had ties to The Damned.

16 One of whom was Jordan and, as he would at Butler's Wharf, Rotten attracted attention by tussling with her.

17 As with Rat's pre-London SS path, the most reliable source for the chronology of Captain's oft-told-of earliest musical adventures is the family

tree on the inner sleeve of Johnny Moped's *Cycledelic* album – for the same reason as Rat: it's the source capturing the information closest to when it happened.

18   Dave White was never heard from again. Rat think he was a hairdresser from east London that McLaren knew.

19   A nascent Buzzcocks had played on April 1, 1976 at Bolton Institute of Technology. It was at "the textile students do," says singer Howard Devoto. "We started off, and immediately [David Bowie's] 'Diamond Dogs' was half the speed it was supposed to be and we got the plug pulled. Was it embarrassing? Absolutely, we would have been cringingly appalling." Devoto and guitarist Pete Shelley retreated for a rethink – but this was, arguably, the first time a band formed in the wake of the Sex Pistols had been seen live. Pre-Damned and pre-Clash then. Buzzcocks' *official* live debut was July 20, 1976 at Manchester's Lesser Free Trade Hall as support to the Sex Pistols.

20   Reminiscent of the main refrain of The Yardbirds' 1965 single 'Evil Hearted You'.

21   The set list was: '1 Of The 2', 'New Rose', 'Alone', The Beatles' 'Help', 'Fan Club', The Stooges, '1970' aka 'I Feel Alright', 'Feel The Pain', 'Fish', 'I Fall', The Who's 'Circles', 'See Her Tonite', 'I Fall', 'So Messed Up'. A month later at Mont-de-Marsan, 'Alone' and 'Circles' had been dropped but the live set was otherwise the same, and played in the same order. The shelved 'Alone' was later revived to fill out the *Music For Pleasure* album.

22   At this time, Bradley had the nom-de-punk Shanne Scratch. Later, when she was in The Nipple Erectors, she was known as Shanne Hasler.

23   When these three tracks were first issued in 2005, they were credited as having been recorded in June. This has remained the case for subsequent releases. They must have been recorded after the July 15 Nashville show as this is when Armstrong and Carroll first saw them. In their first interview, in *Sniffin' Glue 3* (conducted during July), the band talked about the Nashville date and said Chiswick's Roger Armstrong approached them after the show to express his interest in them. The band's then-manager Andrew Czezowski noted the recording date as July 23 in his diary.

24   Czezowski had met staff from both labels at The Ramones' Dingwalls show.

25   Perry began work on the first issue after seeing The Ramones' Dingwalls show. He had appropriated the title of The Ramones' song 'Now I Wanna Sniff Some Glue' for his fanzine.

26   Indeed, in 1978, after punk was systemised, the astute cultural analyst Simon Frith wrote, "It was in the interests of the music papers to help hype

punk rock because if it did become popular, partly thanks to their efforts, they would benefit from new readers turning to them as sources of news, enthusiasm and knowledge – the papers' and the record companies' interests in rock sales are identical."

27 Dadomo died in 1996 and remains a generally unsung pivotal figure in what became known as punk rock. He began writing for *Sounds c* September 1975 and would be a great supporter of The Damned. He also wrote under the name Joe Varnish.

28 He was not 17. At the time Ingham was writing, he was 19. David's 20th birthday was October 12, 1976. He wasn't the only member of The Damned fiddling their age. Promoting 'New Rose' on London's Capital Radio in December 1976, Rat said he was 19 when he was actually 21. During April 1977 in *Melody Maker*, Captain said he was born April 24, 1956 as opposed to April 24, 1954; Brian said he was born February 18, 1955 as opposed to February 18, 1951; Rat said he was born July 30, 1957 instead of July 30, 1955. At that point, David had gone for October 12, 1958 (which, if true, would have made him 18 not 17 when Ingham was writing) rather than October 12, 1956.

29 The Damned's manager Andrew Czezowski was ahead of the curve. For their July 15 Nashville Rooms show, he had written a press release saying "Yes this is punk rock. Get down to The Nashville Rooms at Eight Thirty and listen to the punkiest sound around." This, though, was a behind-the-scenes missive.

30 Earlier in 1976, McLaren had tried to get Hell over to London to form the basis of a band with Chrissie Hynde. It was to be called Zeroboys.

31 In 1978, Ron Watts said of the London-wide ban on punk bands by venues that "it was very bizarre how everyone, they didn't come to a corporate decision amongst the clubs. They just did it." Watts contended that the individual actions by promoters and venues was just that: a domino effect as a result of incidents he pointed to at the 100 Club, Dingwalls, The Marquee and The Nashville Rooms.

32 The Stranglers' management also worked for the Albion agency, which booked shows on the pub circuit so the band had ready access to London's stages. Ron Watts, then managing The Damned, booked shows in High Wycombe's Nags Head as well as the 100 Club – they could play there while the Oxford Street venue cleansed itself of punk.

33 A separate contract was signed with EMI publishing on October 12.

34 The release date of the single is usually given as Friday October 22: singles were indeed issued on Fridays (which the 22nd was), but the November 6 *Music Week* was specific and said 'New Rose' was "released last Tuesday, 26

October". It is this, the only contemporaneously cited release date, which is used here. The only other press notice of the release was the issue of *Sounds* dated October 23 which said "they [The Damned] release their debut single this week" but no actual release date was given – the October 22 date was the Friday before the date carried by the paper, hence the subsequent interpretation of this as the release date. As 'New Rose' was mail order only at this point, conforming to a standard music business release date was unnecessary. *NME* and *Melody Maker* did not carry release notices for the single, though in the issue dated November 13 *NME* said 'New Rose' was released on November 5.

35 Caroline Coon had a heads up on 'New Rose' as she had been at Pathway during the recording session and took photos while there.

36 He had been given them by Nick Lowe who had a photo session for a reissue of his Bay City Rollers cash-in single ('Bay City Rollers We Love You', supposedly by The Tartan Horde and initially issued in June 1975). Lowe asked Rat to pose with him and other Stiff-related people for the new sleeve. Rat did not play on the record.

37 "The Flexibility of Stiff", November 20, 1976, *Music Week*, 81. On November 13 , *NME* had reported that The Damned were due to sign with Stiff on November 5 but they did not put their names to a contract that day.

38 Ron Watts was still The Damned's manager at this point

39 In this period, David was still experimenting with his look. In August at Mont-de-Marsan and September at the 100 Club (the shows from which, to date, most published photos had been seen) he had swept-back hair and the style which became familiar. At Coatham Bowl, he wore black-framed sunglasses and his hair was backcombed into a shorter version of a Johnny Thunders do.

40 *NME* also said Suzie & the Banshees were also on the bill.

41 The Damned were mentioned in passing once. The Sex Pistols were interviewed and seen live; The Clash were interviewed; Sex Pistols followers Siouxsie and Steve Spunker/Severin were interviewed, as were producer Guy Stevens and the 100 Club's Ron Watts. There was little editorial space for The Damned.

42 The best accounts of the *Today* farrago are in Jon Savage's 1991 book *England's Dreaming: Sex Pistols and Punk Rock* and Fred and Judy Vermorel's 1978 book *Sex Pistols: The Inside Story* (see bibliography).

43 Rogers worked for Stiff.

44 Where, on stage, David wore a *Rocky Horror Show* T-shirt: an explicit acknowledgement of a prime influence on his style.

45   *Sounds'* Jonh Ingham became Generation X's next manager.

46   He left in February as The Damned's commitments were increasing. Initially, two guitarists replaced him: Simon Fitzgerald of Rat's former band Tor (as Slimey Toad) and Chrissie Hynde (as Sissy Bar). Hynde left in March, leaving Fitzgerald/Toad as Johnny Moped's sole guitarist. Thus, Johnny Moped and The Damned each drew members from both Captain and Rat's pre-Damned bands.

47   Following this brief brush with Stiff, Motörhead next went to Chiswick Records and then Bronze. Over a longer time line, The Damned did the same, in the same order (with, for them, a dalliance with NEMS falling between Chiswick and Bronze). The connections between the two bands were many: Motörhead first played with The Damned in 1977; Lemmy played bass with the reformed Damned at the Les Punks one-off in 1978 (he appeared on stage with them on other occasions); a joint single was proposed in 1979; The Damned were taken on by Motörhead manager Doug Smith in 1979; both bands recorded at Rockfield (Motörhead in 1975, The Damned at various junctures from 1980); they each appeared in separate episodes of the BBC TV series *The Young Ones* in 1984. Early on, and coincidentally (without knowing of Brian's band), Lemmy had considered Bastard as the band's name. Motörhead were the band most close to The Damned. The Ruts – over *c* 1979 to 1981 – would be the second closest. At different periods and to varying degrees The Adverts, Anti-Nowhere League and Dead Boys were also close to The Damned.

48   Czezowski was owed £400. Once that was recouped, they were paid for playing The Roxy: £100 against a 50% guarantee of the door takings on January 31; £200 for each of their February shows (twice what The Vibrators got that month for playing there. The Jam got £40, the same as Eater).

49   In total, The Damned played The Roxy seven times: January 13, 17, 24, and 31; February 14, 21 and 28. A March 31 show was cancelled. At one date – which is not pinned down – only Brian and Captain turned up so an audience member drummed and Alan Anger of *Live Wire* fanzine sang 'New Rose'. Over January and February, The Damned were The Roxy's most frequent visitors: The Adverts played six times, Eater, Slaughter & The Dogs and The Vibrators each played four times and The Jam three. The source for these figures is Marko (2007), the most in-depth work on The Roxy (see bibliography). For the record, the venue's Susan Carrington and Andrew Czezowski, in their 2016 book (see bibliography) give the figures as follows for January and February: The Damned (five shows); The Adverts (five); Chelsea (five); The Boys (three); Eater (three); The Vibrators (three). While accuracy on who played The Roxy and when they did is unlikely to

be achieved, it is certain The Damned were regularly booked. Beyond the January 1 venue-opening date, The Clash did not play there again. The Sex Pistols never played there.

50   Captain first wore the nurse's dress on January 17 at The Roxy. It belonged to the nurse girlfriend of Sex Pistols' soundman Dave Goodman. He had intended to wear it while introducing that night's support band, Eater (he produced them, and they recorded for his label, The Label). Captain wore it instead as his then-girlfriend was also a nurse. He hoped sporting it would tell her that all the time spent with The Damned was worth it.

51   The connection came through Nick Lowe: he was playing with Dave Edmunds in Rockpile. As a solo artist, Edmunds was signed to Led Zeppelin's Swan Song label.

52   The *Live At The Roxy* album, released June 1977, featured recordings of bands playing live at the venue. The Damned were not featured as Jake Riviera did not want them associated with bands he considered rubbish. If the Sex Pistols and The Clash had been included, he would have allowed The Damned to be too. Johnny Moped were heard on the album though: the first time they made it to vinyl (they had signed to Chiswick in April and their first single was issued in July). Amongst those also on the album were The Adverts, Buzzcocks, Eater and Slaughter & The Dogs, all bands which had been on Damned bills. Despite the absence of top-drawer names, *Live At The Roxy* is an essential, unvarnished document of the many forms of what passed for early British punk.

53   Distribution was through Island's distributor, EMI.

54   The contention that the album tapes were sped up is scotched by listening to the first Peel session, broadcast on December 10, 1976. Garry was making mischief. Likewise, there are live performances that also show this for the lie it is: the July 6, 1976, 100 Club debut and the Mont-de-Marsan August 20, 1976, show have been issued; so has a BBC *In Concert* taped on May 19, 1977.

55   Then, Gravelle used the working name Peter Kodick for music commissions to differentiate from his work as fashion photographer.

56   For the sleeve, Bubbles claimed the credit as "Big Jobs Inc." Bubbles (born Colin Fulcher) began working for Stiff in late 1976. His work had been seen in the underground magazine *OZ*, and his first art-design for a record was *In Blissful Company*, the 1969 debut album by Quintessence. He worked extensively with Hawkwind and was well known to Dave Robinson as he painted the artwork for the 1970 United Artists' *Brinsley Schwarz* album. Jake Riviera knew him from Chilli Willi & The Red Hot Peppers: Bubbles created their graphic identity. His first design for Stiff was the 'Neat Neat Neat' sleeve (Dave Robinson had cobbled together the 'New Rose' sleeve).

Damned Damned Damned was worked on next. Of course, as Bubbles had a long history his involvement with the band further suggested they were in bed with a past which punk was apparently eradicating.

57   The collectability was enhanced by these first copies of the album coming in a plastic sleeve to which was stuck a sticker of the title.

58   The deliberation behind the supposed error was shown by Bubbles' sketch for the rear of the sleeve: it included his hand-drawn representation of the Eddie & The Hot Rods photo, lined-up in their appropriately rat-like poses. Indeed, the picture was taken specially by Brian's girlfriend, the photographer Erica Echenberg. All of which indicates the band had foreknowledge of the sales-generating ruse.

59   Regrettably, British TV and The Damned had few interactions in 1977 and, after *Supersonic*, those which did happen were not broadcast. 'Stretcher Case Baby' was filmed for the Michael Aspel-hosted *Blast Off* in June and the Lu Edmonds/Jon Moss line-up performed 'Neat Neat Neat', 'Problem Child' and 'Fan Club' on *Supersonic* director Mike Mansfield's *Impact* in November. Both were pilots and never screened. The best 1977 footage is from The Old Refectory, Sussex University, Brighton on June 15 – the whole fantastic show was caught on video in black and white by media students with a multiple camera set-up. The main reason for the paucity of footage of the 1976/1977 Damned is that Jake Riviera would not allow filming unless it was paid for, the reason they did not appear in Don Letts' *Punk Rock Movie*.

60   Though Tony James had a hand in 'Fish's antecedent 'Portobello Reds', a song which had been rehearsed by The London SS.

61   The two Patti Smith albums issued to date, *Horses* and *Radio Ethiopia*, used photos as arty as their music to help present her as an artist.

62   See Chapter Five.

63   Of the records released in 1977, two suggest a Damned influence: May's 'Sick Of You'/'(I'm) In Love Today' by The Users (a Cambridge band formed in September 1976) and June's 'I Wanna Be Free'/'Automobile' by The Rings (their singer was former Pink Fairies drummer Twink). In September 1977, the Manchester satire-rock band Alberto Y Los Trios Paranoias issued the *Snuff Rock* EP on Stiff: its opening cut 'Kill' was a lumpen, unfunny parody of The Damned.

64   The *New Elizabethans* report is valuable. Not only is it a relatively considered report on punk, it also includes clips of the recording of 'God Save The Queen' and the Sex Pistols' first live show with Sid Vicious at Notre Dame Hall on March 21, 1977. The interview segments feature Glen Matlock with the band: evidence for how long this had taken to complete. It has not, in full, leaked onto the internet.

65   He had also seen them play live in 1976 at Hammersmith's Red Cow. The launch of his *Dandy In The Underworld* album was held at The Roxy on March 9, 1977. The Damned were there, as was American actor Doug McClure, who was introduced to Brian by Bolan.

66   Both made to Cameron Crowe: the former in *Rolling Stone* in 1975 and the latter in *Playboy* in 1976.

67   In late 1976, Stiff and the New York production company Instant had discussed a reciprocal arrangement. Instant was a partnership between former New York Dolls manager Marty Thau, producer Craig Leon and music industry veteran Richard Gottehrer. Gottehrer provided the finances. Instant was behind Richard Hell's *Blank Generation* EP (issued in the US on the Ork label), which Stiff picked up for UK release: the first in the planned two-way trade. Suicide, Talking Heads and Television were potential candidates for the tie-in with Stiff. However, the deal foundered as Gottehrer withdrew his support as he was not convinced of the worth of the bands Leon and Thau were touting. Also, Hell's signing with Sire in January 1977 drew a line under the proposed Instant-Stiff alliance.

68   Considering that Phonogram, Sire's UK outlet, had rejected The Damned in July 1976 it was hardly surprising they were rebuffed by the US label this time. Furthermore, as The Damned were on Stiff in the UK, Sire would have achieved no UK sales if they had signed them. Any thoughts Sire would sign them were unrealistic.

69   In 1978, in their book *The Boy Looked at Johnny*, *NME*'s Julie Burchill and Tony Parsons claimed "both Scabies and Sensible had scrounged drinks [while out at shows] with anecdotes of their sexual assault upon a New York groupie with a Fender bass".

70   He was 23 that day.

71   Lowe was about to release his next solo record for Stiff, the *Bowi* EP issued in May 13.

72   The Damned and The Adverts first played together on February 14, 1977 at the Roxy.

73   May 19, 1977. Quoted in Cobley, Paul, *Leave the Capital,* in Sabin 1999

74   Though, to a limited degree, Stiff selling *The Damned Disciples Song Book* by mail order was. Printed up by *Zigzag* magazine, it included images of hand-written song lyrics (some with guitar chords), pics and short biographies. Rat said he was "tall, good looking, arrogant and conceited". Captain's hobbies included "drinking [the real ale] Fuller's ESB". Brian had "no comment to make on anything at all". Of their singer, it was noted that "Nothing very much is known about Dave."

75   The compilation album *A Bunch Of Stiff Records* had been issued between *Damned Damned Damned* and *My Aim Is True.*

76 Indeed, as Lu Edmonds says, there was money in songwriting. That is, money which only the songwriter received. This was, and remains, one stream of a band or performer's income.

The nature of income streams are crucial to The Damned's story (as they are to any band or performer). What follow summarises this and lurks in the background for much of the story.

Publishing income – money paid to the writer/composer of a song (as in words and music) – is *one* aspect of a band's potential earnings. The band's management has to/needs to keep on top of all this. This is, increasingly so as the 21st century progresses, what they are paid to do. Any management which does not, especially in the wild and woolly post-internet era, is neglecting their responsibilities to their client: i.e. to the artist they are contracted to represent. In the pre-internet era of much of this book, the manager was more important as access to the music business was harder. The Damned finding Jake Riviera was a massive break: he was embedded in the music industry.

And, as noted here, it is not called the music business for nothing.

Typically, in outline (caveat: actual situations are much, much more complex and require proper professional advice/inputs – the below is a thumbnail summary and for information), any band has six revenue streams (which can feed into each other), all subject to individual contracts, terms and conditions and/or pan-music industry agreed standards:

- Money received from the sales of records (the artist royalty): a percentage of money made from the sales of records, CDs, downloads, streaming or the licensing of their recordings to other labels. If a band has been paid an advance by their label to, say, make a demo or record, it is possible they may not receive any income from sales until their label has recouped this advance. It is the owners of the rights to recordings – the artist has signed a contract with them – who pay out.
- Money from songwriting: paid to the writer of a song (known formally in relation to the product [record, CD, etc.] as the "mechanical royalty"). These can – as Lu Edmonds noted – be contentious as one band member may receive more than another, potentially setting them apart. Which is why John Lennon and Paul McCartney agreeing to credit their songs to Lennon-McCartney, irrespective of who actually wrote them, was far-sighted, far-reaching and, in the medium term, helped create stability.
- Fees paid for live performances. Anything paid for this may be subject to the deduction of a percentage by the concert promoter, by fees paid to a tour manager and/or a booking agent as well as production/staging costs. In lean times, when no current record was out, The Damned often played live to generate income.

- Money made from the sales of merchandise (T-shirts, posters, programmes, band-branded clocks, socks or tea trays, etc). A band can organise this themselves or depute the task to an agency who – like everything else – will take a cut for their work.
- Synchronisation ("sync") rights: the use of recordings on film or television soundtracks, for ads, for gaming. This can be serviced by a sync agency, the band's music publisher or their label (who, most likely, has the rights for the recordings: the label may contract sync to a specialist agency). In the film industry, "music supervisors" are tasked by directors/producers to find songs and deal with this aspect of making the film. There are two permissions: the recording copyright owner, and the songwriter or their representative. Typically, this is the record label and the publisher and both have to agree, separately, to any proposed deal. In the 2016 documentary *Don't You Wish That We Were Dead*, Captain expresses his frustration that The Damned's own recordings of their songs were not being heard in ads. In 1995, American band The Offspring's cover of 'Smash It Up' was used in the soundtrack to *Batman Forever*. The Clash's 'Should I Stay Or Should I Go' being used in a 1991 Levi's jeans ad was crucial to breaking down the ideological wall preventing punk-era material from being used in this fashion.
- Money from songs being broadcast: on the radio, in shops, in television performances. This is, typically, collected by an agency through agreements made with broadcasters and then distributed to members of this collection agency: there are (like the product) two income streams – for the song (to the songwriter) and for the performance (to the performer).

Everything above is further complicated if a band is working internationally. For example, money due from, say, broadcast on Swedish radio, will always be welcome. This can all apply on a territory by territory basis.

All of the above was and is germane to The Damned at various junctures in their wayward progress.

For The Damned, early on, Brian James was pretty much the sole songwriter. This meant, after *Damned Damned Damned* came out, he would receive more money overall than the other band members. In part, this is why cover versions can be contentious: the specific songwriter receives the publishing money, not the band or their other songwriter(s).

Anyone not taking on board at least part or all of the above (perhaps Lesson Number Two in the music business: Lesson Number One is on how to choose a manager) before setting sail through the music business' choppy waters may, subsequently, have gripes.

Or, at least, feel jolly hard done by. As The Damned have on occasion.

77 Later the LA2.

78 For Burchill and Parsons, Dury was "the waggish barrow-chappie" and Costello "the resentful, impotent myopic who appeared out of nowhere (and didn't spend years slogging away at pubs and folk-clubs, cross our hearts)". Nick Lowe was a "middle-aged, multi-chinned senile cynic".

79 It was with Allan Jones on the "Stiffs Greatest Stiffs Live" tour. Lowe spoke about The Damned on October 6 in Bristol.

80 At this time, Moss was calling himself "John Moss": how he was credited while in London. Due to his later fame as the more familiar Jon Moss in Culture Club, he is called Jon here.

81 These were manufactured in Germany but distributed in the UK, so the single counts as a home-country release.

82 Referring to the Los Angeles incident *Zigzag* had reported.

83 While this was exaggeration, Captain had written a moody instrumental on the day Marc Bolan died, September 16, 1977. It surfaced in November 1979 on *Machine Gun Etiquette* as 'Smash It Up (Part 1)'.

84 Initial copies came with a free seven-inch: one side was a version of The Damned's 'Neat Neat Neat' recorded at Lancaster University on October 22 during the "Stiffs Greatest Stiffs" tour. Costello is heard dedicating it to Chris Millar: Costello was moved to do so in the wake of the then-recent coverage of Rat leaving The Damned.

85 The ironic title was borrowed from the budget record label of the same name (known as MFP) which reissued material drawn from the EMI catalogue.

86 For the French release of the album, the images from each side of the inner sleeve became the inside of a fine gatefold sleeve.

87 Each part of Rat's kit was distinctly audible.

88 And arguably, with its cover artist too. Although Barney Bubbles was Stiff's house designer and would have worked on the album come what may, he was a veteran of the psychedelic and post-psychedelic/freak periods. The Damned did not reject his to-all-intents-and-purposes mind-expanding *Music For Pleasure* sleeve.

89 This show, on June 18, was conceived to promote Sphinx, former Hawkwind member Nik Turner's new band. A multi-media event, it had a stage set designed by Barney Bubbles, a light show and dancers from Ballet Rambert in bandages and blindfolds (a Bubbles concept). With this appearance, Brian firmly closed the door to punk.

90 Lords Of The New Church issued three albums over 1982 to 1984, gained an international profile and almost breaking through into the mainstream. The 1983 single 'Dance With Me' was their best-seller in America.

91 Mercedes went on to form the proto-hardcore band The Stimulators.

92   After being tasked by Stiff to be The Damned's road manager on the Anarchy tour and then being sacked, Rogers went on to work as Chiswick Records' press officer and had recently set up Trigger Publicity, based next door to the Rock On shop – Chiswick's base – above the Holt's shoe shop in Camden Town.

93   'California Sun' was actually first released by Joe Jones in 1961, but all the punk-era covers were of The Rivieras' 1964 version.

94   The Whitecats and The Rich Kids had the same manager.

95   'Burglar' was also strongly reminiscent of the peculiar songs John Entwistle wrote for the 1965–8 Who.

96   Quote from a 2016 interview undertaken by Peter Watts. Used with permission.

97   Julian Isaacs aka Auntie Pus knew Rat. They had attended the same school – though not at the same time, as Isaacs was older than Rat.

98   They performed his band's 'She's No Angel'.

99   Which was actually rescheduled for a week later.

100   In Britain, the winter of 1978-79 had seen the members of trade unions striking after the Labour government imposed pay caps in an attempt to control inflation. Most of the strikes were by workers in public service jobs. In the media, it was dubbed the Winter of Discontent (a nod to Shakespeare's *Richard III*) and was a prime ingredient in the Conservative party's 1979 election victory.

101   Quote from a 2016 interview undertaken by Peter Watts. Used with permission.

102   Taylor's record had an impact on Strummer and his entry point was most probably the Chiswick reissue.

103   This was agreed in 1978: a distribution license running for three years. As part of the deal. EMI paid Chiswick an advance against future sales. Working with EMI had no effect who Chiswick did or did not sign.

104   According to the sleeve of the Spanish 'Smash It Up', 'Love Song' was the fastest-selling single EMI had worked on since The Beatles. Ahem.

105   Of which, *Sounds'* Pete Silverton commented on the "silly misogyny of changing The Sweet's 'Ballroom Blitz' to 'Great Big Tits'." He also noted the Lyceum show "proved that they don't have to live on the memories of 'Neat Neat Neat' alone."

106   When The Sweet's 'Ballroom Blitz' was recorded in May 1979, its original lyrics were altered to include a line featuring the word "boiler". Members of The Damned were not alone in referring to women as boilers (at its basic: vernacular for ugly woman): Nick Lowe used the term in an *NME* interview in the issue dated July 30, 1977; Johnny Moped had the song 'V. D. Boiler' (credited to Moped/Toad), heard on March 1978's *Cycledelic*

album. The early 1982 Rhoda With Special A.K.A. single 'The Boiler' offers a harrowing insight into the impact on women's self-perception of being referred to by men as "boilers".

107　'Anti-Pope' was written in 1977 by Captain's brother Phil Burns for his band The Cowards, who played it live the once at The London School Of Economics supporting Johnny Moped. Two Phil Burns co-writes with Moped were in Johnny Moped's set: '3D Time' and 'Hard Lovin' Man', both played when Captain was in the band.

108　In time, the repeatedly worn okapi suit not only became dirty, but was also subjected to infestation from Captain's crabs.

109　First worn on stage at The Lyceum on April 8, 1979.

110　The Stooges cover was apt: this show is The Damned's equivalent of the Iggy Pop & Co's provocative February 9, 1974 Michigan Palace performance captured on the live album *Metallic KO*.

111　Smith had managed Hawkwind, was a friend of Barney Bubbles and also (later) managed Anti-Nowhere League, Girlschool and Tank.

112　The single of 'Smash It Up' was actually 'Smash It Up Part 2', the second element of a proposed four-part composition (along the lines of The Who's 'A Quick One While He's Away'). 'Smash It Up Part 1' preceded 'Part 2' on the album. 'Part 3' was only recorded as a demo, and 'Part 4', though completed, was not issued at the time. A reconstruction of 'Smash It Up Parts 1 to 4' was released for the first time in 2004.

113　The B-side of 'Smash It Up' was 'Burglar'. Two studio versions had already been recorded (for the late 1978 Peel session and as the flipside of the Dodgy Demo 'Love Song' single), but this new, third version (recorded 21–23 May and 16–19 July) was different and an overt musical parody of Public Image Ltd's debut single 'Public Image'.

114　Viz: "We've been crying now for much too long, And now we're gonna dance to a different song, I'm gonna scream and shout 'til my dying breath, I'm gonna smash it up 'til there's nothing left" was the first verse; "smash it up, smash it up, smash it up, smash it up, smash it up, smash it up" the chorus. The third verse was more noteworthy: "Smash it up, you can keep your Krishna burgers, Smash it up, and your Glastonbury hippies, Smash it up, you can stick your frothy lager, Smash it up, and your blow wave hairstyles." It was, as Captain has said, "saying bollocks to everyone". Musically, in part, the song drew from Small Faces' 'I Feel Much Better', the 1967 B-side to 'Tin Soldier'.

115　After the problem with 'Smash It Up' securing BBC radio airplay, Chiswick prepared a special radio-only edit of 'I Just Can't Be Happy Today', which was supplied to Damned-shy DJs to help the single into the charts.

116   The Misfits had met The Damned at the New York Hurrah dates in June 1979 and subsequently came to London. Their own label, Plan 9, was (like 'Channel 7 Plan 9') named after the Ed Wood film *Plan 9 From Outer Space*. The label, though, was up and running in 1978, before 'Channel 7 Plan 9' was written. The Misfits shared many of David's preoccupations but the band ran in parallel with, rather than strictly being influenced by, The Damned.

117   Their drummer, Jeff Beattie, took Rat's place during The Damned's set to allow him to go stage front to sing 'Burglar'.

118   On the sleeve, this looks like a 2D collage. It was not. Smee – for the front and back of *Machine Gun Etiquette*'s sleeve – had pasted photographs to board and assembled them as a diorama. This was then photographed. The same technique was used for the sleeve of The Beatles' *Sgt Pepper's Lonely Hearts Club* band album.

119   Dadomo was more than a music journalist and early punk propagator. In 1977 he was in the Arthur Comics and The Snivelling Shits (pretty much the same band) with fellow *Sounds* contributors Dave Fudger (who had been in the pre–Vibrators band Despair, with the former's Knox) and Pete Makowski. In 1978, he was in The Engineers who issued one single on Beserkley. Three years earlier, Dadomo had recorded a single as Dr. Dark. He also wrote the lyrics for *Raindogs*, a 1975 album by Japanese percussionist Stomu Yamashta. Another of his credits was the lyric for 'Red Hot Passion', a 1977 B–side by South African outfit the Otis Waygood Band. In Dadomo, The Damned had a more than able collaborator.

120   Played by Jack Howarth.

121   With Captain's furry, Womble-like togs already dubbed the okapi suit, the quote was a natural fit for *Machine Gun Etiquette*. It came from the introduction to episode six of Douglas Adams' *The Hitchhiker's Guide To The Galaxy*, first broadcast by BBC radio on April 12, 1978. The voice heard was that of Peter Jones, the narrator of the series: a character designated "The Book". It was extracted from: "…the Earthman Arthur Dent, to whom all this can be of only academic interest, as his only brother was long ago nibbled to death by an okapi, is about to be plunged into a real intergalactic war".

122   Vampira (Maila Nurmi) had appeared in Ed Wood's 1959 film *Plan 9 From Outer Space* (the 'Plan 9 Channel 7' promo video explicitly lifts from the film with David's wife Laurie as a proxy Vampira). Nurmi had hosted/introduced horror films on television in the Los Angeles area from 1954 . She and Dean were publicly linked after his September 1955 death in an issue of the gossip magazine *Whisper* dated February 1956. Ed Wood, Vampira and associated subjects only became of widespread cult interest from the early 1980s: David was way ahead of the curve here.

123 Also in 1980, the French label New Rose issued its first record. Founders Patrick Mathé and Louis Thévenon had named it after The Damned's debut single. New Rose also had the Damned-referencing sub-labels Fan Club and Lively Art.

124 The few (single figures) never-circulated British test-pressings of the single count as the rarest Damned vinyl artefact.

125 The bill for the May 25 to June 14, 1980 booking came to £10,858.97.

126 The first of the *Pebbles* compilation albums was issued in 1979. They were named in tribute to the Lenny Kaye-compiled *Nuggets* double album and initially featured similar – but much more obscure – American Sixties garage and psychedelic bands. As the series continued, it also collected similarly minded British and continental European material. There were 28 volumes, the last issued in 1988. Rather than being licensed from the rights holders, the albums were bootlegs with original singles used as the master sources instead of tapes. Each was compiled and issued by Bomp Records' Greg Shaw: The Damned visited the label's Los Angeles shop in 1977. The Flamin' Groovies, with whom The Damned briefly toured in 1976, were, at that time, managed by Shaw. Despite being American albums, early volumes were on a supposedly Australian label. The *Pebbles* albums were influential and brought much previously obscure and frequently wonderful music to widespread attention. When Naz Nomad & The Nightmares – the alternate Damned – recorded their album in late 1983, four of the tracks covered had been collected on *Pebbles* albums: 'Action Woman' (also covered by Echo & The Bunnymen), 'I Can't Stand This Love, Goodbye', 'She Lied' and 'The Trip' (the version head on *Pebbles* was by Godfrey, rather than the original Kim Fowley recording).

127 In America, sides one and two were issued as single album by the IRS label. This was The Damned's first US release. In its review of the US *Black Album*, the music trade magazine *Billboard* said, "This latest version [of the band] may be the most pop-oriented yet. The band now comes up with structured and harmonic tunes with new wave hooks and understandable lyrics."

128 Like 'Dr. Jekyll And Mr. Hyde' and 'I Just Can't Be Happy Today', 'There Ain't No Sanity Clause' was written with Giovanni Dadomo. The Damned had recorded an unreleased version with him under the title 'There Ain't No Sanity Claus' which was first issued in 2002 on a compilation of Dadomo's band The Snivelling Shits.

129 The support band throughout the tour was south London band The Straps. They paid £3,000, in music business speak the "buy-on", to play the dates. The bill was footed by their drummer, ex-Public Image Ltd member Jim Walker.

130 With demo sessions at RMS Studios.

131   With Hans Zimmer's work on 'The History Of The World (Part 1)' at Nova Sound Recording Studio

132   With inflation factored in, *c.* £72,570 in 2016.

133   Their 1979 version was first heard on the 1990 archive compilation *The Curse Of The Hot Rods.*

134   Back then, the Macclesfield-born Hart was living in LA and known as Farrah Fawcett-Minor. The subject of the X song 'Los Angeles', she came to Britain after seeing The Damned. Captain told July 1977's *Zigzag*, "I met Farrah Fawcett Majors [sic]… she's wasted hundreds of dollars on phone calls since we got back. She's coming to see me soon. She wears clear plastic see-through mini skirts." After arriving in the UK, she became what was dubbed the "tour nurse" and named "Farrah Fuck-It Minor" during 1977's "Stiffs Greatest Stiffs" tour and wrote the jaunt's newsletter. She went on to marry The Attractions' Steve Nieve.

135   In the punk era, Billy Karloff – John Osborn – had formed the bands The Goats, The Supremes and The Extremes and had been playing London since the mid-Seventies. He knew Rat: Billy Karloff & The Extremes had supported The Damned on tour in July 1980. For 'Wait For The Blackout', Karloff's share of the songwriting money equalled that of all the other members combined: recognition of his degree of input into the song.

136   As Chiswick themselves did when they reissued the album in 1982.

137   Anti-Nowhere League paid The Damned £200 to be on the bill.

138   Captain had already produced (and played on) one under-the-radar single in 1979: 'Disco Girls' by Maxims Trash aka Max & The Sunset Boys. He discussed it in an interview appearing in the January 1981 issue of *Zigzag*. A member of the band was Will Rippingale, later of musical absurdists I Ludicrous. Rippingale had recorded The Damned's debut live show at the 100 Club in 1976: the source tape for releases of the show.

139   'Been Teen' was followed in 1982 by 'Everything And More', another Captain/Paul Gray-produced single for Respond. On his own, Captain also produced their 1983 single 'Remember This', which was issued on Dolly Mixture's own label.

140   Roman Jugg was not on either of their singles: he joined the band later. He was, though, in the band when they supported The Damned in Cardiff in April 1979.

141   The show was a sell-out, so a second was booked for the next Sunday.

142   Henry Rollins recalled that The Damned's driver wouldn't let Black Flag on the coach as he said it was full.

143   The production of *Hype* closed after attracting an opening-night audience of 17.

144 Connelly had been in Fox's pre-Ruts band Hit & Run.

145 Both Girlschool and Motörhead were managed by former Damned manager Doug Smith.

146 These were later issued on the *Damned But Not Forgotten* album

147 Issued as a single in July 1982.

148 Rap – and, to varying degrees, hip-hop – was an increasing fascination for some who had roots in the pre-1977 punk era. Captain was not alone. America was first. There, Blondie's 'Rapture' was released in January 1981 and Talking Heads' spin-off outfit Tom Tom Club issued 'Wordy Rappinghood' in June 1981. In Britain, The Clash's 'The Magnificent Seven' came out as a single in April 1981 (its parent album *Sandinista!* was issued in December 1980), Adam & The Ants, 'Ant Rap' in December 1981, and Malcolm McLaren's crackers 'Buffalo Gals' in November 1982. Late to the party, John Lydon joined forces with Afrika Bambaataa and Bill Laswell in December 1984 for 'World Destruction', credited to Time Zone. However, of all these records, Captain's 'Wot!' was the one most explicitly indebted to 'The Message'.

149 Quote from a 2016 interview undertaken by Peter Watts. Used with permission.

150 'Ignite', 'Dozen Girls', 'Gun Fury', 'Pleasure And The Pain', 'Life Goes On', 'Bad Time For Bonzo', 'Don't Bother Me' and 'Dozen Girls'.

151 August 19 and September 2, 1982.

152 The French success came on the back of Captain appearing at January's MIDEM music business conference in Cannes, where he sang to backing tracks.

153 Quote from a 2016 interview undertaken by Peter Watts. Used with permission.

154 Bronze went under in 1986.

155 Gray had already played a three-week series of continental European dates with UFO.

156 Merrick had been in Victimize since its formation in early 1978 as Red Alert & The Rejects, and had appeared on both their singles (he co-wrote three of the four tracks). Roman had joined the band after the singles were recorded and was not heard on anything that was issued. Both were in Victimize when it changed its name to The Missing Men. Their last gig as Victimize was in February 1980. The Missing Men folded when Roman joined The Damned and Merrick went on to Storm Queen.

157 Adapted as a film in 1994.

158 Titled 'Gun Fury' on the album's sleeve and label, but 'Gun Fury (Of Riot Forces)' on the lyric sheet.

159   The sleeves of Queen's second, third, fourth and fifth albums had a similar "no synthesisers" credit.

160   And, with a little tweaking, could have passed for a late-period Jam offering.

161   As confirmed by the pre-Christmas 1982 solo tour which was announced and then cancelled.

162   The album also featured a track by Short Commercial Break, the band formed by Captain's girlfriend Christiane Kistner. They played versions of songs heard in adverts. For *The Whip*, their 'Weetabix And Bran Flakes' was produced by Captain.

163   Lords Of The New Church played their first live show on January 16, 1982 at the Hope & Anchor. The singer was Brian James' friend and former Dead Boy Stiv Bators, their bassist Dave Tregunna (ex-Sham 69: before the Lords, he had been in The Wanderers with Bators). The drummer was Nick Turner, ex-of London-based garage-surf band The Barracudas.

164   On Rat's own Paradiddle Music label and available from July 1983, 'Let There Be Rats' was accompanied by 'Wiped Out' and 'Drums, Drums, Drums'.

165   The Craig's rare 1966 single 'I Must Be Mad' is one of the wildest British records of the Sixties: sounding like The Who as if they were playing at five times their normal tempo while pilled out of their heads. In 1984, when Roman was inspired by it, 'I Must Be Mad' had just been reissued on the Bam-Caruso label's compilation album *The Psychedelic Snarl*. The label was co-run by Phil Smee, who designed the *Machine Gun Etiquette* sleeve and often worked for Chiswick Records. 'I Must Be Mad' had also been heard (its first reissue), in lesser fidelity, on the 1981 compilation album *Chocolate Soup For Diabetics Volume 2*. 'Cold Turkey' by Big Boy Pete was also on that album and covered on Naz Nomad & The Nightmares' *Give Daddy The Knife Cindy* – at least one member of The Damned must have had a well-worn copy of *Chocolate Soup For Diabetics Volume 2*.

166   Quote from a 2016 interview undertaken by Peter Watts. Used with permission.

167   The sleeve was designed by Phil Smee under the pseudonym Harvey S. Williams (a reference to William S. Harvey who designed the Elektra label's sleeves).

168   Chris Slade, from Manfred Mann's Earth Band and Uriah Heep – both former NEMS label-mates of The Damned – became the band's drummer.

169   The 12-inch version of 'Thanks For The Night' included 'Do The Blitz', recorded at the same time as 'Nasty'. Like 'Thanks For The Night', it had been written for *Strawberries*. Furthermore, it was co-written by the departed Paul Gray.

170 A session was recorded for John Peel on July 7: 'Nasty', 'Thanks For The Night' and a cover of The Rolling Stones' 'We Love You' were taped along with the new song 'Is It A Dream?'

171 Although Steve Kutner has a long career in the music business, he is also known as the agent representing footballers Frank Lampard and Ian Wright.

172 Quote from a 2016 interview undertaken by Peter Watts. Used with permission.

173 The set list for The Damned's first show without Captain was: 'Love Song', 'Ignite', 'Disco Man', 'Wait For The Blackout', 'Stranger On The Town', 'Born To Kill', 'Do The Blitz', 'Nasty', 'The Limit Club', 'Melody Lee', 'Neat Neat Neat' and 'Looking At You'. They returned for two encores: firstly 'Smash It Up', 'Noise, Noise, Noise', 'New Rose' and 'We Love You'; then 'Love Song,' 'Thanks For The Night' and 'Pretty Vacant'.

174 Seven tracks were taped and logged on September 8: 'Deadbeat Dance', 'Edward The Bear', 'Grimly Fiendish', 'Missing Man', 'Nightshift', 'There Will Come A Day' and the untitled 'Track With No Name'.

175 Baxendale had created Grimly Feendish for the *Eagle Eye Junior Spy* strip in the Sixties children's comic *Wham!*

176 In fact, at this point, Andy Cheeseman was The Damned's 15th manager: taking Rat's two spells as manager into account as one, and telescoping Doug Smith's joint managership with Tommy Crossan into one spell overall.

177 Captain had recorded a version of Frankie's 'Relax' as the B-side of his November 1984 'One Christmas Catalogue' single, his penultimate for A&M.

178 There was no promo video for 'Eloise'. It was reported that then-hot director Tim Pope was to make one, but it never happened.

179 David was not the only Damned member with a yen for Paul and Barry Ryan. Captain had covered their 1966 single 'I Love Her' on his second and final A&M album *The Power Of Love* in 1983.

180 The Bags' bassist was David's future wife and Damned member Patricia Morrison.

181 A period during which their most public manifestation was as the Captain-free Naz Nomad & The Nightmares.

182 This became the *Flashmag*. Eight issues were mailed out, the last in late 1987.

183 Quote from a 2016 interview undertaken by Peter Watts. Used with permission.

184 *Billboard* September 13, 1986, 94.

185 *The London Gazette*, October 8, 1986, 13019.

186 Roman and Bryn stood down as directors of Fanpack Ltd in March 1992.

187 The titles in the tape logs were all vocal-free backing tracks, except where noted here, and were: 'Bedazzled', 'Fade Away' (with a very rough guide

vocal from David), 'Godfather Revisited', 'McGrogan Park' (on which David's vocal is tentative but suggests what a finished version might have been like: 'Anything' crossed with Billy Idol's 'White Wedding'), 'Mountain Woman', the synth-as-trumpets punctuated 'Quiet Man', 'Rosemary's Tears' (on which Roman is heard singing an intermittent guide vocal), 'Top Cat' and 'Voodoo Woman' (also with a few vocal lines and, overall, reminiscent of Echo & The Bunnymen's 'The Cutter'). Further very sketchy, unfinished and untitled backing tracks were also recorded.

188   Director Gerard de Thame was specially flown to Australia.

189   'In Dulce Decorum' had also been included on the *Miami Vice II* album, released in America in December 1986.

190   The Ramones were also on the bill: Joey Ramone joined The Damned for a run-through of 'Blitzkrieg Bop'.

191   Amongst them were an International AIDS Day concert which had been set for Wembley Arena on May 29 and then cancelled; the Nelson Mandela benefit at Wembley Stadium on June 11; The Prince's Trust concert on June 6 at the Royal Albert Hall. The only one to feature The Damned and any 1976-era bands was Milton Keynes.

192   Though Adam Ant had appeared at Live Aid.

193   Though he agreed with who was there, what happened and how David had delivered his "I'm leaving" bombshell, Bryn Merrick later said the band met at their accountant's office rather than a café or Rat's house.

194   Lords Of The New Church bowed out after a final show at London's Astoria on May 2, 1989. Though Brian knew their end was coming, the dovetailing of the two dates (The Damned's split announcement was in the music press dated May 27, 1989) confirms how speedily the reunion had come together.

195   *NME* reported the split as a brief news item under the heading "It's the end – and about Damned time".

196   The first set of these shows was Brian, Captain, David and Rat doing 1976-era songs; the second set was Captain (on guitar), David, Paul Gray and Rat revisiting *Machine Gun Etiquette* and *The Black Album*.

197   The October Naz Nomad shows featured the standard Sixties cover versions, a few Stooges songs, the MC5's 'Looking At You' but no Damned material. There had also been some February 1989 dates which uncomfortably combined the Sixties songs with the rock'n'roll/Fifties covers debuted at the bizarre Damned Limelight show in September 1988 – and a cover of The Stray Cats' 'Runaway Boys'.

198   Moon was the guitarist in the Link Wray-style band The Volcanoes (the support band at the September 1998 Damned Limelight Club show). Dempsey was a friend of his.

199 On M&G Records: a Polygram backed label. Steve Kutner was behind the deal with the label: an imprint run by Michael (later Lord) Levy, who had run Magnet. An album was recorded for M&G in 1990 but shelved, as was a second single planned for release in February 1992. It was nixed due to the poor sales of 'Johnny Remember Me'. After The Phantom Chords were dropped by M&G, the album was self-issued on cassette in 1992.

200 From the 1961 film of the same name. The song has been covered a lot, but the most familiar version is Gene Pitney's original recording made for the film.

201 Titled *Big Beat Presents David Vanian and the Phantom Chords*.

202 Recording of a third A&M album had begun but it was not completed.

203 Captain's life as well as musical partner.

204 Both the title track and 'The Coward Of Treason Cove' were the versions heard on Captain's final A&M single. Keyboard player Andy Boucher, later in Norman Cook's Beats International, and Eddy Grant also appeared on the album.

205 Named after a type of diesel locomotive.

206 A previously unissued 1982, *Strawberries*-era recording which featured Robert Fripp guesting on guitar. The B-side was a track from Captain's *Revolution Now* solo album. A 12-inch version included two further solo Captain tracks. Not entirely a Damned single then.

207 *The Clash: A Visual Documentary* was published in 1984 but was a slim picture book. As was, though not as slim, 1980's earlier and marvellous *The Clash: Before and After*. *Sex Pistols File*, an essential collection of photographs and reproductions of clippings had been published in 1978 but was also not a biography. Paolo Hewitt's *The Jam: A Beat Concerto – The Authorised Biography* had been published in 1983, but as they pre-existed 1976 this was not strictly a book about a punk band.

208 The book swiftly went out of print and second-hand copies fetch around £200.

209 Matlock's words were helped to the printed page by former *Sounds* contributor Peter Silverton.

210 Compiled and ghosted by Keith and Kent and Zimmerman.

211 In this, Lydon's words were brought to the printed page by British music journalist Andrew Perry.

212 Who says he did it for the money.

213 A single titled 'Prokofiev' was sold at these dates. It was a 1990 recording created by Rat. Brian superimposed a guitar part over elements of The Stooges' 'Gimme Danger'. A vocal by David was then added.

214 Their 'Ain't It Fun' was actually a pre-punk composition first recorded by precursor band Rocket From the Tombs (which also spawned Pere Ubu).

215 From September 1991 to July 1992.

216 Shaw had released a solo single in 1974 but was a familiar figure to obsessive followers of the UK punk scene. He had been a member of the 1977 band The Rings (one single: 'I Wanna Be Free' – they supported The Damned at The Marquee in 1977) and had then passed through The Maniacs (one single: 'Chelsea 77' – they were billed with The Damned at Mont-de-Marsan in 1977), The Physicals (one EP in 1978 and a single in 1980) and Brian James' Brains. In 1990, Shaw had appeared on Brian James' eponymous first solo album (Brian's old friend Malcolm Mortimore was also on the album).

217 In post-production, Glen Matlock overdubbed bass on 'Never Could Believe' and 'Tailspin'.

218 Shaw has also said the album was originally conceived as one where each of the four original members of The Damned would write three songs apiece.

219 The title was a phrase Rat liked: used by a couple of his friends of his.

220 The best, and most trenchant, commentary on this state of affairs is by Alex Ogg in his 2006 book *No More Heroes* (see bibliography).

221 Sometimes given as Monty Oxy Moron.

222 They were married later in the year. Patricia Morrison's musical background is fascinating. From California, she had been at the Orpheum, Los Angeles show in 1977 where Captain jammed with The Weirdos and first (briefly) encountered David there. She was then the bassist in LA punk band The Bags, subsequently in Legal Weapon (from 1980 to 1981) and, in 1982, went on to The Gun Club (with whom she moved to Britain). After this, there was a 1985 spell with Gun Club offshoot The Fur Bible and then, from 1987 to 1989, she was in The Sisters Of Mercy.

223 Formerly of the three-piece band Wardance, who issued one album: 1993's *We're All Niggas… But Not Your Boys*. Before this, he was (1984 to 1986) in the punk band Alternative Attack (named after the two tracks on a 1982 Exploited single) who issued a single and an album on cassette. Then, in 1987, he was briefly in English Dogs, after which he was in metal band Sacrilege in their doom metal phase. After The Damned he was in rock band Jolt with former Senseless Things member Mark Keds.

224 Like Smith, Pinching had also been in English Dogs but was a founder member and with them for the long haul. Smith was his replacement in 1987. In The Damned, it was the other way round, English Dogs formed in Grantham, Lincolnshire in 1982 and evolved to (despite looking as if they were an Exploited-type band) deal in a crossover between punk and speed metal, heard most overtly on the 1984 *To The Ends Of The Earth* EP. Over the next few years, metal won out over punk. English Dogs had many line-up changes, would split in 1987 and reform (with Pinching)

but fell apart after the 1995 *All The World's A Rage* album. There would, though, be reunions.

225 In 1995, The Offspring had recorded their own version of 'Smash It Up'. It appeared on the soundtrack to the *Batman Forever* film.

226 West had been in English Dogs over 1994 and 1995. Before that, he was in Peterborough punk band The Uprising.

227 By this point, Rat's profile had increased through the May 2005 publication of *Rat Scabies and the Holy Grail*, a book by music journalist Christopher Dawes (who had written under the name Push), which documented exactly this: Rat's search for the Holy Grail. It was very funny and cast Rat in an entirely new light.

Index